TOOLS for TEAMS

Building Effective Teams
in the WORKPLACE

TOOLS for TEAMS

Building Effective Teams
in the WORKPLACE

Leigh Thompson
Eileen Aranda
Stephen P. Robbins
and others

Edited by **Craig Swenson**

Pearson Custom Publishing

Congratulations,

with this text you gain access to a valuable website that will open many doors for you! The University of Phoenix has chosen to enhance and expand this book with a dynamic website that contains an abundance of rich and beneficial web links specifically designed to help you achieve success! You can begin to access these tremendous resources immediately!

To access the website, simply type in the following web address:

http://www.pearsoncustom.com/link/uop/teamtools

At the UserID prompt, enter the following:

swenson

At the password prompt, enter the following password:

uopwrench

This will launch the online link library, which includes key terms that are linked to the World Wide Web. Use this page to launch websites selected to reinforce your learning experience.

Please note that a free CD-ROM to accompany this book will be available mid-September 2000. If your book does not already include this CD-ROM and you would like to order a complimentary copy, please visit the website as instructed above and click on the order CD-ROM tab.

Take the first step on the road to success today!

Excerpts taken from:

Making the Team: A Guide for Managers, by Leigh L. Thompson
Copyright © 2000 by Prentice Hall, Inc.
A Pearson Education Company
Upper Saddle River, New Jersey 07458

Teams: Structure, Process, Culture, and Politics,
by Eileen K. Aranda, Luis Aranda, with Kristi Conlon
Copyright © 1998 by Prentice Hall, Inc.

Organizational Behavior: Concepts, Controversies, and Applications, Sixth Edition,
by Stephen P. Robbins
Copyright © 1996 by Prentice Hall, Inc.

Training in Inter-Personal Skills: TIPS for Managing People at Work, Second Edition,
by Stephen P. Robbins and Phillip L. Hunsaker
Copyright © 1996, 1989 by Prentice Hall, Inc.

The Art and Science of Leadership, Second Edition, by Afsaneh Nahavandi
Copyright © 2000, 1997 by Prentice Hall, Inc.

The Facilitative Leader: Behaviors That Enable Success, by R. Glenn Ray
Copyright © 1999 by Prentice Hall, Inc.

Supervision: Diversity and Teams in the Workplace, Ninth Edition,
by Charles R. Greer and W. Richard Plunkett
Copyright © 2000, 1996, 1994, 1992, 1989, 1986, 1983, 1979, 1975 by Prentice Hall, Inc.

Understanding Behaviors for Effective Leadership, by Jon P. Howell and Dan L. Costley
Copyright © 2001 by Prentice Hall, Inc.

Project Management: Engineering, Technology and Implementation,
by Avraham Shtub, Jonathan F. Bard, and Shlomo Globerson
Copyright © 1994 by Prentice Hall, Inc.

Interpersonal Skills for Leadership, Second Edition, by Susan Fritz, F. William Brown, Joyce Poulacs
Lunde, and Elizabeth A. Banset
Copyright © 1997 by Simon and Schuster Custom Publishing (now Pearson Custom Publishing)

Team Building: Current Issues and New Alternatives, Third Edition, by William G. Dyer
Copyright © 1995 by Addison-Wesley Publishing Company

Leadership: Essential Steps Every Manager Needs to Know, Third Edition,
by Elwood Chapman and Sharon Lund O'Neil
Copyright © 1997 by Prentice Hall, Inc.

The Prentice Hall Self-Assessment Library: Insights into Your Skills, Abilities, and Interests, Edited by
Stephen P. Robbins. Copyright © 2000 by Prentice Hall, Inc.

Printed in the United States of America

10 9 8 7 6 5 4 3 2 1

Please visit our web site at www.pearsoncustom.com

ISBN 0–536–61750–3

BA 992609

PEARSON CUSTOM PUBLISHING
75 Arlington Street, Boston, MA 02116
A Pearson Education Company

Contents

Section 2: Getting Started 49

Section 3: Getting to Results 81

Section 4: Conflict Happens 213

Preface

*T*his is *not* a textbook. It is, as its title suggests, a toolkit. Every craftsman and artisan knows that to do a job right, you must choose the right tool. Successful professionals—managers, educators, counselors, and nurses—have had to learn this lesson and follow the same practice.

These days, organizations of all kinds use teams to get things done. For all the promised benefits, however, doing those things as teams is very different than doing them the way most of us are used to. Doing teams well is not necessarily an instinctive skill—particularly in western cultures where the value and importance of the individual has been emphasized, often at the expense of the collective. While we applaud the virtues of teamwork and cooperation, our heroes remain the self-made person and rugged individualist who succeeds in the face of seemingly insurmountable odds. John Wayne and Gary Cooper aren't dead but have been reincarnated as Bruce Willis and Harrison Ford.

Little wonder that when it comes to making teams work we often come off frustrated and disillusioned. Where, after all, are we supposed to learn the skills and attitudes—create the tools, in other words—to help build teams that reach the potential we're told they have. Many of us didn't attend primary and secondary schools where teamwork and cooperation were valued and taught in the classroom. How, then, do we overcome years of schooling where what we now call "cooperation" was considered "cheating?"?

Learning to work effectively as a team member and leader is a critical organizational competency that University of Phoenix works to develop across the curriculum in all academic programs. That is why the faculty of University of Phoenix decided to create this book. We want you, our students, to have access to tools that will increase your success at teaming. We are positive it can help you make your UOP Learning Teams more effective. Our ultimate hope, however, is that you'll use this toolkit in your jobs to help your organizations improve the quality and effectiveness of teams there.

*I*ntroduction—Team Learning at University of Phoenix

Since University of Phoenix was founded nearly a quarter of a century ago, learning teams have been an essential element of its Teaching/Learning Model. UOP's Founder, Dr. John Sperling, recognized the value of teams in both academia and the workplace long before these benefits became widely known and accepted. Dr. Sperling believed—and subsequent research has confirmed—that learning teams fill several essential functions that are especially beneficial to working adult learners. Learning teams can:

- Create collaborative learning environments in which working adults can share the practical knowledge that comes from their life and work experience.
- Improve the quality of shared projects and assignments.
- Serve as vehicles for the kind of shared reflection through which adult students make sense of and apply new knowledge.
- Provide a sense of community and support that is invaluable in helping working adults cope with the challenge of balancing school with other life demands.

*T*he Importance of "Team" Competence at Work

There is another equally important function that should be served by learning team participation. More than ever, organizations require their employees to work effectively as members of teams. The University's institutional research, supported by virtually every national education study of the past decade, confirms that employers expect colleges and universities to help develop this competency. Research into the attitudes of University of Phoenix students tells us that they expect the University to help them develop these skills too.

Based on these findings, the faculty of University of Phoenix has mandated the use of learning teams as "laboratories" for developing team effectiveness skills. Further, it requires that learning teams be used across the curriculum throughout every student's program of study.

Some might suggest that there are students whose preferred learning styles lean away from learning in groups and that other formats should be available. To that argument, we give two responses. First, learning styles should not be allowed to become straightjackets—to become effective lifelong learners, we will each need continuously to expand our learning repertoires. Second, creating an educational experience that prepares learners to contribute to the effectiveness of their organizations is central to the mission of University of Phoenix. Developing team competence is critical enough to our students, their organizations, and society as to justify our insistent emphasis.

*A*ssembling a Toolkit for Effective Team Building

Just as a skilled carpenter gathers the right tools for the job at hand, a skilled leader and manager also fills his or her toolbox with critical knowledge, skills, and attitudes that fit the job to be done. When that job involves building effective teams, the manager's toolbox must contain knowledge about what teams are, when and why they should be used, and how they can be organized to maximize their effectiveness. It should also contain tools that will help develop the interpersonal and organizational skills, and professional attitudes, that are prerequisites for team success.

In creating **Team Tools,** our goal was to create a toolbox filled with just what you need most to become an effective team member or leader—a team "builder"—in your organization. The content of **Team Tools** was drawn from various business and organizational sources, both scholarly and practical. Each section deals with a different critical aspect of teaming. Often, we've included more than one source in the discussion of a particular topic. Just as different craftsmen and artisans approach the same job from a slightly different perspective, so do those who study and write about management. We think the varied perspectives you'll experience will broaden and deepen your knowledge and skills.

Section One discusses "Team Basics." What are teams? How do they differ from simple groups? Why do organizations use teams? Are there different kinds of teams? When should teams be used—and when should they not? How big should they be? How should members be chosen? These are the kinds of questions covered in this section, meant to provide a foundation for your team efforts at work.

"Getting Started" is the title of Section Two. Understanding the process by which teams tend to function—or fail—is essential to building effective teams. This section looks at team and group processes from multiple points of view. The importance and process of creating a charter and how to hold effective team meetings are important elements of Section Two.

Most teams are formed to accomplish a specific goal. Section Three, "Getting to Results," provides essential information about project management, decision making, and problem solving in a team environment. Additionally, it deals with one of the most crucial management and leadership skills in this age of information—how to use technology to team when members are dispersed geographically.

"Conflict Happens!" That conflict is a normal and natural part of the teaming process comes as no surprise to anyone who has worked in teams. Effective leaders and managers have learned that you can't avoid team conflict, but you can learn to manage it. Section Four provides two different perspectives and processes for this essential skill.

The last section—Team Learning: Marrying Task and Process—provides knowledge to help team leaders and members build and renew their teams. It also discusses another essential, but often overlooked, aspect of building effective teams: the requirements for effective "followership."

Finally, the appendices contain numerous inventories, checklists, assessments, forms and exercises you can use to help evaluate, diagnose, build, and plan for effective teams.

In the CD-ROM version of **Team Tools**, you'll notice that various terms are highlighted. When you are connected to the Internet, these hyperlinks will direct you to various resources available to expand your knowledge and skill at teaming.

*T*eam Basics

Introduction

During the last decade of the Twentieth Century, nearly every company in North America caught the team bug. If the hype was to be believed, workplace teams would solve virtually every corporate problem, ratchet up quality, increase productivity and profits, improve organizational culture, and cure the common cold. Teams were good. Teams were in. Hierarchy was bad. Hierarchy was out.

Try this thought experiment: The boss comes back from a conference (always a dangerous thing) carrying a big binder they handed out at the conference and announces that the organization is going to "institute teams." Clearly he or she expects everyone else to share the zeal and, so, forms an executive team to plan the "teaming effort."

Soon, teams are being formed across the company. There's a big kickoff meeting or videoconference broadcast. An eye-catching logo and clever motto are flashed on the screen and emblazon the T-shirts, baseball caps, and buttons that are distributed to everybody in the company.

The training department gets into the spirit and training classes, Web sites, manuals, and posters are popping up all over the place. There are teams meeting everywhere, employees carrying notebooks, gathering data and making presentations to management with their proposals.

It's now 18 months later. The posters are gone; the buttons are junk in the back of that pencil drawer in your cubicle and the word "team"—if spoken at all—is whispered or elicits a sneer.

Ring a bell? It would in lots of cubicles and offices across America. So what happened? Was the idea to try teams a bad one? The answer, I believe, is a clear and resounding NO! The problem was not with teams. This is a description of what can happen in any organizational change effort and isn't about teams.

The truth is, the boss probably didn't understand the complexity of the task, failed to count the costs and pay the price. Building effective teams is complex, takes a lot of thought and work, and requires long-term commitment. Just as there are different kinds of tasks, there are different kinds of teams, it's not a "one size fits all" kind of thing. A team isn't the right structure for every task and sometimes may even be counterproductive.

But done right, with people who know how to do it, management who knows how to support it, and leaders who understand the process, teams can be a superior organizational structure and tool. People in teams *can* (not necessarily *do*) accomplish much, much more than those same individuals working separately. Companies that have realized the complexity, counted the costs, and paid the price have reaped the benefits.

Smart leaders and managers know this. That's why virtually every study of the skills organizations expect their employees to develop places interpersonal competence in a team setting near the top of the list.

Understanding the basics is the first step. This section starts at the beginning. It covers the why, when, how, how big, and who of teams.

*W*hat *Is a* Team?

*C*haracteristics of Teams

Groups have worked together to accomplish organizational goals for many years. However, the concept and use of teams as a central element of decision-making and performance are more recent. Table 1.1 outlines the differences between groups and teams.

One of the most celebrated examples of the use of teams is the Johnsonville Sausage Company, where team management and empowerment have shown dramatic results. Other organizations, such as AT&T, have reaped the benefits of using teams as decision-making and implementation tools. The company has used cross-functional teams to address the needs of its customers. Team members have the responsibility to solve problems and manage themselves. The results have been quicker response times and more satisfied customers. At Rubbermaid, 20 cross-functional teams assigned to product development are credited with the company's continued success (Farnham 1994). Kodak uses cross-functional teams oriented toward customers' needs. They identify best business practices that can then be implemented in other parts of the organization ("Kodak's Picture" 1996). Pharmacia Upjohn, a pharmaceutical giant, revamped its organizational structure to establish self-managed teams that include experts from different parts of the organization as team members and gives them wide latitude to make decisions about how to provide service. The objective is to allow those closest to the customer to make decisions that affect customer service (Smith 1996).

TABLE 1.1 DIFFERENCES BEWEEN GROUPS AND TEAMS	
Groups	**Teams**
Members work on a common goal.	Members are fully committed to common goal and mission they developed.
Members are accountable to manager.	Members are mutually accountable to one another.
Members do not have clear stable culture and conflict is frequent.	Members trust one another and team has a collaborative culture.
Leadership assigned to single person.	Members all share in leadership.
Members may accomplish their goals.	Members achieve synergy: 2 + 2 = 5,

Sources: J.R. Hackman, *Groups That Work (and Those That Don't)* (San Francisco: Jossey-Bass); and J.R. Katzenbach, and D.K. Smith, *The Wisdom of Teams: Creating the High Performance Organization* (New York: Harper Business, 1993).

The successful use of teams is also at the cornerstone of management in many health care organizations where teams are used as planning tools and as the key to quality patient care. Teams made up of not only internal employees but also external community constituents have become central to the success of many institutions (Allen 1991; McCool 1992). The bases for effective use of teams are the same in the private and public sectors.

The first distinguishing characteristic of a team is its members' full commitment to a common goal and approach that they have often developed themselves. Members must agree that the team goal is worthwhile and agree on a general approach to that goal. Such agreement provides the vision and motivation for team members to perform. The second characteristic is mutual accountability. To succeed as a team, members must feel and be accountable to one another and to the organization for the process and outcome of their work. Whereas group members report to the leader or their manager and are accountable to them, team members take on responsibility and perform because of their commitment to the team.

The third characteristic of a team is a team culture based on trust and collaboration. Whereas group members share norms, team members have a shared culture. Team members are willing to compromise, cooperate, and collaborate to reach their common purpose. A collaborative climate does not mean the absence of conflict, however. Conflict can enhance team creativity and performance if handled constructively. Related to the team culture is shared leadership. Whereas groups have one assigned leader, teams differ by sharing leadership among all members.

Finally, teams develop synergy. Synergy means that team members together achieve more than each individual can. Whereas group members combine their efforts to achieve their goals, teams reach higher performance levels.

LYNN MERCER'S TEAMS AT LUCENT

Lynn Mercer is the cellular-phone factory manager at Lucent Technologies. She is dedicated to the concept of self-managed teams and has worked hard to make it a success. The teams in her operation decide how the work should be done, what improvements are needed, and who should perform them. She notes that she just sets the mission of the factory, and the rest is up to the teams: "If I give you an endgame you can find your way there" (Petzinger 1997, B1). Lucent's teams elect their own leaders and are exceptionally flexible so they can adapt to the ever-changing needs of the cellular-phone industry, and members truly understand their customers' needs.

Mercer explains that, although all instructions are still written down in her team-managed factory, every individual can make on-line changes to a procedure if the individual's team agrees. Not only do teams have the power to change procedures, others can also learn from them and do not have to reinvent the wheel. Team members learn many tasks and skills and can perform them well. Teams decide on local solutions to problems, and as one manager notes, "We solve problems in hallways rather than conference rooms" (Petzinger 1997, B1).

The results have been remarkable: Mercer's factory has not missed a deadline in over two years, and labor costs remain a very low percentage of total costs.

Source: T. Petzinger Jr. "How Lynn Mercer Manages a Factory That Manages Itself," *Wall Street Journal*, March 7, 1997, B1.

$\mathcal{S}$elf-Managed Teams

Whereas traditional managers and leaders are expected to provide command and control, the role of leaders in teams is to facilitate processes and support team members. The leader sets general direction and goals; the team members make all other decisions and implement them. This new role for leaders is most obvious in self-managed teams (SMT), teams of employees who have full managerial control over their own work (for some examples, see Barry 1991; Crum and France 1996; Spencer 1995).

Numerous organizations such as Toyota, General Foods, and Procter & Gamble have used self-managed teams successfully for decades. In fact, Procter & Gamble once claimed its self-managed teams were one of the company's trade secrets (Fisher 1993). Self-managed teams have the following five characteristics:

- *The power to manage their work.* Self-managed teams can set goals, plan, staff, schedule, monitor quality, and implement decisions.

- *Members with different expertise and functional experience.* Some members may be from marketing, finance, production, design, and so on. Without a broad range of experience, the team could not manage all aspects of its work.

- *No outside manager and the power to implement decisions.* The team does not report to an outside manager. Team members manage themselves, their budget, and their task through shared leadership. Stanley Gault, chairman of Goodyear, the largest tire manufacturer in the United States, says that "the teams at Goodyear are now telling the boss how to run things. And I must say, I'm not doing half-bad because of it" (Greenwald 1992).

- *Coordination and cooperation with other teams and individuals affected by the teams' decisions.* Because each team is independent and does not formally report to a manager, the teams themselves rather than managers must coordinate their tasks and activities to assure and achieve integration.

- *Internal leadership based on facilitation.* Leadership often rotates among members depending on each member's expertise in handling a specific situation. Instead of a leader who tells others what to do, sets goals, or monitors achievement, team leaders remove obstacles for the team and make sure that the team has the resources it needs. The primary role of the team leader is to facilitate rather than control. Facilitation means that the leader focuses on freeing the team from obstacles to allow it to reach the goals it has set.

The success of the team depends on a number of key factors. First, the members of a team have to be selected carefully for their complementary skills and expertise. The interdependence among the members makes creation of a right combination critical. The "right" combination depends as much on technical as on interpersonal skills. Second, the team members need to focus on and be committed to the team goal. For example, individuals from different functional departments such as marketing or production, although selected because of their expertise in particular areas, need to leave the department mind-set behind and focus on the task of the team. Third, the team task has to be appropriately complex and the team has to be provided with the critical resources it needs to perform the task. Finally, the team needs enough power and authority to accomplish its task and implement its ideas. The sources of team power are available to the team to allow it to perform its job.

Building an effective team is a time-consuming process that requires both interpersonal team building and extensive technical support. The development of trust, a common vision, and the ability to work well together depend on appropriate interpersonal skills. Tackling complex tasks, once the trust and goals are established, requires timely technical training. Many of these interpersonal and technical functions traditionally fall on the leader's shoulders. However, leadership in teams is often diffused, a factor that puts further pressure on individual team members to take on new tasks and challenges.

*W*hat Is a Team?

Not everyone who works together or in close proximity belongs to a team. A **team** is a group of people who are interdependent with respect to information, resources, and skills and who seek to combine their efforts to achieve a common goal. As is summarized in the box titled: Five Key Characterisics of Teams, teams have five key defining characteristics. First, teams exist to achieve a shared goal. Simply put, teams have work to do. Teams produce outcomes for which members have collective responsibility and reap some form of collective reward. Second, team members are interdependent regarding some common goal. Interdependence is the hallmark of teamwork. *Interdependence* means that team members cannot achieve their goals single-handedly, but instead, must rely on each other to meet shared objectives. There are several kinds of interdependencies, as team members must rely on others for information, expertise, resources, and so on. Third, teams are bounded and remain relatively stable over time. *Boundedness* means the team has an identifiable membership; members, as well as nonmembers, know who is on the team. *Stability* refers to the tenure of membership. Most teams work together for a meaningful length of time—long enough to accomplish their goal. Fourth, team members have the authority to manage their own work and internal processes. We focus on teams in which individual members can, to some extent, determine how their work gets done. Thus, although a prison chain gang may be a team in some sense, the prisoners have little authority in terms of managing their own work. Finally, teams operate in a larger social system context. Teams are not islands unto themselves. They do their work in a larger organization, often alongside other teams. Furthermore, teams often need to draw upon resources from outside the team and vice versa.

Editor's Note:
Here's another take
on the characteriscs
of teams

FIVE KEY CHARACTERISTICS OF TEAMS
(Alderfer, 1977; Hackman, 1990)

- Teams exist to achieve a shared goal.
- Team members are interdependent regarding some common goal.
- Teams are bounded and stable over time.
- Team members have the authority to manage their own work and internal processes.
- Teams operate in a social system context.

A *working group,* by contrast, consists of people who learn from one another and share ideas, but are not interdependent in an important fashion and are not working toward a shared goal. Working groups share information, perspectives, and insights, make decisions, and help people do their jobs better, but the focus is on individual goals and accountability. For example, consider the operators who staff the phone lines at 1-800-MATTRESS. They share, via their computer network, specifications on hundreds of mattresses and bed frames. They may also share information among themselves on sales techniques, consumer demographics, or tie-in items. Yet they are individually evaluated based on their sales performance. These phone operators share resources, but not results. A team is a type of group, but not all groups are teams.

Why Should Organizations Have Teams?

Teams and teamwork are not novel concepts. In fact, teams and team thinking have been around for years at companies such as Procter & Gamble and Boeing. In the 1980s, the manufacturing and auto industries strongly embraced a new, team-oriented approach when U.S. firms retooled to combat Japanese competitors who were quickly gaining market share (Nahavandi & Aranda, 1994). During collaboration on the B-2 stealth bomber between the U.S. Air Force, Northrop, and some 4,000 subcontractors and suppliers in the early 1980s, various teams were employed to handle different parts of the project. "As new developments occurred or new problems were encountered during the program, the Air Force/Northrop team formed ad hoc teams made up of [their] own experts and specialists from other companies and scientific institutions" (Kresa, 1991).

Managers discovered the large body of research indicating that teams can be more effective than the traditional corporate hierarchical structure for making decisions quickly and efficiently. Even simple changes like encouraging input and feedback from workers on the line can make a dramatic improvement. For instance, quality control (QC) circles and employee involvement groups are often vehicles for employee participation (Cole, 1982). It is a mark of these programs' success that this kind of thinking is considered conventional wisdom nowadays. But, although these QC teams were worthy efforts at fostering the use of teams in organizations, the teams needed for the restructuring and reengineering processes of the future may be quite different (Nahavandi & Aranda, 1994). This point is brought home even more clearly in light of A. T. Kearney's findings that nearly seven out of ten teams fail to produce the desired results ("*The Trouble with Teams,*" 1995).

At least three challenges of the future suggest that building and maintaining effective teams will be of paramount importance. The first has to do with *specialization*. As the economy expands and organizations grow accordingly, firms become ever more complex, both in their tasks and in the markets they serve. Thus, the activities of individuals in these firms are necessarily becoming more specialized. An increasingly global and fast-paced economy requires people with specialized expertise. Yet the specialists within a company need to know how to work together. Moreover, as acquisitions, restructurings, outsourcing, and other structural changes take place, the need for coordination becomes all the more salient. Changes in corporate structure and increases in specialization imply that there will be new boundaries between the members of an organization. Boundaries both separate and link teams within an organization (Alderfer, 1977; Friedlander, 1987), although the boundaries are not always obvious. These new relationships require team members to learn how to work with others to achieve their goals. Team members must integrate through coordination and synchronization with suppliers, managers, peers, and customers.

The second challenge has to do with *competition*. In today's economy, a few large firms are emerging as dominant players in the biggest markets. These industry leaders often enjoy vast economies of scale and earn tremendous profits. The losers are often left with little in the way of a market—let alone a marketable product (Frank & Cook, 1995). Think, for example, of Microsoft's Windows operating system and Office Products market share dominance. The division that develops the Office Products software—which includes Word, Excel, PowerPoint, Outlook, and Access—employs thousands of people. Those products share a lot of code with each other, and so teamwork is critical to coordinate the activities of the various component groups that make up the Office Products Division (Anonymous, 1996). With so much at stake, firms are aggressively competing in a winner-take-all battle for market share. Thus, bringing out the best in individuals within the firm has become ever more important. This means that people can be expected to specialize more and more in their areas of expertise, and these areas of expertise will get ever more narrow and interdependent. Both firms and individuals will have to increasingly rely on others to get access to their expertise. This is the core structure of a team-based approach to work.

A third factor is the *emergence of the information age*. Computer technology extends the firm's obligations and capacity to add value to its customers. For example, Toyota has a Monday-to-Friday design-to-delivery program, in which a customer "designs" a car on a computer terminal on Monday, and the factory automatically receives the specifications and has manufacturing completed by Friday of the same week (Cusumano, 1985). With ever-improving ability to communicate with others anywhere on the planet (and beyond!), people and resources that were once remote can now be reached quickly, easily, and inexpensively. This has facilitated the development of the virtual team—groups linked by technology so effectively that it is as if they were in the same building. Technology also gives managers options they never had before, in terms of which resources they choose to employ on any particular project. The role of management has shifted accordingly; they are no longer primarily responsible for gathering information from employees working below them in the organizational hierarchy and then making command decisions based on this information. Their new role is to identify the key resources that will best implement the company's objectives and then to facilitate the coordination of those resources for the company's purposes. The jobs of the team members have also changed significantly. This can be viewed as a threat or a challenge. Millions of jobs have been altered dramatically or have disappeared completely since the advent of computers. For example, George David, CEO of United Technologies Corp., believes that 18 million U.S. workers (almost one in six) are "at risk" because their jobs are "prone to automation" (Zachary, 1996). Decisions may now be made far from their traditional location; indeed, sometimes even by contractors who are not employees of the firm. This dramatic change in structure requires an equally dramatic reappraisal of how firms structure the work environment.

What Kinds of Teams Are There?

Types of Teams in Organizations

Organizations have come to rely on team-based arrangements to improve quality, productivity, customer service, and the experience of work for their employees. Yet not all teams are alike. Teams differ greatly in their degree of autonomy and control vis-à-vis the organization. Specifically, how is authority distributed in the organization? Who has responsibility for the routine monitoring and management of group performance processes? Who has responsibility for creating and fine-tuning the design of the group (Hackman, 1987)? Consider the four levels of control depicted in Figure 1-1.

The most traditional type of team is the **manager-led team**. In the manager-led team, the manager acts as the team leader and is responsible for defining the goals, methods, and functioning of the team. The teams themselves have responsibility only for the actual execution of their assigned work. Management is responsible for monitoring and managing performance processes, overseeing design, selecting members, and interfacing with the organization. Manager-led teams provide the greatest amount of control over team members and the work they perform; they allow the leader to have control over team members and the work they perform; they allow the leader to have control over the process and products of the team. In addition, they are efficient, in the sense that the manager does the work of setting the goals and outlining the work to be done. In manager-led teams, managers don't have

Making the Team: A Guide for Managers, by Leigh L. Thompson. Copyright © 2000 by Prentice Hall, Inc.

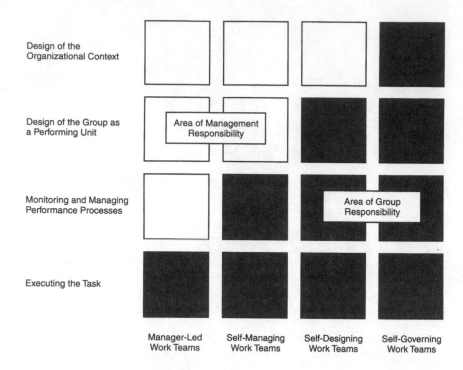

FIGURE 1-1

Authority of Four Illustrative Types of Work Groups
Source: Hackman, J.R. 1987, "The Design of Work Teams." In J.W. Lorsch (Ed.), *Handbook of Organizational Behavior.* Upper Saddle River, NJ: Prentice Hall.

to sit by and watch the team make the same mistakes they did. Manager-led teams also have relatively low start-up costs. The key disadvantages are diffusion of responsibility and conformity to the leader. In short, members have less autonomy and empowerment. Such teams may be ideally suited for simple tasks in which there is a clear overriding goal, such as task forces or fact-finding teams. Specific examples include military squads, flight crews, and stage crews.

In **self-managing or self-regulating teams**, a manager or leader determines the overall purpose or goal of the team, but the team is at liberty to manage the methods by which to achieve that goal. Self-managed teams are increasingly common in organizations. Examples include executive search committees, managerial task forces, and so on. For example, at Whole Foods Markets, the largest natural-foods grocer in the United States, the culture "is premised on decentralized teamwork. The team, not the hierarchy, is the defining unit of activity. Each of the 43 stores is an autonomous profit center composed of an average of 10 self-managed teams—produce, grocery, prepared foods, and so on—with designated leaders and clear performance targets" (Fishman, 1996). Self-managing teams build commitment, offer increased autonomy, and often enhance morale. The disadvantage is that the manager has much less control over the process and products, making it difficult to assess progress. Self-managing teams can also be more time-consuming.

Self-directing or self-designing teams determine their own objectives and the methods by which to achieve them. Management has responsibility only for the team's organizational context. Self-directed teams offer the most potential for innovation, enhance goal commitment and motivation, and provide opportunity for organizational learning and change. However, self-directed or self-designing teams are extremely time-consuming, have the greatest potential for conflict, and can be very costly to start up. (For a step-by-step guide to setting up self-designing teams, see Orsburn, Moran, Musselwhite, & Zenger, 1990). Furthermore, it can be extremely difficult (or impossible) to monitor their progress. Other disadvantages include marginalization of members and lack of team legitimacy. Self-designing teams may be ideally suited for complex, ill-defined, or ambiguous problems and next-generation planning. At the Harley-Davidson Motor Company, there is a "commitment to making the company a high-performance work organization, where the people closest to a job have the authority and responsibility to do it the best way they can. Part of the company's management approach is freedom and teamwork—it encourages each plant to solve its problems in its own way" (Imperato, 1997, p. 104). According to CEO Rich Teerlink, "The issues are always the same . . . quality, productivity, participation, flexibility, and cash flow. But each plant deals with them in a different way. We don't have cookbooks because there isn't a cookbook. We're on a journey that never ends. And the day we think we've got it made, that's the day we'd better start worrying about going out of business" (p. 104).

Self-governing teams and boards of directors are usually responsible for executing a task, managing their own performance processes, designing the group, and designing the organizational context. They are the extreme in terms of control and responsibility. In many companies, the president or chief operating officer has been replaced with an executive, self-governing team (Ancona & Nadler, 1989). Examples of this approach are John Reed's structuring of Citicorp's senior management when he succeeded Walter Wriston, and Walter Shipley's creation of the "three president" structure at Chemical Bank in the 1980s. When British Steel took the construction industry by storm by developing a unique, patented steel-skinned concrete panel system called the bi-steel system, it did so with the use of "a semi-autonomous team within a giant conglomerate not widely credited for encouraging innovative virtually self governing teams" (Greek, 1997, p. 19).

In certain cases, firms want to set up a self-governing (autonomous) team, similar to the independent counsel's office, to investigate serious problems, such as the sexual harassment case at Mitsubishi (e.g., the team headed up by Lynn Martin; Holland, 1996). The way the military has handled problems with sexual harassment stands in sharp contrast, not only in terms of the kinds of teams set up to examine the problems, but also in terms of the results they have achieved. In other cases, these kinds of teams could be disastrous, such as a committee composed of boards of directors—employees could be intimidated by the authority of these individuals and, therefore, unwilling or unable to provide a critical perspective on the status quo.

There are trade-offs involved with each of these four types of teams. Self-governing and self-directed teams provide the greatest potential in terms of commitment and participation, but are also at the greatest risk of misdirection. When decisions are pushed down in organizations, team goals and interests may be at odds with organizational interests. Unless everyone in the organization is aware of the company's interests and goals, poor decisions (often with the best of intentions) may be made. An organization that chooses a manager-led group is betting that a manager can run things more effectively than group members can. If it is believed that the group can do the job better, a self-governing or self-designing team may be appropriate. One implication of this is that the manager's traditional role as a collector of information is less and less important. If shared control over the performance situation and processes is preferred, a self-managing group is chosen.

*T*ypes of Teams

Editor's Note:
Here's a different
view on the types of
teams.

There are three general kinds of teams that organizations use:

Work teams:	teams that form natural work units, doing the day-to-day work of the organization
Task teams:	teams that address a specific problem or opportunity
Management teams:	teams drawn from people who direct operational or organizational units

Each type of team has an appropriate application and specific requirements and issues to consider. Membership, skill development, stability needs, and overall implications for the use of teams in the organization need to drive the team design decision. Care must be taken at this early point in the team's life to enhance its chances of success.

WORK TEAMS

Natural work groups are the most logical teams to create within the organization. These teams might come from existing organizational units such as sections or departments, or they might be regional units such as small field offices. While they are the most natural of teams in the organization, these units have normally worked as a collection of individuals rather than as a team. Frequently, work unit members do not visualize or share a common goal for the unit; seldom are they rewarded for unit performance. On the other hand, these groups often perform common, interdependent work, and so it often makes sense for organizations to start a team initiative with work teams.

In considering a current department or function as a likely base for a work team, important changes taking place in organizational structure need to be considered so that appropriate work teams are chosen. Across industries increasing emphasis is on creating cross-functional or process teams. When deciding how to develop work teams, one of the most important concerns is who should be part of the work team. The organization needs to have a clear view of its desired long-term structure as it brings teams on as common organizational units. For example, if the organization is working toward cross-functional and process teams, it needs to be cautious about encouraging unnecessary cohesion among functional groups.

A concrete example of a situation where an organization had to choose the type of work team it wanted might be helpful to elaborate this point. An organization wanted to improve its order processing and delivery performance. Order processing in the organization was traditionally structured with departments for order entry, credit, packaging, inspection, and shipping. Each function was responsible for managing its particular issues for all of the company's customers.

As the company grew it added more people to each department to handle the work. As is typical, each department developed procedures that suited its needs, drew boundaries around its responsibilities, and focused on internal issues and efficiencies. The larger the departments became, the less they knew what the people were doing in their units and in related units, and the easier it was for things to be left undone. Customers became increasingly dissatisfied because they were never able to talk to the same customer service person twice; each phone call required telling the employee the history of the account. Customers also were often given inaccurate information because information was not easily shared within the department. In addition, since order processing consisted of several steps involving different departments, customer files could be unavailable, out of the department that needed them when a call came in. The employee could not know the current state of the order. As a result, customers were constantly being transferred from department to department in an effort to locate their orders.

As a response to customer complaints, the company decided the customer would be better served if the employees worked together better. The company decided to create teams. But what kind of team did it want to create? There were at least three choices:

1. *Create teams for each department.* That is, establish an order entry team, a credit team, a packaging team, an inspection team, and a shipping team. Have each of the groups learn to work together and share information within the team.

2. *Build a team for the entire order processing function.* That is, create a team which would bring together all the employees from the different departments currently involved in order processing.

3. *Build a team for the entire delivery process.* This team would include people within the company, but outside the traditional order processing departments, who had great influence on the delivery process, specifically accounting and manufacturing.

The issue here is not that the company make the **correct** choice. None of the choices is intrinsically right or wrong. However, each has tradeoffs. The key to a wise decision is defining how the teams fit within the larger organizational structure and how they can function best.

If the choice is to build the teams within the current departments (choice 1 above) it will be relatively easy to get some quick efficiency improvements. Each person knows the work of the department and can probably offer good suggestions for improving the way work is done. However, in the long term this may not help the customer. Each unit may work better and still neither speed up the overall process nor necessarily provide the customer with better information on the current state of an order—all because the team is not cross-functional.

If the choice is to build a cross-functional team of the current order processing department (choice 2 above), teamwork will be more difficult. The members of the cross-functional team will not readily understand the work of the other departments. It is even possible that the different departments have been blaming one another for the current problems and that team members therefore will be defensive about suggestions to change their part of the process. Such teams traditionally take longer to establish and in the process will change the way the company does business.

Also, the number of people included in this team will be too large. This may be the case in the first choice as well since the departments are getting larger and larger.

In the next section we will discuss more about the appropriate size of teams. Suffice it to say at this point that a team made up of all the departments would somehow have to be broken down into smaller subgroups.

The up side of the cross-functional team choice is that the customer is likely to see improvement. Working together, the entire order process can be improved. Since the general work of the unit is relatively similar, there would also be the opportunity for cross-training, thus enhancing the overall capability of the team.

The choice to bring together an overall process team (choice 3 above) would be the most challenging to achieve. The team would now have people who speak different organizational languages, do different kinds of work, and may have conflicting performance goals. Not only will this team take more time to understand each other's views and values, it will require the organization to share information at a new level and to break down its assumptions about separation of tasks and control. For example, management would have to decide to whom this team would be accountable and what decisions the team could make.

However, if this team can perform well, the customer will likely receive the most benefit because this team can deal with effectiveness (doing the right things), as well as efficiency (doing things right). The first two teams are limited to dealing primarily with efficiency issues.

Thus, the critical first step in developing teams is to understand the impact of the team on organization. If the company makes choice 1, the organizational structure can stay the same; improvement occurs within the current unit. Choice 2 requires the organizational structure and reporting relationships to change somewhat. People are brought together differently, necessitating adjustments in supervision and management, though the nature of the work stays the same. Choice 3 not only changes the reporting relationships, but brings people together with entirely different responsibilities and goals for the organization. Choice 3 requires a radical change in organizational power and decision-making.

The organization described in the example above selected choice 2. It designated subgroups around account size and region. Since the organization had a very traditional structure and very conservative management style, combining similar functions was seen as enough of an initial change. Once those teams are working well, however, management might be encouraged to spread the lateral interaction and responsibility further. Management must put the creation of a team in context to consider how this team will impede or reinforce management's desire for the evolution of the overall organization's structure.

TASK TEAMS

Because they are by definition temporary, task teams do not present the same structural problems found in work teams. With a task team there is no sense that the team needs a different organizational structure to manage it. However, since task teams are often among the first teams brought into the organization, it is wise for management to consider all the implications of bringing them on board. Task teams are not without problems—two of the most important being valuing other perspectives and managing implementation.

Task teams are usually cross-functional. The whole idea of the team is to get as many different ideas about a given problem or opportunity as possible. But we often think that just bringing the group together is enough to benefit from its heterogeneous membership. Experience has taught us otherwise.

Let's look at a common scenario for a task team. The organization wishes to draw together representatives from different departments to solve a problem. In this case, the organization is relocating and a team has been charged with deciding on the layout and design of the internal space, selection of new furniture and accessories, and the location of people and equipment in the new building. Without a deliberate effort to manage the different points of view represented on the team, those differing perspectives will likely lead only to conflict. Each person will feel that it is his/her responsibility on the team to be an advocate for his/her own department and protect its interests. Successful membership on the team will be viewed as getting the "best" for one's constituency. With this view, the team is off on a downhill slope, for there is no sense of common goal for the team nor common good for the organization, and therefore, no way for everyone to feel successful.

As the organization brings a task team together, it must carefully design the team so it can work together. Some of the design issues to address are:

1. *Power level and mix of people in the team.* The more implementation-oriented the task, the more levels needed.

2. *Disposition of members toward problem solving and collaboration.* The more controversial and the greater the time pressure, the more important to have able problem solvers on the team.

3. *The amount of time allowed to address the issue.* The more innovative (requiring thinking outside current mindsets), the more dedicated blocks of time are needed.

4. *Specificity of task.* The more controversial and/or strategic, the more the desired outcome needs to be well defined.

For example, one design decision might be how to balance the position power in the team; that is, should team members all come from the same level of the organization so that "bosses" in the group do not pressure "subordinates" to see things their way? Or, should management spread the levels represented on the team to get multiple views? This mixed-level design is useful if the organization wants to foster communication and respect at all levels of the organization. Techniques that encourage participation and minimize power need to be part of the mixed-level team process.

Another design decision might be how to put people on the team who are known for their ability to reach agreement rather than people known for stubbornness. A task team needs multiple perspectives to realize its potential, but it does not need people who are unable to learn or to see the value in another point of view. Rather than choosing team members on the basis of extent of specific knowledge, it might be better to base the membership on understanding of the overall implications of the team task or on long-term organizational needs.

The point of this discussion is that, because task teams are brought together expressly to resolve issues, it is necessary to consciously design the team in terms of membership, time commitment, and direction to better be able to work together. Organizations seldom think about the problem-solving approaches and people needed on the task team for it to be successful. They assign people simply on the basis of proximity or availability.

Once the team begins to work together, another problem for the task team can arise. The more the team builds cohesiveness, the less it looks outside its group for input. Therefore, acceptance of its ideas is usually a serious issue for a task team to address.

Take the building design team we discussed earlier as an example. Once the team begins to work together, it will need to resolve issues and begin to make decisions. The more team members are able to come to agreement, the less likely they will be to get information from outside the group. The building task force is likely to get very involved in its task, to develop cohesive relationships, and to spend a lot of time together. The organization will assume the team effort is working well because the team is getting along well together and making progress.

Then, when the "solution" is presented by this "effective team" to the entire organization, it is met with resistance. The team members and management are surprised and annoyed that the rest of the employees do not like the team recommendation, nor appreciate the team's effort. The problem is not that the solution is a poor one, for teams seldom come up with irresponsible or silly solutions, but rather that those outside the team had increasingly little input into the decision. The rest of the employees feel that they are being sold a "bill of goods," and they are suspicious. In fact, the task force often makes the situation worse because it begins the problem-solving process by getting information from its constituents and making promises about future contact. The expectation for sharing information has been set, but as time goes on and the team gets more comfortable with one another, there is less interaction with those outside the team.

The first response of those left out of the process is to argue with the solution and pick out its shortcomings. Since no solution is perfect, there are always plenty of things to argue about. Team members defend their recommendation, get angry at their fellow employees, and say they will never represent the department again. Management decides that teams do not work and resorts to individual decision-making.

To get good ideas from a team is not the same as having those good ideas accepted by the rest of the organization. Later in the book we will discuss how to improve the chances of getting good ideas from the team and how to get those ideas accepted.

MANAGEMENT TEAMS

Perhaps the most difficult teams to develop are management teams because they have the least obvious purpose. Work teams usually have goals and objectives or fairly well-defined "work to be done." Task teams are created for a given purpose, though that purpose needs to be important and well defined. But management teams are often not sure why they meet together as a team.

A management team will often say that its goals are those of the organization. But organizational goals are not the same as the management team's goals. Organizational goals relate to the functional responsibilities that the members of the management team have and are focused downward in the organization. Those goals are more closely tied to the manager's relationship with his/her work team than to colleagues on the management team.

A management team needs its own goals defining what it will hold itself collectively responsible for. There needs to be a value-added dimension to the management team itself. The management team often says the value added is improved communication about organizational issues. To that end, the management team has staff meetings where members report on the work/problems/achievements in their departments, and the team sometimes makes operational decisions affecting those departments.

While information sharing may be a useful process, it does not constitute a substantive goal that can bring management together as a team, nor does it result in an achievement that adds value to the organization. Katzenbach and Smith, in *The Wisdom of Teams*, found that simply to report and make occasional operations-level decisions is not an engaging enough purpose to form a team. The level of most staff meeting discussion tends to keep the team members deeply entrenched in their individual responsibility and not focused on the overall good of the organization. The real purpose of a management team is to provide synthesis to organizational goals and activities. Team members must leave their functional identities at the door and deal with the organization as a whole if they are to develop into a team.

Katzenbach and Smith also found that to become a team, management groups must do real work together. Real work for management teams revolves around development of the entire organization. We are learning from organizational studies, especially those in the area of Total Quality Management and reengineering, that viewing the organization as a collection of separate parts is ineffective. Even if all the parts run well individually, the organization will not run well if the units are not integrated. In fact, the better each separate unit runs, the less well the entire organization runs because each unit will optimize at the expense of the others.

Thus, management teams must take on tasks that inspire and integrate the work of the organization. This work usually comes in the form of building a vision, refining the culture, carrying out major change initiatives, or improving the morale/image of the organization or unit. These are tasks that go beyond reporting and deciding functional/operational issues. They require management teams to understand the organization's vision and each other, to set aside their functional views, and to work together on a common purpose. As Peter Senge states in *The Fifth Discipline*, a major obstacle to team learning and good collective thinking is the attitude that "I am my position." This is an especially serious disability for a management team.

In summary, then, there are three different kinds of teams that the organization can use: work teams, task teams, and management teams. Often the organization uses all three. Each of the three kinds of teams has very different needs and implications; and if the organization is going to develop effective teams, it must address the differences within and among these teams. It is not enough just to bring people together or to treat all teams the same.

Are Teams Always Better?

A Contrary View of Teams

Teams are not the answer for all management problems or a silver bullet for improved performance. Unfortunately, the term "teamwork" is often misused. Sometimes it is used as a euphemism for suppressing legitimate disagreement with the manager's viewpoints or submitting to the will of others at all costs. Donald G. Smith has pointed out a number of problems with this common but dysfunctional view of teamwork:

> Positive-thinking gave business . . . the idea of the *team player,* which is a wonderful euphemism for someone who looks the other way when the Cossacks plunder the village. . . . When I entered corporate America directly out of college, I was given some invaluable advice by an older employee . . . [management] did not want to see boat rockers, and such people were immediately marked with an indelible stamp and considered unpromotable. The basic idea was to swallow one's integrity during business hours and to be a part of the "team." . . . I participated in programs that cost twice as much as they should have because of mismanagement, and I slavishly followed the

Supervision: Diversity and Teams in the Workplace, Ninth Edition, by Charles R. Greer and W. Richard Plunkett. Copyright © 2000, 1996, 1994, 1992, 1989, 1986, 1983, 1979, 1975 by Prentice Hall, Inc.

orders of some of the most incompetent and mentally deficient human beings I have ever encountered. I saw and tolerated waste and bungling that staggered the imagination. I saw
boat rockers hung out to dry, with none of their peers having
a kind word to say about them . . . with the only thought ever
expressed being that they should "have known better." (Smith,
1994, p. 93)

The points of this discussion are that supervisors should avoid misusing
the term teamwork and that they should not stifle constructive dissent for
the purpose of teamwork. In addition, some employees do not want to take
on some of the responsibilities of self-managed teams. While self-managed
teams are the means by which many companies have empowered their
employees, some find that they do not fit the system. For example, self-managed team members give each other feedback. Some employees find this very
stressful because other team members pay great attention to how they do
their jobs (Aeppel, 1997). In addition, with self-managed teams some employees feel that they have many bosses instead of one boss. At Eaton's plant in
South Bend, Indiana, one employee said the following:

"They say there are no bosses here," says Randy Savage, a longtime devoted employee, "but if you screw up, you find one
pretty fast." Indeed, with everyone watching everyone else, it
can feel like having a hundred bosses. . . . Worker mishaps that
might hamper production or tarnish the plant's reputation
are considered an affront to everyone and prompt a sort of
communal confession. (Aeppel, 1997, p. A1).

In addition to these concerns, some team members do not like to give
negative feedback to other team members and find that their communications
or interpersonal skills are inadequate for such functions. For example

Similarly, some workers refuse to speak at meetings called to
point out problems with a co-worker's performance. . . . And
others say they would never go in front of the rest of the work
force to apologize for a mistake . . . With workers expected to
sort out problems among themselves rather than have managers intervene, strong interpersonal skills are vital. . . . But
Mr. Gordon [team member] didn't like the frequent meetings
on communication. For instance, new workers are required
to give speeches before new employees and managers and to
attend training seminars about saying "we," never "I" or "you,"
when being critical to avoid sounding accusatory. (Aeppel,
1997, A13)

Some Observations about Teams and Teamwork

There is a lot of folklore and unfounded intuition when it comes to teams and teamwork. We want to set the record straight by exposing some of the observations that managers find most useful.

COMPANIES THAT USE TEAMS ARE NOT MORE EFFECTIVE THAN THOSE THAT DO NOT

When companies are in trouble, they often restructure into teams. However, putting people into teams does not solve problems; if not done thoughtfully, this may even cause more problems. For every case of team success, there is an equally compelling case of team failure, as indicated by this chapter's opening example. Teams can outperform the best member of the group, but there are no guarantees. Admitting the inefficiency of teams is hard, especially when most of us would like to believe in the Gestalt principle that the whole is greater than the sum of its parts! As we discuss in later chapters, teams can suffer from many drawbacks, such as too much emphasis on harmony or individualism, causing a feeling of powerlessness and creating discord (Griffith, 1997). Teams are not a panacea for organizations; they often fail and are frequently overused or poorly designed. In the best circumstances, teams provide insight, creativity, and cross-fertilization of knowledge in a way that a person working independently cannot. In the wrong circumstances, teamwork can lead to confusion, delay, and poor decision-making.

Making the Team: A Guide for Managers, by Leigh L. Thompson. Copyright © 2000 by Prentice Hall, Inc.

MANAGERS FAULT THE WRONG CAUSES FOR TEAM FAILURE

Imagine yourself in the following situation: The wonderful team that you put together last year has collapsed into lethargy. The new product line is not forthcoming, conflict has erupted, and there is high turnover. What has gone wrong? If you are like most managers, you place the blame on a clash of personalities: Someone is not behaving as a team player, or petty politics are usurping common team goals.

Misattribution error is a tendency for managers to attribute the causes of team failure to forces beyond their personal control. Leaders may blame individual team members, the lack of resources, or a competitive environment. By pointing to a problem team member, the team's problems can be neatly and clearly understood as emanating from one source. This saves the manager's ego (and in some cases the manager's job), but stifles learning and destroys morale. It is more likely that the team's poor performance is due to a structural, rather than personal, cause. Furthermore, it is likely that several things are at work, not just one.

MANAGERS FAIL TO RECOGNIZE THEIR TEAM-BUILDING RESPONSIBILITIES

Many new managers conceive of their people-management role as building the most effective relationships they can with each individual subordinate; they erroneously equate managing the team with managing the individual (Hill, 1982). These managers rarely rely on group-based forums for problem solving and diagnosis. Instead, they spend their time in one-on-one meetings. Teamwork is expected to be a natural consequence. As a result, many decisions are based upon limited information, and decision outcomes can backfire in unexpected and negative ways.

EXPERIMENTING WITH FAILURES LEADS TO BETTER TEAMS

It may seem ironic, but one of the most effective ways to learn is to experience failure. Evidence of this is provided by the fallout that accompanied the Los Angeles Police Department's (LAPD) handling of the riots that broke out following the Rodney King beating verdict in 1992. A *Los Angeles Times* editorial following the incident stated that "successful policing is a team effort; likewise, unsuccessful policing of the magnitude that occurred the night the riots broke out is a team failure" (*Los Angeles Times*, 1992, p. B4). The aftermath of the criticisms levied upon the LAPD and the people who run the department caused an overhaul within the management ranks of the department. A failed team effort should be viewed as a critical source of information from which to learn. The problem is that failure is hard to take: Our defense systems go into overdrive at the mere inkling that something we do is not above average. The true mark of a valued team member is a willingness to learn from mistakes. However, this learning can only come when people take personal responsibility for their actions.

The truth is, teams have a flatter learning curve than do most individuals; it takes teams longer to "get on their feet." However, teams have greater potential than do individuals.

CONFLICT AMONG TEAM MEMBERS IS NOT ALWAYS A BAD THING

Many managers boast that their teams are successful because they never have conflict. However, it is a fallacy to believe that conflict is detrimental to effective teamwork. In fact, conflict may be necessary for effective decision-making in teams. Conflict among team members can foment accuracy, insight, understanding, and development of trust and innovation.

STRONG LEADERSHIP IS NOT ALWAYS NECESSARY FOR STRONG TEAMS

A common myth is that to function effectively, teams need a strong, powerful, and charismatic leader. In general, leaders who control all the details, manage all the key relationships in the team, have all the good ideas, and use the team to execute their "vision" are usually overworked and underproductive. Teams with strong leaders may succumb to flawed and disastrous decision-making.

A leader has two main functions: A *design* function, meaning that the leader structures the team environment (working conditions, access to information, incentives, training, and education); and a *coaching* function, meaning that the leader has direct interaction with the team (Hackman, 1996).

GOOD TEAMS CAN STILL FAIL UNDER THE WRONG CIRCUMSTANCES

Teams are often depicted as mavericks: Bucking authority, striking out on their own, and asking for permission only after the fact. Such cases do occur, but they are rare and tend to be one-shot successes. Most managers want consistently successful teams. This is particularly important in industries where considerable tooling up is required for team members.

To be successful in the long run, teams need ongoing resources and support. By resources, we mean more than just money. Teams need information and education. In too many cases, teams tackle a problem that has already been solved by someone else in the company, but a lack of communication prevents this critical knowledge from reaching the current task force.

To lay the best groundwork for teams before the problems begin, it is important to consider such factors as the goals and resources of the team: Are the teams' goals well defined? Does everyone know them? Are the goals consistent with the objectives of other members of the organization? If not, how will the inevitable conflict be managed? Does everyone on the team have access to the resources necessary to successfully achieve the goal? Is the organizational hierarchy set up to give team members access to these resources efficiently? If not, it might be necessary to reconsider the governance structure within which the team must operate. What are the rights of the team members in pursuing their duties, who can they contact, and what information can they command? It is also important to assess the incentive structure existing for team members and for those outside the team with whom team members must interact. Does everyone have the right incentives (to do the things they are supposed to do)? Are team members' incentives aligned with those of the group and the organization; for instance, to cooperate with one another and to fully share information and resources? There is no cookie-cutter solution to team structure. For instance, it may be appropriate for team members to compete with one another (in which case, cooperation may not be an achievable feature of the group dynamic). Choosing the structure of the group and the incentives that motivate the individuals inside it are essential factors contributing to the success of any team.

RETREATS WILL NOT FIX ALL THE CONFLICTS BETWEEN TEAM MEMBERS

Teams often get into trouble. Members may fight, slack off, or simply be unable to keep up with their responsibilities, potentially resulting in angry or dissatisfied customers. When conflict arises, people search for a solution to the team problem. A common strategy is to have a "team-building retreat" or "corporate love-in," where team members try to address underlying concerns and build trust by engaging in activities—like rock climbing—that are not part of what they ordinarily do as a team.

A team retreat is a popular way for team members to build mutual trust and commitment. A retreat may involve team members spending a weekend camping and engaging in cooperative, shared, structured activities. This usually results in a good time had by all. However, retreats fail to address the structural and design problems that plague the team on a day-to-day basis in the work environment. Design problems are best addressed by examining the team in its own environment while team members are engaged in actual work. For this reason, it is important to take a more comprehensive approach to analyzing team problems. Retreats are insufficient because they allow managers to blame team interpersonal dynamics on the failures, rather than deeper, more systemic problems, which are harder to identify.

*W*hen Should Teams Be Used?

*L*eader-Participation Model

Back in 1973, Victor Vroom and Phillip Yetton developed a **leader-partici-pation model** that related leadership behavior and participation to decision-making. Recognizing that task structures have varying demands for routine and nonroutine activities, these researchers argued that leader behavior must adjust to reflect the task structure. Vroom and Yetton's model was norma-tive—it provided a sequential set of rules that should be followed for deter-mining the form and amount of participation desirable in decision-making, as dictated by different types of situations. The model was a complex decision tree incorporating seven contingencies (whose relevance could be identified by making "Yes" or "No" choices) and five alternative leadership styles.

More recent work by Vroom and Arthur Jago has resulted in a revision of this model. The new model retains the same five alternative leadership styles but expands the contingency variables to twelve, ten of which are answered along a five-point scale. Table 1.2 lists the twelve variables.

The model assumes that any of five behaviors may be feasible in a given situation—Autocratic I (AI), Autocratic II (AII), Consultative I (CI), Con-sultative II (CII), and Group II (GII):

- *AI*. You solve the problem or make a decision yourself using infor-mation available to you at that time.

Organizational Behavior: Concepts, Controversies, and Applications, Sixth Edition, by Stephen P. Robbins. Copyright © 1996 by Prentice Hall, Inc.

> **Editor's Note:**
> This section isn't specifically about teams—it concerns when participation should be used in decision-making. However, because we use teams to make decisions, it can help determine when teams are and are not indicated.

TABLE 1.2   CONTINGENCY VARIABLES IN THE REVISED LEADER-PARTICIPATION MODEL

QR: Quality Requirement

How important is the technical quality of this decision?

1	2	3	4	5
No Importance	Low Importance	Average Importance	High Importance	Critical Importance

CR: Commitment Requirement

How important is subordinate commitment to the decision?

1	2	3	4	5
No Importance	Low Importance	Average Importance	High Importance	Critical Importance

LI: Leader Information

Do you have sufficient information to make a high-quality decision?

1	2	3	4	5
No	Probably No	Maybe	Probably Yes	Yes

ST: Problem Structure

Is the problem well structured?

1	2	3	4	5
No	Probably No	Maybe	Probably Yes	Yes

CP: Commitment Probability

If you were to make the decision by yourself, is it reasonably certain that your subordinates would be committed to the decision?

1	2	3	4	5
No	Probably No	Maybe	Probably Yes	Yes

GC: Goal Congruence

Do subordinates share the organizational goals to be attained in solving this problem?

1	2	3	4	5
No	Probably No	Maybe	Probably Yes	Yes

CO: Subordinate Conflict

Is conflict among subordinates over preferred solutions likely?

1	2	3	4	5
No	Probably No	Maybe	Probably Yes	Yes

SI: Subordinate Information

Do subordinates have sufficient information to make a high-quality decision?

1	2	3	4	5
No	Probably No	Maybe	Probably Yes	Yes

TC: Time Constraint

Does a critically severe time constraint limit your ability to involve subordinates?

1	5
No	Yes

GD: Geographical Dispersion

Are the costs involved in bringing together geographically dispersed subordinates prohibitive?

1	5
No	Yes

MT: Motivation-Time

How important is it to you to minimize the time it takes to make the decision?

1	2	3	4	5
No Importance	Low Importance	Average Importance	High Importance	Critical Importance

MD: Motivation-Development

How important is it to you to maximize the opportunities for subordinate development?

1	2	3	4	5
No Importance	Low Importance	Average Importance	High Importance	Critical Importance

Source: V.H. Vroom and A.G. Jago, *The New Leadership: Managing Participation in Organizations* (Englewood Cliffs, NJ: Prentice Hall, 1988), pp. 111-12. With permission.

- *AII.* You obtain the necessary information from subordinates and then decide on the solution to the problem yourself. You may or may not tell subordinates what the problem is when getting the information from them. The role played by your subordinates in making the decision is clearly one of providing the necessary information to you rather than generating or evaluating alternative solutions.

- *CI.* You share the problem with relevant subordinates individually, getting their ideas and suggestions without bringing them together as a group. Then *you* make the decision, which may or may not reflect your subordinates' influence.

- *CII.* You share the problem with your subordinates as a group, collectively obtaining their ideas and suggestions. Then you make the decision that may or may not reflect your subordinates' influence.

■ *GII.* You share the problem with your subordinates as a group. Together you generate and evaluate alternatives and attempt to reach an agreement (consensus) on a solution.

Vroom and Jago have developed a computer program that cuts through the complexity of the new model. But managers can still use decision trees to select their leader style if there are no "shades of gray" (that is, when the status of a variable is clearcut so that a "Yes" or "No" response will be accurate), there are no critically severe time constraints, and subordinates are not geographically dispersed. Figure 1-2 illustrates one of these decision trees.

Research testing of the original leader-participation model was very encouraging. Because the revised model is new, its validity still needs to be assessed. But the new model is a direct extension of the 1973 version and it's also consistent with our current knowledge of the benefits and costs of participation. So, at this time, we have every reason to believe that the revised model provides an excellent guide to help managers choose the most appropriate leadership style in different situations.

Two last points before we move on. First, the revised leader-participation model is very sophisticated and complex, which makes it impossible to describe in detail in a basic OB textbook. But the variables identified in Table 1.1 provide you with some solid insights about which contingency variables you need to consider when choosing your leadership style.

Second, the leader-participation model confirms that leadership research should be directed at the situation rather than the person. It probably makes

QR	Quality requirement:	How important is the technical quality of this decision?
CR	Commitment requirement:	How important is subordinate commitment to the decision?
LI	Leader's information:	Do you have sufficient information to make a high-quality decision?
ST	Problem structure:	Is the problem well structured?
CP	Commitment probability:	If you were to make the decision by yourself, is it reasonably certain that your subordinate(s) would be committed to the decision?
GC	Goal congruence:	Do subordinates share the organizational goals to be attained in solving this problem?
CO	Subordinate conflict:	Is conflict among subordinates over preferred solutions likely?
SI	Subordinate information:	Do subordinates have sufficient information to make a high-quality decision?

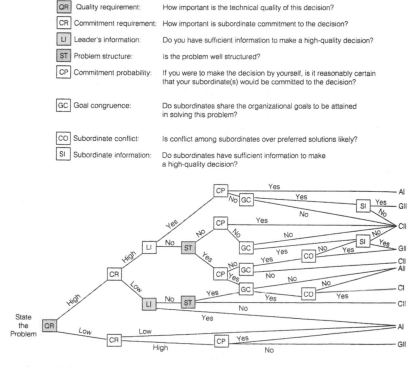

FIGURE 1-2

The Revised Leader Participation Model (Time-Driven Decision Tree-Group Problems)

more sense to talk about autocratic and participative *situations* than about autocratic and participative *leaders*. As did House in his path-goal theory, Vroom, Yetton, and Jago argue against the notion that leader behavior is inflexible. The leader-participation model assumes that the leader can adjust his or her style to different situations.

*W*hen Should Participation Be Used?

Participation is a continuum. On one end, the leader makes all the decisions without any consultation or even information from the subordinates; on the other end, the leader may delegate all decision-making to an individual or to the group and let members have the final say. Few leaders use extreme autocratic or delegation styles; most use a style that falls somewhere in between. Longitudinal research about employee involvement conducted by researchers at the University of Southern California indicates that organizations can reap many benefits from a variety of types of employee participation and involvement (Lawler, Mohrman, and Ledford 1995). These programs include such methods as information sharing, group decision-making, and the use of teams, empowerment, profit sharing, and stock option plans. All these programs increase employee involvement and participation in the organization. The study results show that the adoption of such programs has clear positive impact on performance, profitability, competitiveness and employee satisfaction (Lawler, Mohrman, and Ledford 1995).

Editor's Note: Here's another view of the same issue— when should teams be used and when should they not.

Consider how US Air, the sixth-largest air carrier in the United States, used a team to design a new low-fare airline, initially called US2 (Carey 1998). Rakesh Gangwal, president of US Air, asked two dozen of its employees without any start-up experience to find the best way to compete with Southwest Airlines. A catering truck driver and baggage handler in Baltimore, an aircraft cleaner in Pittsburgh, and a ramp supervisor were among the two dozen other airline specialists who joined the design team that spent four months investigating the competition. The team traveled extensively on Southwest, Shuttle by United, Alaska Airlines, and Delta Express with the goal of learning what makes each competitor efficient and effective. The members then assembled in Arlington, Virginia, and worked on their start-up's name. Gangwal announced that MetroJet would take off June 1, 1998. After the announcement, the team was disbanded and members sent back, reluctantly, to their regular jobs. "It's kind of like letting your child be married off," notes ramp supervisor Greg Solek (Carey 1998, B2). By using a team to make an important decision, Gangwal received input from many employees who would otherwise not be involved and in so doing, built their commitment to the success of the new operation.

CRITERIA FOR PARTICIPATION

Despite its many potential benefits, participation is not a cure-all. There are some situations when its use is more appropriate than others. After many years of debate and research about participative management in both social sciences and management, there are clear criteria for when it is most effective to use groups in decision-making (see Table 1.3).

Overall, if the organization, its leaders, and its followers are ready for participative management and there is no strong time pressure, the task is complex, and employee commitment is important, leaders should rely on employee participation in making decisions. However, if there is genuine time pressure or the leader, followers, or organization are not ready, then participation is not likely to yield many benefits. For example, if a leader has a high need for control, is highly task oriented, and has been successful in using an autocratic-style leadership, he or she is unlikely to be able to implement participation easily. And if followers have either little need to participate or are willing to trust the leader, participation may not be required or at least may not lead to better results. Similarly, some organizational cultures are more supportive of participation than others.

Another factor in using participation is whether the task or the structure limits its use. If followers cannot easily interact with one another and with the leader, either because of task or geographic restrictions, participation may not be appropriate. In some instances, legal and confidentiality requirements may preclude participation, for example, in personnel decisions.

The case of Kiwi Airlines presents an interesting example of the potential pitfalls of mismanaged participation (Bryant 1995). When Kiwi Airlines was founded in 1992, it quickly became the symbol of all that is good about participative and egalitarian leadership. Created by a group of ex-Eastern

TABLE 1.3 CRITERIA FOR USE OF PARTICIPATION	
Criteria	**Description**
• When the task is complex and multifaceted and quality is important	Complex tasks require input from people with different expertise; people with different points of views are more likely to deliver a quality decision.
• When follower commitment is needed in successful implementation	Follower participation increases commitment and motivation.
• When there is time	Using participation takes time; legitimate deadlines and time pressures precludes seeking extensive participation.
• When the leader and followers are ready and the organizational culture is supportive	Participation can only succeed if both leader and followers agree to its benefits, are trained in how to use it, and are committed to its success. The organizational culture has to encourage or at least tolerate employee participation.
• When interaction among leader and followers is not restricted by the task, structure, or environment	Participation requires interaction among leaders and followers; such interaction is only possible if there are no restrictions due to factors such as geographic location, structural elements, or task requirement.

SHARING UNIQUE INFORMATION

How can groups benefit from the unique knowledge and information of each of their members? Research suggests that group discussions typically focus on "shared information," which is information that every group member has, instead of making use of "unshared information," which is knowledge that is uniquely held by individual members. However, groups need access to that unshared information to make effective decisions.

Researchers Larson, Foster-Fishman, and Franz studied the leadership style that promotes the sharing of unshared information. In accordance with previous research results, these researchers found that shared information was introduced and used significantly more than unshared information, explaining why group discussion can be a less-than-optimal way of soliciting unique contributions from group members. However, leaders played a key role in information management. Whereas participative leaders encouraged more shared information to surface, it was the directive leaders who brought more unshared information to light both when it was their own and when it came from other group members, even when it disagreed with their own point of view. The directive leaders actively used the unshared information to convince their group members. When directive leaders held correct unshared information, they helped their group make effective decisions; however, when these leaders did not have the best information, their directiveness affected the groups' decision negatively.

The result of this study echo the proposition of resource-utilization contingency models and draw attention to the role of leader in encouraging and managing group members to participate actively in decision-making.

Source: J. R. Larson Jr., P. G. Foster-Fishman, and T. M. Franz, "Leader Style and the Discussion of Sharing and Unshared Information in Decision-Making Groups," *Personality and Social Psychology Bulletin* 24, no. 5 (1998): 482–495.

Airline pilots and other employees, Kiwi promised not to repeat any of Eastern's mistakes and aimed at creating a family atmosphere for all its employees. The employees were all owners with varying degrees of shares and the corresponding pride and desire for involvement, control, and commitment that come from ownership. All decisions were made with full participation. All employees, regardless of levels, pitched in to get the job done and deliver the quality service that soon earned Kiwi honors in surveys of airline quality. The airline quickly grew to more than 1,000 employees with over 60 daily flights. One of the pilot-founders and then chairman of Kiwi, Robert W. Iverson, attributed the stunning growth and success to the employees' commitment and the organization's egalitarian culture. Kiwi was truly a symbol of the benefits of participation and involvement.

In 1994, the bubble burst. Kiwi's board, which included fellow founders and owners, booted Iverson out of office. This event revealed serious management and organizational deficiencies within the airline. The dark side of participation was an amazing lack of concern for management decisions. Many employee-owners failed to follow management directives if they did not agree with them. Employees demanded input in every decision, a factor that led to stagnation in decision-making and an inability to act to solve problems. Iverson admitted, "One of the stupidest things I ever did was call everybody owners. . . . An owner is somebody who thinks he can exercise gratuitous control." The case of Kiwi Airlines demonstrates the ineffective use of participation. Many of the decisions in which employees participated could have been handled more effectively and efficiently by a few managers.

THE ROLE OF CULTURE

An additional factor when considering the use of participation is national cultural values. Factors such as collectivism, power distance (Hofstede 1996) and cross-cultural organizational cultures (Trompenaars 1994) impact whether leaders can use participation successfully. For example, Japanese culture, with its strong emphasis on conformity, consensus, and collectivity at the expense of individual goals (Chen 1995), supports the use of participative management despite relatively high power distance. Participation in Japan is a mix of group harmony and consensus, with elements of directive leadership (Dorfman et al. 1997). Mexico is also relatively high on collectivism, power distance, and masculinity. The Mexican culture, however, has a well-established tradition of autocratic leadership without a history of participative leadership (Dorfman et al. 1997). In such a cultural context, neither the leader nor the followers find participation desirable. Similarly, in cross-cultural organizational cultures that Trompenaars labels the Eiffel Tower—France, for example—the focus is on performance through obedience and respect for legitimate authority (Trompenaars 1994). In such an environment, a leader is ascribed great authority and is expected to know much; asking for subordinate participation may easily be perceived as weakness and lack of leadership ability.

Cultures such as the United States and Australia that have relatively egalitarian power distributions but are also highly individualistic pose a different challenge. The low power distance allows for participation, but the value placed on individual autonomy and individual contribution may be an obstacle to cooperation in a team environment. In addition, what are considered appropriate team behaviors may also vary considerably from one culture to another (Kanter and Corn 1993). An effective team member in Japan is above all courteous and cooperative, members avoid conflict and confrontation (Zander 1983). In the United States, effective team members speak their mind, pull their weight by contributing equally, and participate actively. German employees are taught early in their careers to seek technical excellence. In Afghanistan, a team member is obligated to share his or her resources with others, making generosity an essential team behavior. In Israel, values of hard work and contribution to the community drive kibbutz team members. The Swedes are comfortable with open arguments and will publicly disagree with one another and with their leader. Each culture expects and rewards different types of team behaviors.

These cross-cultural differences in team behavior create considerable challenges for the leadership of culturally diverse teams. Success depends on accurate perceptions and careful reading of cross-cultural cues. Leaders must be flexible and patient and willing to not only listen to others but question their own assumptions. They also need to consider that many behavioral differences have individual rather than cultural sources. The only constant in the successful implementation of teams is the leader's sincere belief in the team's ability to contribute to the organization (Marsick, Turner, and Cederholm 1989). Such belief is necessary regardless of the cultural setting.

What Is the Optimum Team Size?

Team size varied dramatically, from 3 to 25 members, with an average of 8.4. The modal team size was 5. These numbers can be compared to the optimum team size: As we discuss later in the book, teams should generally have fewer than 10 members—more like 5 or 6.

Through our experiences in the industrial age we have learned that bigger is not always better. People cannot relate to large numbers of people, and they often get lost in the impersonality of big organizations. Throughout all business sectors, we now see large organizations beginning to form smaller groups to gain the focus, energy, relationships, and communication found in small companies.

This same issue of size holds true for teams. To be effective, teams need to be small enough to allow people to develop relationships, to provide for participation at meetings, and to engender a feeling of mutual accountability. If the team is too large, members tend to see themselves as having little impact on team outcomes. They feel that it does not matter if they come to the meetings, nor that their particular skills are needed. Or, they may think that the large size of the team makes the process too time consuming or stressful as members vie for air time and recognition.

There are no absolutes for team size, but experience and research have shown that the most effective team size ranges from 4 to 12 people. With

Making the Team: A Guide for Managers, by Leigh L. Thompson. Copyright © 2000 by Prentice Hall, Inc.

Teams: Structure, Process, Culture, and Politics, by Eileen K. Aranda, Luis Aranda, with Kristi Conlon. Copyright © 1998 by Prentice Hall, Inc.

fewer than 4 people, a team lacks perspective. For a complex situation 4 is probably not adequate, though 4 people may form the core of the team. As team membership grows beyond 12 people, it becomes difficult to manage the relationships within the team. Team members break off during meetings and form smaller subgroups. Side conversations predominate, and the group loses focus. Air time also becomes a problem as the team size grows.

Even with only 12 people, each person can speak less than 10 minutes if team meetings last no more than two hours. And, in general, two hours is the maximum a team can meet on a regular basis. After two hours, team members are usually physically tired and intellectually spent. Of course, the reality is that some people speak more than 10 minutes and others speak very little or not at all. The larger the group, the wider the participation gap becomes, and with that, useful communication grows more difficult.

TEAM SIZE

Editor's Note:
Another take on the question of team size. Interesting research in this section.

Does the size of a group affect the group's overall behavior? The answer to this question is a definite "Yes," but the effect depends on what dependent variables you look at.

The evidence indicates, for instance, that smaller groups are faster at completing tasks than are larger ones. However, if the group is engaged in problem solving, large groups consistently get better marks than their smaller counterparts. Translating these results into specific numbers is a bit more hazardous, but we can offer some parameters. Large groups—with a dozen or more members—are good for gaining diverse input. So if the goal of the group is fact-finding, larger groups should be more effective. On the other hand, smaller groups are better at doing something productive with that input. Groups of approximately seven members, therefore, tend to be more effective for taking action.

One of the most important findings related to the size of a group has been labeled **social loafing**. Social loafing is the tendency of group members to do less than they are capable of as individuals. It directly challenges the logic that the productivity of the group as a whole should at least equal the sum of the productivity of each individual in that group.

A common stereotype about groups is that the sense of team spirit spurs individual effort and enhances the group's overall productivity. In the late 1920s, a German psychologist named Ringelmann compared the results of individual and group performance on a rope-pulling task. He expected that the group's effort would be equal to the sum of the efforts of individuals within the group. That is, three people pulling together should exert three times as much pull on the rope as one person, and eight people should exert eight times as much pull. Ringlemann's results, however, did not confirm his expectations. Groups of three people exerted a force only two-and-a-half times the average individual performance. Groups of eight collectively achieved less than four times the solo rate.

Replications of Ringelmann's research with similar tasks have generally supported his findings. Increases in group size are inversely related to indi-

Organizational Behavior: Concepts, Controversies, and Applications, Sixth Edition, by Stephen P. Robbins. Copyright © 1996 by Prentice Hall, Inc.

SOCIAL LOAFING MAY BE A CULTURALLY-BOUND PHENOMENON

Is the social-loafing phenomenon universal? Preliminary evidence suggests not. Let's look at why the social-loafing effect is probably consistent with a highly individualistic society like the United States and not collectivist societies like Japan or the People's Republic of China.

An individualistic culture is dominated by self-interest. Social loafing is likely to occur in such cultures because it will maximize an individual's personal gain. But social loafing shouldn't appear in collective societies since individuals in such cultures are motivated by in-group goals rather than self-interest. Work group members in countries like Japan will work to attain their group's collective goals regardless of the identifiability of their inputs. That is, they view their actions as a component essential to the group's goal attainment.

As noted, the preliminary evidence confirms this logic. A comparison of managerial trainees from the United States and the People's Republic of China found that the social-loafing effect surfaced among the Americans but not among the Chinese. The Chinese didn't demonstrate any social-loafing effect and, in fact, appeared to actually perform better in a group than when working alone.

What this research suggests is that social loafing does not appear in all cultural settings. Predominantly studied by American researchers, it seems to be most applicable to such highly individualistic countries as the United States. As a result, the implications for OB of this effect on work groups need to be qualified to reflect cultural differences. In highly collectivistic societies, managers should feel comfortable in using groups even if individual efforts cannot be readily identified.

---

vidual performance. More may be better in the sense that the total productivity of a group of four is greater than that of one or two people, but the individual productivity of each group member declines.

What causes this social loafing effect? It may be due to a belief that others in the group are not pulling their own weight. If you see others as lazy or inept, you can reestablish equity by reducing your effort. Another explanation is the dispersion of responsibility. Because the results of the group cannot be attributed to any single person, the relationship between an individual's input and the group's output is clouded. In such situations, individuals may be tempted to become "free riders" and coast on the group's efforts. In other words, there will be a reduction in efficiency where individuals think that their contribution cannot be measured.

The implications for OB of this effect on work groups are significant. Where managers utilize collective work situations to enhance morale and teamwork, they must also provide means by which individual efforts can be identified. If this is not done, management must weigh the potential losses in productivity from using groups against any possible gains in worker satisfaction.

The research on group size leads us to two additional conclusions: (1) groups with an odd number of members tend to be preferable to those with an even number; and (2) groups made up of five or seven members do a pretty good job of exercising the best elements of both small and large groups. Having an odd number of members eliminates the possibility of ties when votes are taken. And groups made up of five or seven members are large enough to form a majority and allow for diverse input, yet small enough to avoid the negative outcomes often associated with large groups, such as domination by a few members, development of subgroups, inhibited participation by some members, and excessive time taken to reach a decision.

$\mathcal{H}$ow Should Members Be Selected?

$\mathcal{G}$roup Member Resources

A group's potential level of performance is, to a large extent, dependent on the resources that its members individually bring to the group. In this section, we want to look at two resources that have received the greatest amount of attention: abilities and personality characteristics.

ABILITIES

Part of a group's performance can be predicted by assessing the task-relevant and intellectual abilities of its individual members. Sure, it's true that we occasionally read about the athletic team composed of mediocre players who, because of excellent coaching, determination, and precision teamwork, beat a far more talented group of players. But such cases make the news precisely because they represent an aberration. As the old saying goes, "The race doesn't always go to the swiftest nor the battle to the strongest, but that's the way to bet." A group's performance is not merely the summation of its individual members' abilities. However, these abilities set parameters for what members can do and how effectively they will perform in a group.

What predictions can we make regarding ability and group performance? First, evidence indicates that individuals who hold crucial abilities for attaining the group's task tend to be more involved in group activity, generally contribute more, are more likely to emerge as the group leaders, and are more satisfied if their talents are effectively utilized by the group. Second, intellectual ability and task-relevant ability have both been found to be related to overall group performance. However, the correlation is not particularly high, suggesting that other factors, such as the size of the group, the type of tasks being performed, the actions of its leader, and level of conflict within the group, also influence performance.

PERSONALITY CHARACTERISTICS

There has been a great deal of research on the relationship between personality traits and group attitudes and behavior. The general conclusion is that attributes that tend to have a positive connotation in our culture tend to be positively related to group productivity, morale, and cohesiveness. These include traits such as sociability, self-reliance, and independence. In contrast, negatively evaluated characteristics such as authoritarianism, dominance, and unconventionality tend to be negatively related to the dependent variables. These personality traits affect group performance by strongly influencing how the individual will interact with other group members.

Is any one personality characteristic a good predictor of group behavior? The answer to that question is "No." The magnitude of the effect of any *single* characteristic is small, but taking personality characteristics *together*, the consequences for group behavior are of major significance. We can conclude, therefore, that personality characteristics of group members play an important part in determining behavior in groups.

*C*omposition

Most group activities require a variety of skills and knowledge. Given this requirement, it would be reasonable to conclude that heterogeneous groups—those composed of dissimilar individuals—would be more likely to have diverse abilities and information and should be more effective. Research studies substantiate this conclusion.

When a group is heterogeneous in terms of personalities, opinions abilities, skills, and perspectives, there is an increased probability that the group will possess the needed characteristics to complete its tasks effectively. The group may be more conflict-laden and less expedient as diverse positions are introduced and assimilated, but the evidence generally supports the conclusion that heterogeneous groups perform more effectively than do those that are homogeneous.

An offshoot of the composition issue has recently received a great deal of attention by group researchers. This is the degree to which members of a group share a common demographic attribute, such as age, sex, race, educational level, or length of service in the organization, and the impact of this attribute on turnover. We'll call this variable **group demography**.

Here we consider the same type of factors, but in a group context. That is, it is not whether a person is male or female or has been employed with the organization a year rather than ten years that concerns us now, but rather the individual's attribute in relationship to the attributes of others with whom he or she works. Let's work through the logic of group demography, review the evidence, and then consider the implications.

Groups and organizations are composed of **cohorts**, which we define as individuals who hold a common attribute. For instance, everyone born in 1960 is of the same age. This means they also have shared common experiences. People born in 1960 have experienced the women's movement, but not the Korean conflict. People born in 1945 shared the Vietnam War, but not the Great Depression. Women in organizations today who were born before 1945 matured prior to the women's movement and have had substantially different experiences from women born after 1960. Group demographics therefore, suggests that such attributes as age or the date that someone joins a specific work group or organization should help us to predict turnover. Essentially, the logic goes like this: Turnover will be great among those with dissimilar experiences because communication is more difficult. Conflict and power struggles are more likely, and more severe when they occur. The increased conflict makes group membership less attractive, so employees are more likely to quit. Similarly, the losers in a power struggle are more apt to leave voluntarily or be forced out.

Several studies have sought to test this thesis, and the evidence is quite encouraging. For example, in departments or separate work groups where a large portion of members entered at the same time, there is considerably more turnover among those outside this cohort. Also, where there are large gaps between cohorts, turnover is higher. People who enter a group or an organization together, or at approximately the same time, are more likely to associate with one another, have a similar perspective on the group organization, and thus be more likely to stay. On the other hand, discontinuities or bulges in the group's date-of-entry distribution is likely to result in higher turnover rate within that group.

The implication of this line of inquiry is that the composition of a group may be an important predictor of turnover. Differences per se may not predict turnover. But large differences within a single group will lead to turnover. If everyone is moderately dissimilar from everyone else in a group the feelings of being an outsider are reduced. So, it's the degree of dispersal on an attribute, rather than the level, that matters most. We can speculate that variance within a group in respect to attributes other than date of entry, such as social background, sex differences, and levels of education might similarly create discontinuities or bulges in the distribution that will encourage some members to leave. To extend this idea further, the fact that a group member is a female may, in itself, mean little in predicting turnover. In fact, if the work group is made up of nine women and one man, we'd be more likely to predict that the lone male would leave. In the executive ranks of organizations, however, where females are in the minority, we would predict that this minority status would increase the likelihood that female managers would quit.

roup Processes

The next component of our group behavior model considers the processes that go on within a work group—the communication patterns used by members for information exchanges, group decision processes, leader behavior, power dynamics, conflict interactions, and the like.

Why are processes important to understanding work group behavior? One way to answer this question is to return to the topic of social loafing. We found that one-plus-one-plus-one doesn't necessarily add to three. In group tasks where each member's contribution is not clearly visible, there is a tendency for individuals to decrease their effort. Social loafing, in other words, illustrates a process loss as a result of using groups. But group processes can also produce positive results. That is, groups can create outputs greater than the sum of their inputs. Figure 1-3 illustrates how group processes can impact on a group's actual effectiveness.

Synergy is a term used in biology that refers to an action of two or more substances that results in an effect that is different from the individual summation of the substances. We can use the concept to better understand group processes.

Social loafing, for instance, represents negative synergy. the whole is less than the sum of the parts. On the other hand, research teams are often used in research laboratories because they can draw on the diverse skills of various individuals to produce more meaningful research as a group than could be generated by all of the researchers working independently. That is, they produce positive synergy. Their process gains exceed their process losses.

roup Tasks

Imagine, for a moment, that there are two groups at a major oil company. The job of the first is to consider possible location sites for a new refinery. The decision is going to affect people in many areas of the company—production, engineering, marketing, distribution, personnel, purchasing, real estate development, and the like—so key people from each of these areas will need to provide input into the decision. The job of the second group is to coordinate the building of the refinery after the site has been selected, the design finalized, and the financial arrangements completed. Research on group effectiveness tells us that management would be well advised to use a larger group for the first task than for the second. The reason is that large groups facilitate pooling of information. The addition of a diverse perspective to a problem-solving committee typically results in a process gain. But when a group's task is coordinating and implementing a decision, the process loop created by each additional member's presence is likely to be greater than the process gain he or she makes. So the size-performance relationship is moderated by the group's task requirements.

FIGURE 1-3

Effects of Group Processes

The preceding conclusions can be extended: The impact of group processes on the group's performance and member satisfaction is also moderated by the tasks that the group is doing. The evidence indicates that the complexity and interdependence of tasks influence the group's effectiveness.

Tasks can be generalized as either simple or complex. Complex tasks are ones that tend to be novel or nonroutine. Simple ones are routine and standardized. We would hypothesize that the more complex the task, the more the group will benefit from discussion among members on alternative work methods. If the task is simple, group members don't need to discuss such alternatives. They can rely on standardized operating procedures for doing the job. Similarly, if there is a high degree of interdependence among the tasks that group members must perform, they'll need to interact more. Effective communication and minimal levels of conflict, therefore, should be more relevant to group performance when tasks are interdependent.

These conclusions are consistent with what we know about information-processing capacity and uncertainty. Tasks that have higher uncertainty—those that are complex and interdependent—require more information processing. This, in turn, puts more importance on group processes. So just because a group is characterized by poor communication, weak leadership, high levels of conflict, and the like, it doesn't necessarily mean that it will be low-performing. If the group's tasks are simple and require little interdependence among members, the group still may be effective.

*T*eam Membership

Perhaps the most important decision we make in initiating teams is how we determine the composition of team membership. We often choose team members on the basis of proximity or position, neither of which innately adds strength to the team. A proximity error occurs when we use criteria like seniority, association, or location as the basis for membership. A consequence of such selection criteria is that teams routinely have the same people on them. This results in having those same people using the same perspectives, coming up with the same ideas, and suggesting the same resolutions.

Membership based on proximity also often causes or exacerbates divisions within the organization. For example, the home office usually has more representation on a team because they are close together and do not have to travel. This deprives the home office of views from the field and keeps the field personnel from developing positive relationships with those in the home office. Suspicion, indifference, and sometimes hostility are common feelings across field office and home office boundaries. How teams are put together creates or intensifies these feelings. Teams provide a fine opportunity to bring people with disparate views together to build relationships and develop workable resolutions to problems. We need to maximize that potential in teams by carefully defining team membership.

Position is another composition decision we make when putting a team together. We tend to put people from the same levels in the organization together on the team. Again, this limits our perspective. The rationale often

Editor's Note:
A slightly different view on choosing members. Again, though, diversity is stressed.

used for this composition error is that people are more free to talk when they are at the same level. They may be more free to talk, but have we lessened the value of their conversation? Information from above and below the level of team members is usually vital to the acceptance of the decisions it will make. In addition, the active participation of a senior-level team member often gives credence to the work of the team. Inclusion of subordinates in the team gives important perspectives and provides an opportunity for development of the subordinate team member. If there are power problems within teams comprised of various levels in the organization, we need to learn the process and participation skills necessary to work effectively together. Senior people can learn not to intimidate and dominate in a group, and less-senior people can learn to speak their minds and develop new skills. If we do not learn these skills, teams will only perpetuate a shortcoming of hierarchy and reinforce the suspicion between levels in the organization.

The most important aspect of deciding team composition, then, is to look for *contribution* to the team purpose rather than convenience of meeting or balance of power. As team members are chosen, the key questions to ask are:

- What different kinds of information does the team need to work effectively? *Who can provide that information?*

- What skills does the team need? *Who can bring these skills to the team or who is willing to develop them?*

- What cross-functional bridges can be built with this team? *Who needs to be on the team to make this happen?*

- How can the team be a learning/development tool for members? *Who can facilitate this learning on the team?*

- How can the team build relationships among people who do not often work together? *Who should be included in the team from outside the usual membership pool?*

SECTION 2

Getting Started

Introduction

It may seem obvious to most of us but I'll say it anyway: creating an effective team, one that gets done what it's supposed to get done, doesn't just happen. Yet, considering the way many organizations approach teaming, it appears that very often, management just doesn't get it.

Most often, it is because management is ignorant of how teams work and what it takes for them to be effective. Understanding team "process" is essential if we hope to get the teams we create, lead, or serve on to achieve what they were created to achieve. Numerous researchers and management scientists have attempted to describe the process teams go through. In this section, a few of the better-known process models are presented that range from the simple to the sophisticated.

These models teach several key lessons. For example, teams have a life cycle—identifiable phases or stages they go through. Sometimes teams get stuck early in the process and spend undue amounts of time and effort in "wheel-spinning." When this happens they fail or, at the very least, don't achieve their potential. Either way, the result is the failure of the larger organization to perform at its potential. Finally, and possibly most important, the managers responsible for creating workplace teams can, if they will pay the price, create teams that have a much greater likelihood of achieving their potential.

The way to accomplish this is by making sure the team is properly "chartered." A team charter is the recipe or roadmap for its success. It is the crucial point in the beginning of the process when management spells out the purpose, marks out the boundaries, identifies the resources available, and counts the costs. It is the chance for the team members to align their purposes, identify barriers and potential conflicts, document their commitment, and chart the path ahead.

The importance of this discipline can't be overemphasized. It is clearly the most important step in the team process. The quality of nearly everything that follows will depend in great part on the amount of thought and effort management and team members put into it. Ironically, consciously building a team charter often receives the lowest investment of intellectual effort. Perhaps that is because we see the results we want and desire to "get on with things" and chartering takes time. Or, perhaps, management simply doesn't know there is such a thing or understand how truly critical it is.

The next portion of Section Two deals with the team chartering process. It just may be the most important segment of Team Tools.

Is There a Predictable Process Teams Go Through?

Stages of Group Development

For twenty years or more, we thought that most groups followed a specific sequence in their evolution and that we knew what that sequence was. But we were wrong. Recent research indicates that there is no standardized pattern of group development. In this section, we'll review the better-known five-stage model of group development, and then the recently discovered punctuated-equilibrium model.

THE FIVE-STAGE MODEL

From the mid-1960s, it was believed that groups passed through a standard sequence of five stages. As shown in Figure 2-1, these five stages have been labeled *forming, storming, norming, performing,* and *adjourning.*

The first stage, **forming**, is characterized by a great deal of uncertainty about the group's purpose, structure, and leadership. Members are "testing the waters" to determine what types of behavior are acceptable. This stage is complete when members have begun to think of themselves as part of a group.

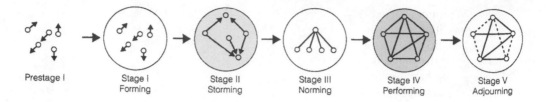

FIGURE 2-1

Stages of Group Development

The **storming** stage is one of intragroup conflict. Members accept the existence of the group, but there is resistance to the constraints that the group imposes on individuality. Further, there is conflict over who will control the group. When this stage is complete, there will be a relatively clear hierarchy of leadership within the group.

The third stage is one in which close relationships develop and the group demonstrates cohesiveness. There is now a strong sense of group identity and camaraderie. This **norming** stage is complete when the group structure solidifies and the group has assimilated a common set of expectations of what defines correct member behavior.

The fourth stage is **performing**. The structure at this point is fully functional and accepted. Group energy has moved from getting to know and understand each other to performing the task at hand.

For permanent work groups, performing is the last stage in their development. However, for temporary committees, task forces, teams, and similar groups that have a limited task to perform, there is an **adjourning** stage. In this stage, the group prepares for its disbandment. High task performance is no longer the group's top priority. Instead, attention is directed toward wrapping up activities. Responses of group members vary in this stage. Some are upbeat, basking in the group's accomplishments. Others may be depressed over the loss of camaraderie and friendships gained during the work group's life.

Many interpreters of the five-stage model have assumed that a group becomes more effective as it progresses through the first four stages. While this assumption may be generally true, what makes a group effective is more complex than this model acknowledges. Under some conditions, high levels of conflict are conducive to high group performance. So we might expect to find situations where groups in Stage II outperform those in Stages III or IV. Similarly, groups do not always proceed clearly from one stage to the next. Sometimes, in fact, several stages go on simultaneously, as when groups are storming and performing at the same time. Groups even occasionally regress to previous stages. Therefore, even the strongest proponents of this model do not assume that all groups follow its five-stage process precisely or that Stage IV is always the most preferable.

THE PUNCTUATED-EQUILIBRIUM MODEL

Studies of more than a dozen field and laboratory task force groups confirmed that groups don't develop in a universal sequence of stages. But the *timing* of when groups form and change the way they work is highly consistent. Specifically, it's been found that (1) the first meeting sets the group's direction; (2) the first phase of group activity is one of inertia; (3) a transition takes place at the end of the first phase, which occurs exactly when the group has used up half its allotted time; (4) the transition initiates major changes; (5) a second phase of inertia follows the transition; and (6) the group's last meeting is characterized by markedly accelerated activity. These findings are shown in Figure 2-2.

The first meeting sets the group's direction. A framework of behavioral patterns and assumptions through which the group will approach its project emerges in this first meeting. These lasting patterns can appear as early as the first few seconds of the group's life.

Once set, the group's direction becomes "written in stone" and is unlikely to be reexamined throughout the first half of the group's life. This is a period of inertia—that is, the group tends to stand still or become locked into a fixed course of action. Even if it gains new insights that challenge initial patterns and assumptions, the group is incapable of acting on these new insights in Phase 1.

One of the more interesting discoveries made in these studies was that each group experienced its transition at the same point in its calendar—precisely halfway between its first meeting and its official deadline—despite the fact that some groups spent as little as an hour on their project while others spent six months. It was as if the groups universally experienced a midlife crisis at this point. The midpoint appears to work like an alarm clock, heightening members' awareness that their time is limited and that they need to "get moving."

This transition ends Phase 1 and is characterized by a concentrated burst of changes, dropping of old patterns, and adoption of new perspectives. The transition sets a revised direction for Phase 2.

Phase 2 is a new equilibrium or period of inertia. In this phase, the group executes plans created during the transition period.

The group's last meeting is characterized by a final burst of activity to finish its work.

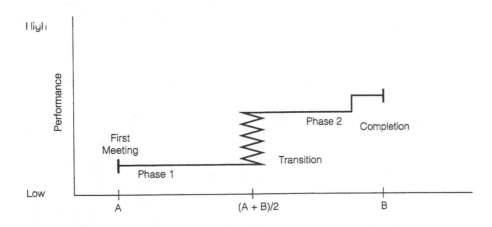

FIGURE 2-2

The Punctuated-Equilibrium Model

We can use this model to describe some of your experiences with student teams created for doing group term projects. At the first meeting, a basic timetable is established. Members size up one another. They agree they have nine weeks to do their project. The instructor's requirements are discussed and debated. From that point, the group meets regularly to carry out its activities. About four or five weeks into the project, however, problems are confronted. Criticism begins to be taken seriously. Discussion becomes more open. The group reassesses where it's been and aggressively moves to make necessary changes. If the right changes are made, the next four or five weeks find the group developing a first-rate project. The group's last meeting, which will probably occur just before the project is due, lasts longer than the others. In it, all final issues are discussed and details resolved.

In summary, the punctuated-equilibrium model characterizes groups as exhibiting long periods of inertia interspersed with brief revolutionary changes triggered primarily by their members' awareness of time and deadlines. Or, to use the terminology of the five-stage group development model, the group begins by combining the forming and norming stages, then goes through a period of low performing, followed by storming, then a period of high performing, and, finally, adjourning.

THE THREE-STAGE MODEL

Developing an effective team process is evolutionary. It begins with the first team meeting and, if the process is effective, continues to evolve and improve. Below is a diagram of the evolution the team process goes through. Note that for an effective team, the process evolves in a circular way, continually renewing into a spiral of increasing performance.

Effective teams go through three basic phases: formation, development, and renewal. In the formation stage, the team does the ground-breaking work of deciding on a task and agreeing to basic rules of operation. The development phase allows the team to make progress toward the task and get comfortable with the meeting process and one another. In the transformation phase, the team uses task information and participant cohesion to move itself into innovation and creative problem solving. The renewal phase allows the team to mature and improve, and it is able to take on more complexity—either within the current task or with a new task. Increased complexity requires the team to reexamine its purpose and process, and the team begins the cycle anew—except on a higher plane. And so the process continues with the effective team growing and developing, able to handle more complex and difficult issues and continuing to add value to the organization.

Between each stage there is a breakpoint (see Figure 2-3). These breakpoints represent plateaus that teams commonly reach in their evolution. Teams have a tendency to stall on these plateaus, continually reworking old issues, solutions, and behaviors. To continue to improve, the team must break through the current phase into the next more demanding one.

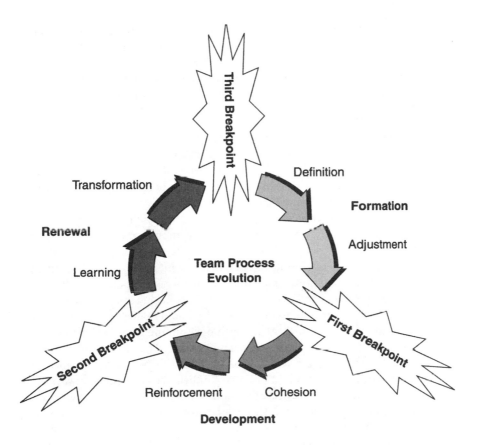

FIGURE 2-3

Evolution of a Team

PHASE 1: FORMATION

Definition

The team begins its evolution at the point of formation. All team members are together for the first time, and their initial task is to define what they want to accomplish and how they will operate as a team. We have discussed the value and method of purposing. We learned that team members need to validate and clarify the reason why they are coming together and what they hope to accomplish. The team then needs to set goals and establish measures to assure both progress and achievement in the team's work. As stressed earlier, teams will benefit if they take the time needed to purpose well, for without a clear task definition the team will not perform well.

In this section of the book we will discuss process definition for the team. Ground rules define the way the team will operate. They focus on developing and maintaining relationships with those outside and inside the team, and on principles and procedures for day-to-day functioning of the team.

Without these ground rules, the team wastes time and energy, and it is faced with deciding how to do things over and over again. In addition, without ground rules team meetings and activities often result in conflict over misunderstandings in expectations. Clear ground rules give all team members a common platform for participation and decision-making.

Adjustment

The second part of the formation phase is adjustment. Both task goals and process rules tend to be made under a mantle of idealism. As the demands of the task and personalities of team members unfold, the team needs to clarify and adjust its expectations. Task issues at this point tend to revolve around deadlines and the scope of the work. Team members have, by this time, put the team charge in context with their other responsibilities. It is time for a reality check to clarify what the team can accomplish and within what time frames.

Adjustment in ground rules takes on an internal focus. Given that the dates and times of meetings and that initial interaction procedures have been set, the team now becomes concerned with managing internal relationships. Preparation for meetings and the quality and quantity of participation in them are common issues. As leadership within the team begins to develop, power and position struggles are not uncommon. The more the team is structured toward being self-led, the more volatile this period can be since there is not a designated leader to resolve conflict. Tension almost always exists among team members during this adjustment period, for team members are struggling to find their place in a new environment. In fact, tension is so natural that absence of tension should be a cause for concern. It may well indicate that team members have withdrawn or that they are disinterested and unwilling to expend the effort to bring this collection of individuals into a team. Apathy is a more dangerous enemy to the team in this phase than is tension.

The adjustment phase of evolution comes to a breakpoint when the team gets mired down in arguments about what to do and who should do what. When team meetings rehash old issues or when people do not meet their deadlines or keep their promises, blaming becomes the norm. Teams need to push through this adjustment phase. They do this by setting clear *short-term* goals, celebrating early successes, putting ground rules in concrete form with a charter and rituals, and by confronting those who violate the common rules. The break-through strategy, then, is one of clarity and firmness. The team must agree that their charge is serious business and that they will hold themselves and one another accountable for the team's success. If the team does not break through this phase, it will deplete its energy by going in circles. Slowly members will stop attending meetings, and the team will remain a team in name only.

PHASE 2: DEVELOPMENT

Cohesion

For those teams that pass through the formation phase, the next phase is development, which focuses on building cohesion and reinforcing team purpose. Having settled the process disputes and experienced some success, the team is making progress. This phase is characterized by interest and energy.

In the cohesion phase, attention focuses on task, teammates accommodate one another's peculiarities, and the team begins to gel. Team members tend to be supportive of one another's ideas. Ground-rule issues revolve around participation. The team wants to improve its internal processes and to make sure that team members feel accepted. In parallel fashion, task issues deal with work methods. Team members are working together, gathering information, and making decisions in a spirit of cooperation and continuous improvement. Life in the team is good. Team members begin to identify with the team, and team members develop important relationships.

Reinforcement

In the reinforcement stage, cohesion builds and homogeneity increases. Team members take on one another's norms, and getting along becomes very important. Ground rules focus on confidentiality and meeting efficiency—anything to protect against stirring up trouble inside the team. Task issues focus on showing a solid front; agreement assures the right course of action. The team's good ideas are remembered and exaggerated.

Reinforcement leads to the second breakpoint for a team. Unlike the first breakpoint that centered on conflict, this one centers on comfort. As the reinforcement stage evolves, it becomes too much of a good thing. The team at this point tends to isolate itself from outsiders—"*they* just don't understand us." The team is likely to suppress disagreement—"we do not have time to disagree," or "we need to get along." The team often loses perspective—"we do not need more information; ours is the best way." With these attitudes, team development comes to a halt. The team loses energy because there are no new things to do; their investment is in self-preservation and self-perpetuation. If the team stays together, it often takes on a siege mentality—"everyone is out to get the team." The result is that the team closes ranks even more and views outsiders suspiciously. Soon the team is lost in irrelevance as the rest of the organization moves on without them.

Teams must break through this second barrier. Team members do this by using their cohesion to take on new issues and to challenge their current problem-solving methods and assumptions. The team lets its confidence foster exploration rather than solidify its position; it lets its trust encourage diversity in ideas. At this point in team development, task goals need to be stretched, outsiders need to be brought into the team, and process goals need to focus on creativity and exploration. The break-through strategy for the development stage is creating the freedom to explore and to change mindsets.

PHASE 3: RENEWAL

Learning

Passing through the second breakpoint, a successful team enters the renewal stage of team evolution. This stage operationalizes the mindset changes that allowed the breakthrough. Since the team is now willing to explore new ways of doing things, it needs to learn new skills. The focus of the team shifts outward, and the new mindset is one of understanding the plethora of issues at hand and embracing the variety of relationships involved in accomplishing its task.

In the learning stage, the team shrugs off the temptation it confronted in the development phase—to reinforce the current way of doing things. The team decides to push beyond its present limits. It may decide to benchmark against a new industry or learn a new technical or process skill. Outsiders become a source of useful information and potential partners, and differing points of view are no longer threatening. Team attention is focused on growing and developing both as individual team members and as a team unit. Positive energy generated in this process brings new comfort and propels the team into developing new ideas and activities, and the team is revitalized. Task assignments take on new life with fresh ideas, and team process becomes more confrontive. Tension in the team returns, but this time it is positive—focused on issues rather than personalities. All this energy is driven by the team for the benefit of the team. Commitment and mutual accountability have become a reality. The team has become high performing, and its potential is awesome.

Transformation

Transformation is the final stage in the cycle of team evolution. The team is at a high energy level with creativity and cohesiveness in sync. Meaningful results are coming from the team's actions. True synergy is displayed in the far-sighted, innovative resolutions the team suggests. In fact, the team seems to have more ideas than it knows what to do with. Once again the team has reached a breakpoint. If the team issues remain the same, the team will get bored. The team tires of working in the same arena; there are only so many meaningful variations to a theme. The team needs a new challenge.

The only way to sustain the energy of the learning stage is to stress and press the team. If the team fails to take on more complex challenges, it will slip back to the comfort of the reinforcement stage. To rally a second time from that comfort is very difficult, so the successful team must take the risk of transformation. Transformation requires challenging all that the team has built: its assumptions, its process, and its purpose. This may mean disbanding the team, changing membership, partnering with a former "enemy," and/or taking on controversial issues. Whatever the new challenge is, it will be a significant departure from the past. It will put the team in a new situation with a new mindset. This is the third breakpoint. If the team can change, it can renew itself and continue to achieve on a higher plane.

An example of a team positioned for transition is the process team described earlier in the book. The order entry team chose to form a cross-functional team from the units involved in order entry. They were in a middle-ground position; that is, they were willing to include all members of the order-fulfillment process but were unwilling to include those departments outside order processing, specifically manufacturing and accounting. For this team, if it is able to get through the evolution process in its unit redesign task, its transformation challenge could be to take on the entire product delivery process. Having accomplished the restructuring of one process, they would likely be ready to take on a larger, more complex task. They might even provide that very traditional organization its first venture into a self-led process team!

In their book *Built to Last*, Jim Collins and Jerry Porras talk about organizations that endure. Their research showed that survivors have several things
in common, including strong core ideologies, an impatience with the status
quo, a willingness to practice self-reflection and to challenge their assumptions, and an eagerness to take on the big issues. "Built to last" companies are
confident, risky, robust entities. The same can be said of teams that endure.
Core ideologies that include trust, mutual accountability, and commitment
drive the team to think well, interact effectively, and take on serious issues. The
team's process enables it to grow and develop. The team that pays close attention to process evolution and has the courage to push through breakpoints,
has the best chance to reach excellence and to endure.

In this section of the book, we will deal with several aspects of an evolv-
ing team process. We will discuss the ground rules that the team must set to
define and protect the practices it wants to follow. These ground rules help
the team to define itself. Ground rules also provide the mechanism for the
team to adjust both its task objectives and progress as well as its process goals.

In the later chapters in this section, we will discuss the rules of participation that help a team balance member contributions. Effective means of
participation allow the team to become cohesive. Team members have a forum
for sharing their ideas, and support and cooperation are fostered. Once the
team has developed a level of trust, participation can allow the team to learn
new conservation skills and to draw out multiple perspectives on an issue.
Effective participation within the team can build the security needed in the
development phase and then permit the break-through into renewal.

Finally, we will explore the key reason for the existence of a team—
decision-making. For successful teams, decision-making is a caldron of controversy, diversity, creativity, and trust. It is not a peaceful process. It is a
rough-and-tumble romp into new ideas and risky goals. The tension is high,
but so is the camaraderie. To reach this level of effective decision-making,
the team must mind its process, develop key problem-solving skills, and foster key attitudes on creativity and innovation. In the next three chapters, we
will discuss both the methods of effective decision-making needed in the
development phase and the new thinking needed for the renewal phase.

A DIFFERENT FIVE-STAGE MODEL

Teams go through predictable stages of development if they are well facilitated. First, in the introducing stage, team members need to get to know each
other. Expectations and needs of all team members must be described and discussed. This discussion can be accomplished with the expectations check
technique, a process in which team members describe what a team success
would look like. At this point team members get a chance to describe their
personal needs concerning the team. Ground rules must also be discussed
and defined to gain consensus on prescribed ways of behaving. Icebreakers are
useful to initiate conversations among team members. Illustrations of these
techniques will be detailed later in the chapter.

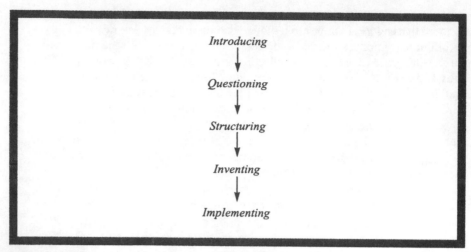

FIGURE 2-4

Stages of Team Development

During the second stage, called questioning, the team defines current problems that need to be resolved. Utilizing a series of questions, the team achieves clarification of the problem. Some of the questions are:

What was observed that told us we have a problem?

How big was the problem?

When was the problem observed?

Where did the problem occur?

What is the effect of the problem on the organization?

PROBLEM STATEMENT

1. What was observed?

   Equipment operators didn't report to work.

2. What is the magnitude of the problem?

   Fifteen percent of the operators are absent, which is a 40 percent increase over last year's absenteeism.

3. When was the problem observed?

   Mondays and Fridays.

4. Where did the problem occur?

   Mixing area and Extrusion area.

5. What is the effect? (Cost to the company the problem creates)

   We had to increase two half-time employees to full-time status to cover these absences. Each employee makes $19/hr ¥ 20 hr/week ¥ 52 weeks ¥ 2 employees = $39,520 per year. Benefits are required for full-time employees and not for part-time employees. Benefits are about 30 percent of the total salary. Full-time salary for one employee is $39,520 ¥ .30 percent ¥ 2 employees = $23,712 benefit cost. The total cost is $63,232 per year.

Poorly constructed problem statement:

We have an absenteeism problem with our employees.

A comprehensive problem statement:

Fifteen percent of the equipment operators did not report to work last month on Mondays and Fridays. This is a 40 percent increase over last year with a cost of over $63,000.

Other tools such as the Know/Don't Know chart and the Is/Is Not chart are useful to help define the problems that the team should address.

Stage three is called structuring. In this stage the team should define the path forward to address the problem. A flow chart is useful to plan the team steps and to identify appropriate problem-solving tools at each step.

In the inventing stage, stage four, the team must determine how to solve the problem they have described. The invention of the solution requires the use of creative problem-solving tools. Then, a specific course of action must be determined from among the alternatives. Finally, the action plan is completed in the implementing stage, when specific action steps, individual responsibilities, time frames, resources needed, and tracking mechanisms must be identified. At this point, the planning becomes reality and desired outcomes can be achieved.

$\mathcal{N}$orms

Did you ever notice that golfers don't speak while their partners are putting on the green or that employees don't criticize their bosses in public? This is because of **"norms."**

All groups have established norms; that is, acceptable standards of behavior that are shared by the group's members. Norms tell members what they ought and ought not do under certain circumstances. From an individual's standpoint, they tell what is expected of you in certain situations. When agreed to and accepted by the group, norms act as a means of influencing the behavior of group members with a minimum of external controls. Norms differ among groups, communities, and societies, but they all have them.

Formalized norms are written up in organizational manuals setting out rules and procedures for employees to follow. By far, the majority of norms in organizations are informal. You do not need someone to tell you that throwing paper airplanes or engaging in prolonged gossip sessions at the water cooler are unacceptable behaviors when the "big boss from New York" is touring the office. Similarly, we all know that when we are in an employment interview discussing what we did not like about our previous job, there are certain things we should not talk about (difficulty in getting along with co-workers or our supervisor), while it is very appropriate to talk about other things (inadequate opportunities for advancement or unimportant and meaningless work). Evidence suggest that even high school students recognize that in such interviews certain answers are more socially desirable than others.

Students quickly learn how to assimilate classroom norms. Depending upon the environment created by the instructor, the norms may support unequivocal acceptance of the material suggested by the instructor, or, at the other extreme, students may be expected to question and challenge the instructor on any point that is unclear. For example, in most classroom situations, the norms dictate that one not engage in loud, boisterous discussion that makes it impossible to hear the lecturer, or humiliate the instructor by pushing him or her "too far," even if one has obviously located a weakness in something the instructor has said. Should some in the classroom group behave in such a way as to violate these norms, we can expect pressure to be applied against the deviant members to bring their behavior into conformity with group standards.

COMMON CLASSES OF NORMS

A work group's norms are like an individual's fingerprints—each is unique. Yet there are still some common classes of norms that appear in most work groups.

Probably the most widespread norms deal with *performance-related processes*. Work groups typically provide their members with explicit cues on how hard they should work, how to get the job done, their level of output, appropriate communication channels, and the like. These norms are extremely powerful in affecting an individual employee's performance—they are capable of significantly modifying a performance prediction that was based solely on the employee's ability and level of personal motivation.

A second category of norms encompasses *appearance factors*. This includes things like appropriate dress, loyalty to the work group or organization, when to look busy, and when it's acceptable to goof off. Some organizations have formal dress codes. However, even in their absence, norms frequently develop to dictate the kind of clothing that should be worn to work. Presenting the appearance of loyalty is important in many work groups and organizations. For instance, in many organizations, especially among professional employees and those in the executive ranks, it is considered inappropriate to be openly looking for another job. This concern for demonstrating loyalty, incidentally, often explains why ambitious aspirants to top-management positions in an organization willingly take home at night, come in on weekends, and accept transfers to cities they would otherwise not prefer to live in.

Another class of norms concerns *informal social arrangements*. These norms come from informal work groups and primarily regulate social interactions within the group. With whom group members eat lunch, friendships on and off the job, social games, and the like are influenced by these norms.

A final category of norms relates to *allocation of resources*. These norms can originate in the group or in the organization and cover things like pay assignment of difficult jobs, and allocation of new tools and equipment. In some organizations, for example, new personal computers are distributed equally to all groups. So every department might get five, regardless of the number of people in the department or their need for the computers. In another organization, equipment is allocated to those groups who can make the best use of it. So some departments might get twenty computers and some none. These resource allocation norms can have a direct impact of employee satisfaction and an indirect effect on group performance.

THE "HOW" AND "WHY" OF NORMS

How do norms develop? *Why* are they enforced? A review of the research allows us to answer these questions.

Norms typically develop gradually as group members learn what behaviors are necessary for the group to function effectively. Of course, critical events in the group might short-circuit the process and act quickly to solidify new norms. Most norms develop in one or more of the following four ways: (1) *Explicit statements made by a group member*—often the group's supervisor or a powerful member. The group leader might, for instance, specifically say that no personal phone calls are allowed during working hours or that coffee breaks are to be kept to ten minutes. (2) *Critical events in the group's history*. These set important precedents. A bystander is injured while standing too close to a machine and, from that point on, members of the work group regularly monitor each other to ensure that no one other than the operator gets within five feet of any machine. (3) *Primacy*. The first behavior pattern that emerges in a group frequently sets group expectations. Friendship groups of students often stake out seats near each other on the first day of class and become perturbed if an outsider takes "their" seats in a later class. (4) *Carry-over behaviors from past situations*. Group members bring expectations with them from other groups of which they have been members. This can explain why work groups typically prefer to add new members who are similar to current ones in background and experience. This is likely to increase the probability that the expectations they bring are consistent with those already held by the group.

But groups do not establish or enforce norms for every conceivable situation. The norms that the group will enforce tend to be those that are important to it. But what makes a norm important? (1) *If it facilitates the group's survival*. Groups don't like to fail, so they look to enforce those norms that increase their chances for success. This means that they will try to protect themselves from interference from other groups or individuals. (2) *If it increases the predictability of group members' behaviors*. Norms that increase predictability enable group members to anticipate each other's actions and to prepare appropriate responses. (3) *If it reduces embarrassing interpersonal problems for group members*. Norms are important if they ensure the satisfaction of their members and prevent as much interpersonal discomfort as possible. (4) *If it allows members to express the central values of the group and clarify what is distinctive about the group's identity*. Norms that encourage expression of the group's values and distinctive identity help to solidify and maintain the group.

CONFORMITY

As a member of a group, you desire acceptance by the group. Because of your desire for acceptance, you are susceptible to conforming to the group's norms. There is considerable evidence that groups can place strong pressures on individual members to change their attitudes and behaviors to conform to the group's standard.

Do individuals conform to the pressures of all the groups they belong to? Obviously not, because people belong to many groups and their norms vary. In some cases, they may even have contradictory norms. So what do people do? They conform to the important groups to which they belong or hope to belong. The important groups have been referred to as *reference* groups and are characterized as ones where the person is aware of the others; the person defines himself or herself as a member, or would like to be a member; and the person feels that the group members are significant to him or her. The implication, then, is that *all* groups do not impose equal conformity pressures on their members.

The impact that group pressures for **conformity** can have on an individual member's judgment and attitudes was demonstrated in the now-classic studies by Solomon Asch. Asch made up groups of seven or eight people, who sat in a classroom and were asked to compare two cards held by the experimenter. One card had one line, the other had three lines of varying length. As shown in Figure 2-5, one of the lines on the three-line card was identical to the line on the one-line card. Also as shown in Figure 2-5, this difference in line length was quite obvious; under ordinary conditions, subjects made fewer than one percent errors. The object was to announce aloud which of the three lines matched the single line. But what happens if the members in the group begin to give incorrect answers? Will the pressures to conform result in an unsuspecting subject (USS) altering his or her answers to align with the others? That was what Asch wanted to know. So he arranged the group so that only the USS was unaware that the experiment was "fixed." The seating was prearranged: The USS was placed so as to be the last to announce his or her decision.

The experiment began with several sets of matching exercises. All the subjects give the right answers. On the third set, however, the first subject gives an obviously wrong answer—for example, saying "C" in Figure 2-5. The next subject gives the same wrong answer, and so do the others until it gets to the unknowing subject. He knows "B" is the same as "X," yet everyone has said "C." The decision confronting the USS is this: Do you publicly state a perception that differs from the preannounced position of the others in your

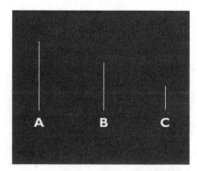

FIGURE 2-5

Examples of Cards Used in Asch Study

group? Or do you give an answer that you strongly believe is incorrect in order to have your response agree with that of the other group members?

The results obtained by Asch demonstrated that over many experiments and many trials, subjects conformed in about thirty-five percent of the trials; that is, the subjects gave answers that they knew were wrong but that were consistent with the replies of other group members.

What can we conclude from this study? The results suggest that there are group norms that press us toward conformity. We desire to be one of the group and avoid being visibly different. We can generalize further to say that when an individual's opinion of objective data differs significantly from that of others in the group, he or she is likely to feel extensive pressure to align his or her opinions to conform with that of the others.

The Key to Team Success: Creating a Team Charter

Who's to Blame?

When something goes wrong in our organizations, the most common response is to find someone to blame. That makes things simple and easy. If we can put the finger on the particular some*one* who messed up, we can go back to doing what we were doing without feeling guilty.

The problem is, of course, that it's not nearly that simple *or* easy. If we were really to understand the situation in all its complexity, we would usually see that no one person is or could be responsible for the failure. There's a saying in the quality improvement field that "every process is perfectly designed to achieve the results it is achieving." This is what Peter Senge was writing about in **The Fifth Discipline**, his now-classic book about the Learning Organization, when he made the point that "structure determines behavior." What Senge meant is that when things are structured in certain ways, the results produced will tend to be the same irrespective of who's in charge or charged with carrying out the task.

When Bad Teams Happen to Good People (with apologies to Rabbi Kushner)

When teams fail in our organizations, we do the same thing. We look around for people or things to blame. People didn't carry their weight. The meetings were a waste of time. We couldn't get past the conflicts. We didn't know what we were supposed to do. Management won't pay any attention to the recommendations anyhow, so why bother. The truth is that when teams fail, the fault often rests with a flawed process for getting them started. We might argue that it is "management's" fault because "they" haven't designed an effective process. But, don't we, as team members, also share responsibility for making our teams successful? By learning the process ourselves, we can go a long way toward building effective teams.

The First Step to Team Success

So what is this first and most important step for creating effective teams? It's called **"Chartering."** Chartering is the process by which the team is formed, its mission or task described, its resources allocated, its goals set, its membership committed, and its plans made. It is the process of "counting the costs" that it will take for a team to achieve its goals and deciding whether the organization is really committed to getting there. A good charter creates a recipe or roadmap for the team as it carries out its charge. It helps members move far more quickly past the "storming" and "norming" phases of the group process and get to the "performing" stage. It can be crucial in helping the group deal with the natural kinds of conflict that can arise at any stage of the team's life. Moreover, it can assist in facilitating the learning of the team and its members as they work to improve the effectiveness of this and future team efforts.

Elements of an Effective Charter

There's a fairly simple logic to building a team charter. Ask yourself questions about all the various conditions, resources, attitudes, and behaviors that will be required in order for the team to accomplish its goals—and answer them. Here's a list of some of the most important questions:

1. **What is the purpose for creating the team?** Research on team effectiveness concludes that the most important contributing factor is a clear and elevating goal. Further, the relationship between goal setting and task performance is probably the most robust finding in the research literature of the behavioral sciences. The more completely the purpose of the team can be identified, the more likely management, team members, and the rest of the organization will support it in accomplishing its objectives.

2. **What kind of team is needed?** One mistake people often make is thinking that a team is just a team. There are different kinds of teams for different kinds of goals. Is the team meant to accomplish a task, manage or improve a process, come up with a new product idea or design, solve a problem, or make a decision?

3. **Will the team be manager led or self-managed?** Who, if anyone, is in charge? That will depend on the task and the maturity of the members. If it is self-managed or leaderless, who will be responsible for facilitating the team's progress toward its goal?

4. **What skills are needed to accomplish the goal?** An inventory of critical knowledge and expertise should be undertaken. It is essential those teams have as members, or have access to others who can be ad hoc resources, and who can supply the necessary competence to achieve the objectives.

5. **How will members be selected?** This is more difficult than it might seem. Often there are internal political, deployment, or logistical barriers. We want the right balance of thinkers and doers. We want people who will follow through. We want to use known resources but develop new competence in the organization. We want enough diversity of opinion to get all the "cards on the table" without creating unnecessary conflict. How will the personalities of the various players fit? Can the company afford to have them take time away from other priorities? Bad choices here can doom the results.

6. **What resources will be necessary to achieve the objectives?** Is management willing to devote the time as well as the financial, human and intellectual capital necessary to get the job done? Counting the costs and deciding that it is worth those costs is crucial. In self-managed or leaderless teams (such as UOP Learning Teams), these are questions that need to be answered by team members both individually and collectively. Are they willing to commit their time, talents, and effort to that goal to the extent necessary?

7. **What are the boundaries?** Management needs to identify the parameters within which the team is expected to operate. How much time will the team be given? How often are the members expected to meet? What is the scope of their concern? (It's sometimes useful when creating process improvement teams to identify change recommendations that are off-limits. For example, it is common for teams to come back with a recommendation that more staff is the solution. By limiting such recommendations, at least at first, the team is forced to look for solutions that deal more with the process.)

8. **What process will the team use to get results?** Once the team has been formed and the members selected, management—and especially the team itself—must determine how it will go about getting the job done. This is the "ground rule" phase and involves deliberately taking charge of the "norming" process. When and where will the team meet? How will it meet (face-to-face or some kind of virtual arrangement)? What maintenance roles will the members agree are important and how will they assign those? How will the members communicate with one another? What happens if a member can't be at a meeting but has an assignment due? What are expectations regarding participation in meetings?

9. **How will we secure equal commitment?** A frank discussion about the level of commitment members are willing to give is key to achieving success. Do they share an equal view as to the importance of the goal? Are they personally willing to expend the effort necessary to get the desired result? What circumstances might limit their ability to perform up to the expectations of others? Getting all this out on the table early on can avoid conflicts down the road.

10. **How will we plan for conflict?** The title of Section Four is *Conflict Happens.* And it does! The best way to minimize the amount of unproductive conflict is to conduct a frank discussion about potential discord. Two of the most common examples of conflict in teams result when members don't pull their weight and follow through on assignments and commitments, or when one or more members try to over-control and dominate the group. By identifying these and other potential conflicts and agreeing beforehand how members will deal with them, a team can minimize the disruption to goal achievement. In essence, you're giving one another permission to do the kind of confrontation that is necessary to get past the conflicts.

11. **What will we do to get the job done? The Project Plan:** Early on, there's a need to analyze the task, break down tasks, establish the timeline, make and accept assignments, and get started. Usually, we make this the first step but it's really the final step of the "chartering" process.

12. **How will we evaluate our success and learn from the process?** How will we know what mid-course corrections need to be made to the process or plan? How will we measure our progress? What can we do to learn from this experience about how not only to make this team better, but future teams: both those we serve on individually and teams the company forms. By planning how and when the team will reflect on the process they are going or have gone through, the individuals, team, and larger organization benefit.

There is a direct proportional relationship between the amount of time and intellectual effort we spend chartering our teams and the likelihood those teams will achieve their goals. Going about this process in a conscious, reflective manner often is the deciding factor in achieving optimal results.

$\mathcal{W}$ork Expectations

The second area for focus with ground rules is work expectations. People join teams with very different ideas about the work involved in being a member of the team. Few people will deliberately perform poorly, but team members need information about the standards of the team. For example, it is common for people to send out information about the topic of a meeting and then never reach that topic at the meeting or never refer to the information provided. If there is not a positive consequence for meeting preparation, participants will not read materials sent prior to meetings.

On the other hand, some meetings ask for people to give their interpretations, opinions, and recommendations based on the material provided prior to the meeting. In this case, participants are very likely to be prepared. Having had either one of these experiences, or any of the various experiences in between, will define what a team member thinks she or he is accountable for in a team meeting.

Common questions teams address in their ground rules involving work expectations include:

- What is the quality of work expected?
- What is the quantity of work expected?
- How is the timeliness of work defined?
- What does it mean to come prepared to a meeting?

As an example of setting work expectation ground rules, let's look at a team that has been brought together to put on a three-day conference. The team members know each other, but they are forming a task team rather than a work team since they represent different departments and will disband when the conference is over. This task team has a wide range of positions represented around the table, including two first-level supervisors, three middle managers, two senior managers, and an outside consultant. With this kind of task team, it is likely that the work expectations will be quite different.

The first issue the team needs to address is the quantity of work expected. This is usually done through task assignments. For this team, task assignments include securing facilities, contacting speakers, designing the program, and putting together a list of those to be invited. If the team is to work well, all members must get real work to do. If the two supervisors get all the assignments and the more-senior people just get reports, resentment will be the result. Fortunately, in this example, the senior managers used their experience and contacts to secure speakers for the conference. The work assignments might have been better if the senior managers had worked with a supervisor so that that person would begin to develop the network skills and resources of the senior managers.

Quality of work proved to be a more difficult issue for this team to address. A team of three members was asked to put together a design for the program. One of the team members turned out to have work expectations substantially different from the other two. At the meeting to which this subgroup was to bring a rough draft of their ideas for conference topics and format for discussion with the entire team, two of the members brought in typed, complete ideas. The third member, however, brought in handwritten, incomplete ideas that appeared to have been put together just minutes before the meeting. Information from the first two members had been duplicated so every team member could view their suggestions. The third member had only his personal copy. The result was that the first two parts of the conference were thoroughly discussed and planned. The third part, however, was dealt with only vaguely, and at the end of the conference, it was clear that the third part was the weakest of the conference.

Hindsight makes it clear that two things should have happened in this meeting. When the assignments were handed out, the expectations for product should have been made clear. At this point it would have been easy for a team member to ask what kind of format the team wanted so that each person knew what was expected. The less desirable alternative would have been to address the issue after the information had come to the meeting. The team might have suggested that the third member complete his ideas and bring the finished information to the next meeting, being very specific about how the information was to be provided.

Not addressing the issue, which is what this team chose to do, does not help the team grow and develop. The members that provided the complete work resented the member who had arrived unprepared, and the rest of the team members probably judged the person harshly as well. In defense of the third member, he may not have understood what the norm was for draft work. Maybe on other teams, handwritten, vaguely formed ideas were the norm. It is always wise to reaffirm work expectations at both the overall team level and with each assignment. It is better to err on repeating what everyone knows is the level of work expected than to have misunderstandings of expectations.

An effective way for ground rules to be reinforced is for the team to reflect regularly on the effectiveness of the current meeting. For example, at the conclusion of meetings, the team can spend a few minutes reflecting on the work level of the meeting. Did the team address the right issues? Did the team possess sufficient and appropriate information to carry on a useful meeting and make necessary decisions? Was everyone able to give their point of view? Did the team explore rather than immediately judge the ideas brought to the table? Is everyone satisfied with the progress and process of the meeting?

The answers to these questions can help to improve the work of the team. From the answers, the team should identify one thing that went well in the meeting and decide how team members could make sure it becomes common practice. On the other hand, team members should also identify one thing that hampered the team's work and decide how to prevent it from happening again. To restate an earlier conclusion, team work does not work effectively without attention and learning. Successful teams continually monitor their performance and make regular adjustments so that they make improvements before the team has serious problems.

*C*onfidentiality

The last issue for team ground rules that we will discuss concerns confidentiality and support. Nothing can destroy trust as quickly in a team than to have team discussions shared with those outside the team. When team members hear summaries of what occurred in the team, they often feel that their comments are misrepresented or misinterpreted or, at the very least, that they would like to speak for themselves. To avoid these problems, team members need to decide how they will represent the meeting discussion to others.

Some teams choose a spokesperson for the team. This is probably wise if the work of the team is both highly complex and highly controversial and if there are specific constituencies that need to receive regular reports. Other teams identify instances when the information they are discussing is confidential and not to be shared outside the team. The expectation is that fellow team members will not share any information on this topic outside the meeting.

As with other ground-rule topics, team members often have very different expectations about confidentiality. Teams, as well as the individual members personally, vary widely in how open they want their discussions to be. Yet it is common for teams to neglect discussing confidentiality until one member has breached the unspoken norm. Dealing with a specific infraction takes the team down the path of accusation and blame, and it is difficult to get back to the guidelines for confidentiality and off the personal conflict. It is necessary to be quite specific when the team sets confidentiality guidelines. It is not sufficient to say that team members should keep the meeting information to themselves. This is too sweeping and presents a dilemma when team member constituents ask questions about the meeting.

To develop useful guidelines the team needs to discuss questions such as the following:

- What topics are to be considered confidential?
- How will team members identify confidential information?
- How should team members treat this information?
- How should team members portray team meetings to outsiders?
- Who should be the spokesperson for the group?
- Who should receive meeting minutes?

The discussion on confidentiality also requires a discussion on enforcement and consequence.

- How will the team address instances where a team member has violated the confidentiality norm?
- What will be the consequence of such an action?

An example of a team that struggled with confidentiality will show the serious impact that these issues can have on team climate and progress. The team in question was charged with designing a new educational program. The team had 10 members drawn from units that would be providing information or presenters to the program. Two of the members were outside the department and were expected to ensure that the new program meshed with other company programs.

The team spent its first few meetings talking about the concepts of the program and how the program was to be implemented. It was agreed that the team wanted to keep the other members of the department aware of its progress. Eventually, the team came to the point of making some decisions about what would be included in the program. Three different models were presented for how the program might be designed. The models were quite different and both the content and delivery of information varied within the models.

As the team discussed the various approaches, it became clear that there was discussion about the various models outside the team. In fact, one unit supervisor wrote a memo to the department head pointedly challenging one of the models on the grounds that his unit would only have a minor representation in the program. One of the outside members came to a team meeting unhappy that he heard that he was the obstacle to accepting one of the models. It was clear the team needed to discuss the issue of confidentiality and information sharing.

While the team had agreed that they wanted to keep members of the department informed, they had not provided a mechanism for doing so. Without a method for providing progress reports, individual team members shared accounts of how the team was doing. Given that each team member had preferences for the content and delivery options being discussed, those accounts were not unbiased. And, given the propensity for people to misunderstand, exaggerate, and add their own opinions, the information about the program development process began to bear little resemblance to what actually occurred in the meetings. In addition, as people outside the team began to take positions, team members were getting pressured from various groups to support one model over another. This pressure led to increasingly hostile team meetings as team members began to take positions and advocate rather than look for ways to build the best program for company needs.

In an effort to preserve both the product and process, the team members came to an agreement on the following ground rules:

1. At the end of each meeting the team would develop a progress report to be distributed to all constituents.

2. The team would immediately develop an options report that set forth the main elements of the three models currently under consideration and that asked all department members for feedback.

3. Once the team came up with a draft program it would hold an open forum to discuss the elements of the proposed program.

4. Outside of the above described information sharing methods, team members would not discuss the different models with outside constituents.

By developing specific methods for dealing with the confidentiality of information, the team was able to protect the support atmosphere of the team. Team members once again felt comfortable voicing opinions, knowing that what they said would remain in the meeting room. By meeting with outside constituencies as a group, the team also developed a sense of mutual accountability for the product and stood together to explain their decisions.

Confidentiality issues are difficult ones for the team to discuss. However, if they are discussed as a regular part of the process of setting ground rules, it is easier for team members to share their views and to set out expectations that will minimize transgressions. If ground rules are clear and agreed to, most people will abide by the rules. If a transgression does occur, the team member is usually contrite and has learned a lesson.

G round Rules

Ground rules are prescriptions for team communication. They must arise from the team and be freely committed to by all team members. First, I offer team members a sheet with a list of common ground rules. I urge the participants to feel free to add their own ground rules and not to be limited by the distributed list. I ask team members to circle two ground rules that are listed or that they make up. My list is as follows:

- Be a good listener.
- Keep an open mind.

- No cheap shots.
- Participate in the discussion.
- Ask for clarification.
- Give everyone a chance to speak.
- Focus on the present and the future, not the past.
- Deal with particular rather than general problems.
- Don't be defensive if your idea is criticized.
- Be prepared to carry out group decisions.
- All comments remain in this room.
- Everyone is an equal in this session (no titles).
- Be polite—don't interrupt.

Once everyone has had a few moments to read the list and make two selections, I ask for a volunteer to share the most important ground rule that he or she chose. In response to the team member's choice, I ask a follow-up question or tell a story that relates to the ground rule. For example, when team members suggest "Be a good listener" or "Keep an open mind," I ask the question, "What do you see when you see someone you judge to be a good listener or open-minded?" I keep asking questions until the team member describes behavioral observations. Some behavioral observations of listening might be, "Looks at me," or, "Writes down what I say." Some behavioral observations for open-mindedness may be, "Makes positive statements about my comment," or, "Gives me some time."

When "No cheap shots" is listed, I mention that there is a difference between having fun with a team member and taking cheap shots. Most team members agree. I also share with the group that I want to have fun at work. Again, generally, the team members agree. Next, I ask, "When does good-natured ribbing turn into a cheap shot?" Someone acknowledges that the turning point is different for each person. However, if we are paying attention, we can see when that turning point occurs. The insulted individual may move back from the table or reduce the number of comments that he or she had been making. If we feel that a peer has taken a comment as a cheap shot, it is our obligation to talk to that person about it, apologize for the insult if necessary, and eliminate that behavior in the future.

Some people know the hot buttons of others in their team and push them regularly. I once knew a mechanic named Timmy in the coal mine who was an expert in locating and pushing others' buttons. One day Timmy, Leroy, and I were eating lunch and Timmy leaned over to me and said, "You know, I can make Leroy throw up." I protested, "So? I don't want to see that." He ignored my protest and proceeded to make some well-planned comments to Leroy. In the matter of moments, Leroy's eyes became big as saucers, and he slapped his hand over his mouth and ran out of the lunch area, true to Timmy's prediction. I was stunned that he could or would do this to Leroy. I exclaimed, "What gives you the right to do this to Leroy just because you can? He is down here just like you and me, trying to make a living for his family." Timmy looked at me and said, "It's not my fault. If he can't take it, he shouldn't be down here." He blamed Leroy for being vulnerable. People who regularly throw cheap shots at others sometimes have the same view of life as Timmy.

They feel no responsibility for the pain they inflict on others. I believe that we have an obligation to consider how others receive our humor and act respectfully based upon their responses.

Another ground rule, asking for clarification, is often suggested. I ask team members if they have ever left a meeting without knowing what was explained or expected of them. I usually see numerous heads nodding, so I follow up with the question, "Why does that happen?" Someone might respond that he or she didn't want to appear stupid. Then I ask, "Where did we learn that asking a question could result in our appearing stupid?" Invariably someone describes being scolded by a teacher or parent for asking a question. Then I share my experience with my third grade teacher, Mrs. Steed. I had just moved from Kentucky to Ohio and this was my first day at Beallsville Grade School. As I hadn't yet been fitted with eyeglasses, I didn't realize that my eyesight was bad and that I couldn't see as well as the other children. When Mrs. Steed wrote an assignment on the board, I made the mistake of asking her about it. I was just brazen enough to ask her to repeat the assignment. She replied, "What is the matter with you, can't you read?" As a result of her remark, I felt about an inch high. I asked very few other questions during the rest of that school year. I still think of that experience from time to time. Most of us have had a similar experience. The problem is that not asking questions can lead to mistakes resulting in bad products or unsafe situations. Team members need to be committed to asking and answering questions of other team members.

"Focus on the present and future, not the past," is a very popular ground rule. The reason this is an issue with many team members has to do with resistance to change. Others suggest that the reason we are unable to meet this ground rule is explained in Bruce Springsteen's song, "Glory Days." The song describes two high school friends who meet and automatically start talking about high school baseball as if it was just yesterday. To some people, the past always seems more real than the present. I had one such employee in a training session in 1986. We were talking about change issues in the company at that time. He kept making comments refuting the possibility of change, such as, "Supervisors will never listen to us. They never have for thirty years. Even if they do, they'll take our ideas and claim them for their own. We'll never get any credit." I listened and paraphrased the thoughts of this employee. The resistant employee asked the rest of the group for illustrations of their experiences with supervisors. Most described being aware of significant changes in the way supervisors interacted compared with their behaviors of five years before. I turned back to the resistant employee and made an observation while posing a question: "I can see that the experience that you are thinking about really hurt you. I can also see that it makes you angry even today when you think about it. When did these events that you've been describing happen?" He thought for a few seconds, rubbing his chin, and then said, "1966 or 1967." He had taken this experience and put it in a safe, warm place deep inside. Every so often, usually in a meeting, he allowed it to surface with the same intensity of emotion that he had felt twenty years earlier. Later, even the resistant employee admitted that supervisory behavior was presently more positive and respectful. In fact, the supervisor that he had been talking about had retired five years earlier.

When "Deal with particulars rather than general problems" is chosen, I tell a story about my son. When he was young, he occasionally claimed that I was unfair. My response was not an argument but rather the question, "What exactly have I done that you are describing as unfair?" The answer to that question really got to the root of the issue and allowed for explanation or problem solving. However, some people use this questioning approach as a denial of the problem being identified. I recommend that you be cautious of the danger of closing down communication with this phrase. Just because someone can't give you an illustration doesn't necessarily mean that there isn't a problem. Give the other person some time to think about and describe the root cause.

The discussion around "Don't be defensive" is usually interesting. I ask if I would see a lot of defensiveness if I were in their organization for a period of time. If the answer is, "Yes," I ask, "How do you know when someone becomes defensive?" Someone usually says, "He shuts up and doesn't say anything," or, "Her voice gets louder." I then self-disclose that the first thing I feel when I get defensive is my face flushing. Next, my jaw tightens and flexes. Finally, my voice rises and my eyes become like piercing lasers. These behaviors are physical manifestations of increasing adrenaline. I call this escalation "climbing the stair steps of adrenaline." I also self-disclose that never have good things happened to me at the top of the adrenaline stairs. One other point I make is that my choices are fewer the further I go up the stairs. That is why it is important to be aware of your nonverbal cues as you are climbing or beginning to climb the stairs. Finally, I ask the group if they know what their stair steps look like. Some do, but many don't. Addressing those who don't know their stair steps, I ask, "Who does know what your stair steps look like?" Answers come fast and furiously: spouses, children, parents, siblings, peers at work, and close friends. I suggest that they go to one of these people whom they trust and get some feedback on what the other people see as they become defensive or get angry. Once they find out this information, they can begin to take control of that part of their behavior.

A significant problem that teams encounter is a lack of follow-through on action items that are agreed on in team meetings. "Be prepared to carry out decisions" addresses this issue. I believe one of the reasons action items are not completed is that no one discusses why they weren't done. The team needs to analyze the contributing reasons why the action did not occur and then put remedial plans into place.

"All comments remain in this room" can be a useful ground rule or a strangling one. The key thing to keep in mind is whether comments repeated outside the room would hurt individuals on the team. Some comments could be useful learning to others outside the group and might be important to share. If the comments would have hurtful consequences, they should not be shared outside the team.

"Everyone is an equal in the room" is a ground rule that is important to many people. The fact is that we are not equal on any variable. You are taller or shorter than I and either heavier or lighter than I. The point of this ground rule is that we each deserve equal opportunity to be heard and treated as a valued member of the group.

Once the list is completed and discussed, I ask the team, "Is there any ground rule on the flip chart that you either can't or won't act in accordance with? If there is, you have veto power and we strike it off the list. This list is a living document. It should hang at every team meeting and members can add to or delete ground rules at any time as long as the team discusses the addition or deletion." I make these statements because the ground rules are only useful as a team tool if the team members own and obey them.

The next exercise in the interpersonal communication module is the Best Communicator Exercise, I ask the participants to think of a communicator whom they would describe as the best communicator they have personally known. Then I ask each team member to write down three behaviors that this person demonstrates that made the team member think of him or her. With this list we are focusing on the team members' perceptions of positive and desirable communication behavior. Once the list is complete, I ask the team members to look at it and choose one behavior they would like to work on personally after the session.

SECTION 3

Getting
to Results

Introduction

$\mathcal{T}$he ostensible reason for creating work teams is because they're supposed to *do* something. That's what this section is about.

We create teams instead of doing a task ourselves because we believe that the members of a team working together can accomplish more than the same number of individuals working separately. While we all know that teams have the *potential* to do more and to do it more quickly, achieving those aims isn't simply a matter of getting together a group of people. It often takes much more skill than doing it on your own.

Teaming takes time, patience, communication, organization, and discipline. This is perhaps the same reason so many managers find it difficult to delegate; it often seems easier to say, "I'll just do it myself."

The chartering process, described in Section Two, is the first and the most important step. But the ultimate goal of building a charter is to get to the "performing" stage of the team process more quickly. Once there's a charter, ground rules, and a plan, it's time to get at it. Section Three concerns the knowledge and skills necessary for actually performing the job.

Meetings, meetings, meetings! Why do we have to have so many meetings? And why do they have to be so long? And unproductive? Most of us who have served on teams have heard, and said, these things many times. We know that presenting, discussing, collaborating, assigning, reporting, and deciding are important things that happen in meetings but, we wonder, how are we supposed to get anything done if we're always meeting? Plus, most of us have other responsibilities besides those that come from our team.

We probably wouldn't mind the time so much if we felt we were spending it productively. Most meetings don't give us that feeling, though. The first portion of Section Three presents some different views on making our meetings, especially team meetings, more effective. It deals with the kind of agenda building, time management, record keeping, and follow-up skills that will help us get our teams on to the task at hand and out of the meeting more quickly.

Good meeting management is important, but if we lack the skill to manage the team's tasks and projects, our meetings won't be very productive. The next portion of Section Three discusses the project management process. You'll find especially useful the information regarding the roles and responsibilities of the team leader in project management.

Teams at work are usually formed because our organizations have a problem to solve or a decision to make. Most of us have taken courses or seminars in decision-making and problem solving. We've learned the steps and techniques. Getting a team to go through those steps and make the right decision requires special skill, however, and you'll find some valuable information about making decisions and solving problems as a team. Team decision makers easily fall into the errors of groupthink or experience the "Abilene Paradox (Harvey 1988)." Knowing how to avoid these and other pitfalls will help ensure a better decision or problem resolution.

Finally, one of the biggest challenges we face in managing our teams these days is that the members are increasingly likely to be spread out across the country or the world—let alone across town. Managing teams in a virtual environment is a growing challenge and is a crucial skill for anyone looking to be a manager or team leader in an information economy organization. Knowing how to get things done in teleconferences or computer conferences, how to share data, how to do things at a distance that are much easier in person, requires that we gain new knowledge and develop new skills. The final portion of Section Three provides insightful information to help you develop these skills.

Getting Things Done Through Meetings

Meeting Management

Meetings are the primary forum for the team's work. While meeting management may seem a rather mundane issue for teams, how the team establishes and manages meeting issues will often portend the overall success of the team. The key ground rules for meetings usually address attendance, representation, and information management.

Attendance represents the first opportunity for the team to put into action some of its values and expectations. It is the first opportunity for the team to practice mutual responsibility.

The first decision the team must make is to define acceptable attendance. Attendance requirements depend on the work and culture of the organization and the requirements of the task. For example, some organizations require their people to travel a great deal. In that situation it is unlikely that the team can require that team members attend every meeting. The team must establish a schedule that allows team members the maximum opportunity to attend and then be clear about what is an acceptable attendance rate. If a team member is not regularly present at team meetings, she or he cannot be an effective team member, certainly not a core team member as described earlier. The team then needs to decide on a secondary role for that team member or assign a new member.

Teams: Structure, Process, Culture, and Politics, by Eileen K. Aranda, Luis Aranda, with Kristi Conlon. Copyright © 1998 by Prentice Hall, Inc.

Common questions for team members to ask around attendance include:

- How often will the team meet?
- For how long?
- Where?
- What is tardiness and how should it be dealt with?
- What is the definition of regular attendance?

A more delicate issue of attendance is the notion of what constitutes "being" at the meeting. Some people bring their bodies not their minds and souls to the meeting. Such team members will bring along other work to do; will constantly leave the room to make phone calls; or will not participate. The team must clearly define what it expects from team members once they arrive at the meeting.

A related problem for teams is tardiness. If members constantly come to the meeting late, it creates a disruption. Sometimes tardiness is a power play for the team member, especially if he or she knows the team waits to begin until the person arrives or that they will repeat what has transpired just for the benefit of the person who is tardy. The guiding principle on attendance is that the team should be careful not to reward poor performance. Team meetings must begin and end within the agreed time frames so that members can plan their own schedules. If team members who are late find that the meeting has begun without them, they are more likely to be on time in the future. If the meeting waits for the person, there is no incentive to come on time. In the same way, if the team is willing to revisit issues once the member has arrived, there is no incentive to be there for the original discussion. Also, when the team revisits an issue for an individual person, that person usually has an increased amount of influence over the topic because that individual has heard only a summarized version of the topic of discussion. It is not uncommon for a late-coming member to challenge a decision and have the team revoke what it had earlier agreed upon. If this team behavior occurs regularly, power-oriented team members will soon use such behavior to manipulate team decisions.

Attendance expectations must be clear and accepted by all team members. It is often helpful for them to write down their expectations so that commitment is clear. To be effective, ground rules have to be specific. To simply say that team members will all participate is too general to evoke a commitment to adherence to the rules. In the Team Charter in the appendix of the book, there is a format that teams can use to record their ground rules.

In addition to setting the ground rules, the team must decide what it will do if a team member does not abide by the rules. It is vital that these ground rules be set at the beginning of team meetings, before transgressions occur. If the team waits until it has to deal with inappropriate behavior, it will not be able to separate the ground rule from the problem person, and resentments are likely to occur.

Enforcement is a very important issue for teams. Addressing ground-rule violations is usually the first opportunity for team members to give one another feedback and to reinforce team values. If the team is unwilling or unable to confront attendance issues, it will not be able to deal with the more challenging decision-making expectations that will arise as the team matures and deals with difficult task issues. Keeping ground rules is the first indication of whether the team is serious about its work.

One of the questions that often arises in relation to attendance in team meetings is whether members should send substitutes to meetings they themselves cannot attend. The current thinking on this question is that they should not send substitutes. While it may be appropriate to send a substitute to a group meeting where people simply report information, it is not appropriate to send a substitute to a team meeting. Each team member plays too intimate a role in the team to suggest that a substitute would be able to take the person's place.

Two underlying concepts lead to this "no substitutes" conclusion, and both are based on trust. In an effective team, the absent member must be able to trust that fellow team members will represent his or her issue in the discussion. In addition, the absent team member must respect and value the decisions of the team and accept that, even though she or he cannot attend, the absent team member feels confident that the team will reach a good decision.

This question of substitution is so serious for teams that it needs to be addressed specifically and concisely. Some things that successful teams can do to manage this situation are:

- Appoint a specific person on the team to represent and speak for the views of the missing person. During team discussion, the spokesperson will straightforwardly present what she or he thinks the views and values of the missing member would be.

- Create a ground rule that if a person knows he or she will miss a team meeting, he or she must notify the meeting manager. The meeting manager and the person going to be absent decide how to provide the absent member's views to the team.

- Establish a ground rule to identify the key people needed for a specific discussion. If any of those people cannot attend the meeting, it is canceled. If the meeting is canceled regularly, the team must then step back and discuss the issues of purpose and commitment.

- If a member is missing from a meeting, someone on the team is designated to meet with that person before the next meeting to advise the person of the decisions made and the discussion supporting the decision.

- If decisions are made during the meeting from which a member is absent, the team will not revisit the decision when the missing member returns. The team may decide to revisit its decision because of new information, or for any other content reason, but not simply because the missing member may not agree with the decision that was made.

Teams can use any one or a combination of these tactics or come up with ground rules that meet a team's particular needs. The intent of these actions is to make sure that the team makes progress while also accommodating the inevitable absences of team members.

The final meeting-management issue concerns information management. Information is the gold that the team mines during its meetings. It must be recorded and safe-guarded if it is to be valuable. Teams must, therefore, have ground rules and processes for recording, transforming, and distributing meeting information.

The way a team records information both greatly impacts participation and the quality of decisions made and influences those persons external to the group. The focus of our discussion in this chapter will be on internal recording of issues.

The team must decide on two recording issues: how to display information for decision-making and how to preserve information for recall. Recording decisions made requires a method that will display clearly the good information and ideas that flow from members in an irregular manner throughout a meeting. Many, many good ideas are left unaddressed during team meetings because there is no mechanism for the team to record them. There are several ways for the team to keep track of ideas. One of the most effective is to have a team member play the role of recorder and to keep track of *all* ideas that are brought to the table. This person could also be sure that each person has an opportunity to talk. This role of recorder/facilitator can be played by an outside member, which is often beneficial in the early life of the team. However, over time the team needs to facilitate its own process. The more each team member can develop the skills of listening and understanding the views and ideas of others, the better off the entire team will be. If the team always uses an outside facilitator, the team abdicates its responsibility to learn this key skill as a team.

There are a couple of guidelines that help this recording/facilitating process work well during team meetings. First, the recorder needs to use a public format for recording information, ideas, and decisions. This format needs to be one where everyone can see it and, if necessary, change it. Flip charts, white boards, overhead transparencies, and interactive computer note taking are all possible. The reason for the visual display for all to see is to establish team ownership for the information and to allow the team to recall what has been discussed. Access to minutes kept in the traditional way is limited and delayed, and therefore does not provide useful information for the discussion process.

A second guideline for the facilitator is always to use the exact language of the speaker. It is a temptation for the facilitator to edit the speaker's words if the facilitator thinks she or he can say it better or wants the comment shortened to record it more easily. Resist the temptation! If the comment needs to be shorter, ask the speaker to rephrase it, or if the person is having trouble, ask the rest of the team to provide more concise language. The purpose of recording is understanding, not correct grammar. To keep the ownership of ideas and discussion vested in the team, it is critical to use the team's own words.

A third suggestion is that the recorder be a member of the team who does not have passionate feelings about the issue being presented. The recorder must be sure that all important comments are recorded. If the recorder has a heavy stake in the issue, he or she can influence, by exclusion or editing, the information recorded. If the issue is very controversial for the team, it may be appropriate to bring in an outside facilitator.

Common questions for the team to address about the information recording process include:

- What information from team discussion should we record/preserve?
- How should we record/preserve this information?
- What information should we share with those outside the team? How much? In what format?

Agenda building is another important recording task. Very often the agenda for the meeting is composed in the absence of the team and will therefore only by accident include what the team wants to discuss. The best time to build an agenda for the next meeting is at the end of the current meeting. What discussion items do the team members wish to pursue next time? What new information do they want to discuss? Where does the next team meeting fall in their time frame of accomplishment—does something need to be completed by the next meeting?

Like meeting notes, the agenda should be built publicly with people volunteering to do research, gather materials, contact other people, or pursue other activities related to the agenda. With the input of all, each team member knows what will be expected of him or her by the next meeting. If issues that need to be addressed occur after the agenda has been set, the team needs to devise a way to share that information with all members and to decide how to put the item on the agenda.

Some teams leave an open space on the agenda for the inevitable new situation. If no new situation arises, team members can expand the discussion of other issues or they can adjourn. Other teams prioritize agenda items so that if something is to be postponed the person responsible for the agenda can make the adjustments. Operate by the guideline that says that if an agenda item is moved three times, the team must decide how important the item truly is and whether they should just omit its discussion. Effective teams construct agendas carefully and are willing to take the time to address issues that will make their meeting time productive.

Teams must be careful not to confuse meeting structure and efficiency with effectiveness. If meetings seem unproductive, team members often respond by setting time limits on discussion and making rules that do not allow changes in the agenda. Seldom do these efforts result in better meetings. The focus of improvement in meetings needs to center around content and the decision-making process.

For example:

- What issues really need to be discussed?
- What time frame makes sense for the issues the team needs to discuss?
- What meeting format makes sense for the issues the team needs to discuss?
- What information do we need to have a useful discussion?
- Who needs to be present in order for appropriate decisions to be made?

Meetings tend to take on a routine that is often quite unrelated to the work that needs to be accomplished. Teams talk about unnecessary issues but fail to give enough attention to serious issues; membership gets fixed, as does the meeting place and format. Eventually, the team finds itself with a process that seldom meets its needs. The team needs to challenge its meeting process on a regular basis and be willing to change the process to meet the issue rather than force the issue into the prevailing process.

A role the team often assigns on a rotating basis is that of the meeting manager. This person is charged with the administrative tasks of the meeting. This may include completing and distributing an agenda, securing a room and equipment, drafting minutes, inviting needed nonteam members, and other tasks, depending on the meeting agenda. These tasks can be burdensome if they always fall to the same person; rotated, they are easy to handle, and they provide for new ways to address team issues.

A final recording duty is that of drafting the meeting minutes. Most teams find that meeting minutes are extremely valuable. However, to be of value they do not need to be extensive or fancy. For example, if the meeting notes are done carefully on the flip charts, they can be transcribed for meeting minutes. Meeting minutes certainly can be done in outline form. If the team wants members and others to read the minutes, they need to be short, relevant, and easy to understand.

Some creative teams even use mindmaps for meeting notes. Mindmaps are brief, nonlinear descriptions of what took place at the meeting. A mindmap of a meeting of the facility planning team we described earlier might look like Figure 3-1.

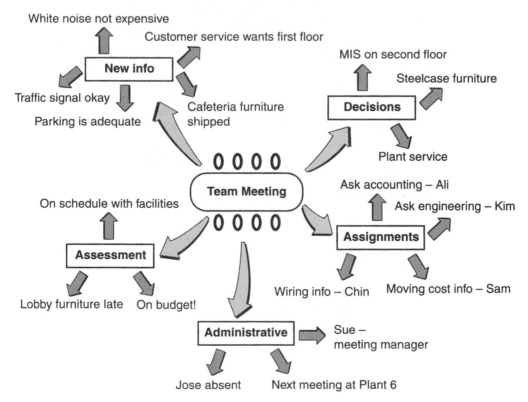

FIGURE 3-1

Example of a Mindmap

Mindmaps are an imaginative way for teams to collect and share information. People reading the mindmap, which is easy to create, get a sense of the dynamics of the meeting. If the team wants the distributed outcome of its meeting to be more formal, the team can still use a mindmap to keep minutes and then translate the mindmap for distribution in a more linear and narrative form.

Managing Meetings: A Toolkit

Holding Effective Team Meetings

The work of teams largely proceeds through meetings. Whether they are regularly scheduled or called out of need, effective meeting management is a key to success. Furthermore, people spend a lot of time in meetings. The average number of meetings jumped from 7 to 10 per week, based on surveys of business professionals between 1981 and 1995 by Mosvick and Nelson, authors of *We've Got to Start Meeting Like This!* (1995). Typical executives spend two-thirds of their time in scheduled meetings, and the amount of time managers spend in meetings increases with organizational level. Middle managers spend about 30 percent of their time in meetings; top management spends about 50 percent of their time in meetings. In addition to scheduled meetings, managers are involved in unscheduled and non-job-related meetings. In a study sponsored by the 3M Corporation, the number of meetings and conferences in industry nearly doubled during the previous decade and the cost of meetings nearly tripled. Most businesses spend 7 to 15 percent of their personnel budgets on meetings.

Perhaps meetings would not be a bad thing if they were economical and effective. Unfortunately, as much as 50 percent of meeting time is unproductive, and up to 25 percent of meeting time covers irrelevant issues. As one senior executive put it, "To waste your own time is unfortunate, but to waste the time of others is unforgivable." Companies are so overburdened with meetings that experts say it's a wonder any work gets done. Meetings also

Editor's Note: Here's another take on how to make meetings work.

trigger stress. The 3M meeting network recently launched a World Wide Web site where workers describe their meeting horror stories. Not surprisingly, managers have resorted to using various tactics, which vary from the radical (removing all chairs to make people stand, locking the doors, requiring people to pay $0.25 before speaking, etc.) to the more tame (the example in the box titled: Announcements, Decisions, and Discussion).

The 4P Meeting Management Model

The 4P model is a method for designing and implementing effective meetings (Whetton & Cameron, 1991). It has four key steps (see Table 3.1): (1) specify the **purpose** of the meeting, (2) invite the right **people**, (3) carefully **plan** the meeting content and format, and (4) effectively manage the meeting's **process**.

Skilled meeting managers do not just sit at the head of the table and call upon people to speak in a round-robin fashion. Nor do they run a "talk show" by simply airing ideas, conflicts, and concerns. Skilled meeting managers do not write down everything that is said; rather, they call out and punctuate key themes. Skilled meeting managers do not verbally paraphrase members' ideas; rather, they record them visually. Skilled meeting managers do not try to induce dominant members to yield the floor by saying, "keep it short" or "we need to hear from everyone"; rather, they use brainwriting at select times. They do not organize the meeting by who is there; rather, by what is to be done (see Box: Announcements, Decisions, and Discussion).

DEALING WITH PROBLEM PEOPLE IN MEETINGS

There is no surefire way to deal with "problem people." As a general principle, having structure helps. It can also be helpful to give group members a list of desirable and undesirable role descriptions prior to the meeting. Table 3.2 is a list of typical group members. Although stated in jest, each description has a ring of truth in it.

ANNOUNCEMENTS, DECISIONS, AND DISCUSSION

Most meetings are organized on the basis of who is there. Reports flow out person by person, department by department, often beginning with the most prestigious person and proceeding down. However, this type of round-robin format is inefficient. It is better to organize meetings by the content. Tropman, author of *Making Meetings Work* (1996), suggests that announcements should come first, then decisions, and finally discussion time, in that order.

TABLE 3.1   4P MEETING MANAGEMENT MODEL

Key Skill	Questions to Ask
Purpose	
• A complex problem needs to be resolved using the expertise of several people.	• What is the purpose of the meeting?
• Team members' commitment to a decision or to each other needs to be enhanced.	• Is the purpose clear to participants?
	• Is a meeting the most appropriate means of accomplishing the goal?
• Information needs to be shared simultaneously among several key people.	• Are key people available to attend the meeting?
	• Is the cost of the meeting in proportion to what will be accomplished?
Participants	
• The size of the team should be compatible with the task.	• Is the size of the meeting appropriate given the problem of coordination costs?
• A balance between people with strong task orientations and those with strong interpersonal skills is desirable.	• What diversity of skills and backgrounds is important to have in the meeting?
Plan	
• Provide for adequate physical space, etc.	• Has an agenda been created?
• Establish priorities by sequencing agenda items and allotting time limits to each item.	• Has the agenda for the meeting been distributed to members prior to the meeting?
• Prepare and distribute the agenda before or at the beginning of the meeting.	• Have members been forewarned if they will be asked to report?
• Organize the agenda by content, not by who is there. Use a three-step approach: announcements, decisions, discussion (Tropman, 1996).	• Has the physical arrangement been considered (e.g., whiteboards, overheads, flipcharts)?
• Think about your visual aids: Visual aids are 43% more persuasive than no visuals (Armour, 1997).	• Has key information been put into proper information displays?
• Choose the most appropriate decision-making structure (e.g., brainstorming, normal group technique).	• Has a note taker been assigned?
Process	
• At the beginning, restate the overall purpose of the meeting and review the agenda and time constraints.	• If this is the first meeting of a team, has an icebreaker been included?
• Make note of the ground rules, such as how decisions will be made (e.g., raised hands, secret ballot).	• Does the icebreaker get people involved in a behavioral or emotional way (at a minimum, a handshake or high-five)?
• Use techniques to ensure equal participation from members.	• Have the ground rules been determined and shared with members in advance of the meeting?
• Conclude the meeting by summarizing key decisions, reviewing assignments, and determining objectives for the next meeting.	

Sources: Adapted from Whetton, D.A., & Cameron, K.S. 1991. *Developing Management Skills* (2nd ed.). Harper-Collins: Armour, S. 1997, December 8. "Business' Black Hole." *USA Today,* p.1A.

TABLE 3.2 TYPICAL GROUPS MEMBERS	
Thelma Talk-a-Lot	("I just have to say this")
Sam Stall	("Let's not rush into this")
Don Domineering	(talks 75% of the time about his own ideas)
Nick Negative	(explains that someone has to be the devil's advocate)
Ted Theorizer	("It's really complex")
Nancy Nuts-'n'-Bolts	(always comes up with an impossible example to deal with)
Jim Just-a Little-Bit-More-Information-on-This-Topic-Please	("I don't feel we should decide until we know more")
Herman Hypochondriacal	(is convinced that any path makes vulnerabilities increase)
Yolanda You're-Not-Going-to-Believe-What-Happened-to-Me	(uses immediate, personal events rather than overarching views to analyze problems)

Source: Tropman, J.E., & Morningstar, G. 1989. *Entrepreneurial Systems for the 1990s: Their Creation, Structure, and Management,* New York: Quorum Books. Reproduced with permission of Greenwood Publishing Group, Inc., Westport, CT.

ADVICE FOR MEETING ATTENDEES

The burden of effective meeting management does not rest solely on the shoulders of the leader. Group members need to engage in the following proactive strategies (Whetton & Cameron, 1991):

- **Determine if you need to attend the meeting.** Don't attend merely because you have been invited. If you have doubts about whether the meeting's agenda applies to you, discuss with the leader why he or she feels your presence is important.

- **Prepare.** Acquaint yourself with the agenda and prepare any reports or information that will facilitate others' understanding of the issues. Come prepared with questions that will help you understand the issues.

- **Be on time.** Stragglers not only waste the time of other participants by delaying the meeting or by requiring summaries of what has happened, but they also hinder effective team building and hurt morale.

- **Ask for clarification on points that are unclear or ambiguous.** Most of the time, you will find that others in the room have the same question but are too timid to speak out.

- **When giving information, be precise and to the point.** Don't bore everyone with anecdotes and details that add little to your point.

- **Listen.** Keep eye contact with whoever is speaking, and try to ascertain the underlying ideas behind the comments. Be sensitive to the

effect of your nonverbal behavior on speakers, such as slouching, doo-
dling, or reading.

- **Be supportive of other group members.** Acknowledge and build on
  the comments of others (e.g., "As Jane was saying . . .").

- **Ensure equitable participation.** Take the lead in involving others so
  that everyone's talents are used. This is especially important if you
  know that some participants' points of view are not being included in
  the discussion. This can be accomplished by encouraging those who
  rarely participate (e.g., "Jim, your unit worked on something like this
  last year. What was your experience like?").

- **Make disagreements principle-based.** If it is necessary to disagree
  with, or challenge, the comments of others, follow the guidelines for
  collaborative conflict management (e.g., base your comments on
  commonly held principles or values; for example: "That's an interesting idea, Bill, but how does it square with the president's emphasis on cost-cutting?").

- **Act and react in a way that will enhance the group performance.** In
  other words, leave your personal agendas at the door and work toward
  the goals of the group.

Common Meeting Diseases and Fallacies

It is almost impossible to predict where most meetings will go awry. The following is a description of the most common meeting diseases and some ideas
on how to combat them.

THE OVERCOMMITMENT PHENOMENON

Symptoms: Many people agree to perform tasks and accomplish goals that
they cannot possibly do in the time allowed. In some cases, this problem is
attributable to the pressures placed on managers to accomplish goals and say
"yes." However, in many more instances, the overcommitment problem stems
from a fundamental inability to estimate how long it will take to accomplish
a task. In addition, people tend to make commitments in advance because
their confidence in their ability to finish is higher when they are further away
from the task (Gilovich, Kerr, & Medvec, 1993). Most people make subjective
mental estimates of how long it will take to accomplish a task, such as writing a report, collecting information, or interviewing a recruit, by imagining
the scenario and then estimating a time line based upon the running of the
scenario. However, individuals' mental simulations fail to take into account
the process losses that will inevitably thwart their efforts. For example, when
they expect to spend 2 weeks writing a report, they fail to anticipate that their
printer will break down and that they will have to spend a day off-site. Consequently, most managers are consistently behind schedule.

In many cases, managers and executives are asked to commit themselves
to perform tasks and events at some time in the distant future. For example,
a team leader might be asked to enroll in a 3-day course next year, travel

abroad to interview other team members, or attend a conference. Many people agree to these future invitations, but when the time approaches, regret that they have to do what they promised (Loewenstein & Prelic, 1991). People fail to adequately weigh the importance of their future opportunities and time constraints, so they commit to things in the future that they would most likely decline to do in the present.

Treatment: The easiest way to deal with the overcommitment problem is to simply double (or triple) the amount of time projected to accomplish a task. For example, publishers typically add 6 months to an author's projected completion time for a manuscript. Another way of combating the bias is to break the task down into its different elements and then estimate the time necessary to complete each part—people are more accurate at estimating the time necessary to accomplish smaller tasks. When someone asks you to do something, such as write a report, travel, or make a presentation, imagine that you are being asked to do this the next week, or even the next day. If you are disinclined, then it may not be a good idea to take it on.

CALLS FOR MORE INFORMATION

Symptoms: Often, teams are uncomfortable making decisions. This is particularly true when the decision matter is complex and value-laden. Under such conditions, teams will do nearly anything to avoid making decisions. The manager faces an avoidance-avoidance conflict: Making a decision is difficult, but not making a decision makes one appear indecisive. Managers often respond to this avoidance-avoidance conflict by requesting more information. In theory, the amount of information relevant to any decision situation is boundless; however, at some point, decisions must be made. One way of avoiding decision-making, but not appearing to be indecisive, is to request additional information. This makes people feel as though they are making progress, but actually, the additional information may not be diagnostic or useful. It is merely gathered so that the team members can better cognitively justify their decision. Decision avoidance is a particular concern when teams make negative decisions, such as downsizing.

Consider, for example, the following scenario (Savage, 1954):

> A businessman contemplates buying a certain piece of property. He considers the outcome of the next presidential election relevant to the attractiveness of the purchase. So, to clarify the matter for himself, he asks whether he would buy if he knew that the Republican candidate were going to win, and decides that he would do so. Similarly, he considers whether he would buy if he knew that the Democratic candidate were going to win, and again, finds that he would do so. Seeing that he would buy in either event, he decides that he should buy, even though he does not know which event obtains. (p. 21)

The preceding rationale is known as the **sure-thing principle** (Savage, 1954). It would seem irrational, or somewhat silly, if the businessperson in this case were to delay purchase until after the election, or to pay money to find out the election results ahead of time. Yet in organizations, decision makers often pursue noninstrumental information—information that appears relevant, but if available, would have no impact on choice. The problem does not end there: Once they pursue such information, people then use it to make their decision. Consequently, the pursuit of information that would have had no impact on choice leads people to make choices they otherwise would not have made (Bastardi & Shafir, 1998).

Treatment: The decision trap of calling for more information can best be dealt with by keeping a clear log that details the history of the decision. For example, a team member might say something like, "You know, this issue was first brought up two years ago, and it was agreed that a competitive analysis was necessary. This competitive analysis was performed and I brought you the results the following spring. Then, it was suggested that a task force be formed. We did this and came to some conclusions in a report circulated last fall. We agreed at that time that we would make a decision at this meeting. I realize that more information is always better, but I am beginning to wonder whether the costs of continuing to search for information are a way of avoiding a decision . . ." This strategy is especially important in teams where membership changes (and, hence, organizational memory is lost) and in teams that must make tough decisions (e.g., employment terminations).

FAILED MEMORY AND REINVENTING THE WHEEL

Symptoms: Many teams face decisions that they make on a repeated basis. For example, merit review decisions, hiring decisions, admission decisions, funding decisions, and so on, are all decisions that must be made repeatedly. However, teams often exhibit a memory loss of sorts, in terms of how they made previous decisions. As a result, they spend precious time arguing with one another as to how they made the decision in the past, and memories prove to be fallible. The failed memory problem is most likely to afflict teams that have not created a sufficient organizational memory. The failed memory problem also haunts teams that experience turnover. Under these situations, team members who take notes, or have some kind of record, have an enormous advantage.

Treatment: The key here is to make the process explicit and then to have it recorded in some fashion so that later it can be retrieved. The problem is that most people trust their memories at the time they are discussing the issue or making the decision; consequently, they don't bother to write down what they believe will be burned into their memory.

Running a Meeting

Editor's Note:
Making meetings
more effective is so
important; here's yet
another take on the
subject.

SELF-ASSESSMENT EXERCISE

For each of the following questions, select the answer that best describes how you *have* or *would* behave in running a group meeting, not how you think you *should* behave.

When Running a Group Meeting, I:

	Usually	Sometimes	Seldom
1. Prepare an agenda beforehand.	☐	☐	☐
2. Ensure ahead of time that all participants are prepared for the meeting.	☐	☐	☐
3. Delay starting the meeting until everyone is present.	☐	☐	☐
4. Make sure that everyone knows the specific purpose(s) of the meeting.	☐	☐	☐
5. Keep disagreements over ideas to a minimum.	☐	☐	☐
6. Encourage participation by all members.	☐	☐	☐
7. Keep discussion focused on the issues.	☐	☐	☐
8. Extend the meeting past its stated finishing time if all items have not been covered.	☐	☐	☐

Scoring Key and Interpretation

For questions, 1, 2, 4, 6, and 7, give yourself 3 points for "Usually," 2 points for "Sometimes," and 1 point for "Seldom."

For questions 3, 5, and 8, give yourself 3 points for "Seldom," 2 points for "Sometimes," and 1 point for "Usually."

Sum up your total points. A score of 22 or higher indicates excellent skills at running a group meeting. Scores in the 16 to 21 range imply some deficiencies in this skill. Scores below 16 denote that you have considerable room for improvement.

SKILL CONCEPTS

If you're a typical manager, you'll spend a large part of your day in meetings. Studies have found that most managers spend between 25 to 30 percent of their time in meetings (Wakin, 1991; Michaels, 1989). And the higher up the the corporate ladder managers climb, the more meetings they attend. Chief executives have been found to spend 59 percent of their time in scheduled meetings and another 10 percent in unscheduled meetings (Mintzberg, 1980).

Many of the hours you'll spend in these meetings will be in a nonleadership role. You'll participate, but it won't be your responsibility to run the meeting. Preparing and contributing appropriately will be your responsibilities. Other times you'll be the person in charge. You'll choose who will attend. You'll set and control the agenda. Most importantly, what you do or don't do will largely influence the meeting's effectiveness. In this chapter, we'll look at group meetings to determine how those in a leadership role can make them as effective as possible.

The Importance of Meetings

It's been calculated that eleven million meetings take place every day in the United States (Jay, 1976, p. 46). Handled properly, these person-to-person encounters are probably the single most efficient mechanism for passing word down and, equally important, up the ranks (Kiechel, 1986). But group meetings are not only devices for disseminating information. They're also effective tools for decision-making, introducing change, and developing a spirit of teamwork. When run *ineffectively*, however, meetings can be costly, time-consuming, and demoralizing to participants. If the dollar cost of a manager's time, including salary and benefits, is $100 an hour (which is fairly typical), ten managers meeting for a couple of hours and accomplishing nothing is a waste of several thousand dollars, plus the time lost from other tasks that could have been accomplished in that time!

The increasing use of telecommunication applications such as teleconferences, and audio, computer-based, and video conferences can save some of these costs by allowing a large number of meetings to take place among members who are physically separated but electronically linked. But telecommunications is not going to eliminate the traditional face-to-face meeting. Such meetings are currently alive and well in almost all organizations and are likely to be thriving for many years to come. Most of the concepts pertaining to the dynamics of group behavior apply to groups' members who are physically together or electronically linked.

How to Run a Meeting*

Meetings are among the most overused and underutilized of all management tools. We have just seen that most managers spend from one-fourth to over two-thirds of their time in scheduled meetings, and the most important organizational decisions are almost always reached in meetings, or as a result of one or more meetings. Given their importance, and the amount of management time they consume, it is indeed a tragedy that so many meetings are so inefficient and, worse, ineffective. When unproductive meetings occur regularly, managers with demanding schedules begin to believe that their primary goal is to get out of the meeting rather than to get the most out of it (Michaels, 1989).

Yet planning and conducting a meeting are not difficult tasks. While there are no magic formulas to guarantee success, there are a number of simple procedures that effective managers employ to improve the quality of their meetings.

*Source: This section was prepared by James P. Ware. Copyright © 1977 by the President and Fellows of Harvard College. By permission of the Harvard Business School.

There are, of course, many different kinds of meetings, ranging from two-person interchanges all the way up to industry-wide conventions with thousands of participants. Most management meetings, however, involve relatively small groups of people in a single organization. This section will concentrate on a number of techniques for running these kinds of management meetings more effectively. For further simplicity, we will focus primarily on scheduled meetings of managers who are at approximately the same level in the organization, and who have known each other and worked together before.

The suggestions that follow are divided into planning activities to carry out before the meeting and leadership activities to engage in during the meeting. Both kinds of work are essential: The most thorough preparation in the world will be wasted if you are careless during the meeting, while even outstanding meeting leadership rarely overcomes poor planning.

Preparing for the Meeting

Perhaps the most useful way to begin is simply to sit down with a blank sheet of paper and think through what the meeting will be like. Write down all the issues that are likely to come up, what decisions need to be made, what you want to happen after the meeting, and what things have to happen before the meeting can take place. Although the circumstances surrounding each meeting are unique, your planning should include the following activities:

Setting Objectives.   Most management meetings are called either to exchange information or to solve organizational problems. Generally, your reasons for calling the meeting are fairly obvious, especially to you. It is worth being very explicit about your purposes, however, because they have major implications for who should attend, which items belong on the agenda, when and where you hold the meeting, and what kinds of decision-making procedures you should use.

An information-exchange meeting can be an efficient mechanism if the information to be shared is complex or controversial, if it has major implications for the meeting participants, or if there is symbolic value in conveying the information personally. If none of these conditions is present, it may be more efficient, and just as effective, to write a memo or make several telephone calls.

Problem-solving meetings provide an opportunity to combine the knowledge and skills of several people at once. The ideas that evolve out of an open-ended discussion are usually richer and more creative than what the same people could produce working individually.

These two different objectives call for very different kinds of meetings. Thus, you should be very explicit about what you are trying to accomplish, both to yourself and to the other meeting participants.

Selecting Participants.   Invite people to the meeting who will either contribute to, or be affected by, its outcome. Select individuals who have knowledge or skills relevant to the problem, or who command organizational resources (time, budgets, other people, power, and influence) that you need access to.

As you build your participant list, you should also give thought to the overall composition of the group. Identify the likely concerns and interests of the individual managers, and the feelings they have about each other. Try to obtain a rough balance of power and status among subgroups or probable coalitions (unless you have clear reasons for wanting one group to be more powerful).

Do everything you can to keep the size of the group appropriate to your objectives. While an information-exchange meeting can be almost any size, a problem-solving group should not exceed eight to ten people if at all possible.

Planning the Agenda.   Even if you are planning an informal, exploratory meeting, an agenda can be a valuable means of controlling the discussion and of giving the participants a sense of direction. The agenda defines the meeting's purpose for participants and places boundaries between relevant and irrelevant discussion topics. Furthermore, the agenda can serve as an important vehicle for premeeting discussions with participants.

Some important principles of building an agenda are listed below:

- Sequence items so they build on one another if possible.
- Sequence topics from easiest to most difficult and/or controversial.
- Keep the number of topics within reasonable limits.
- Avoid topics that can be better handled by subgroups or individuals.
- Separate information exchange from problem solving.
- Define a finishing time as well as a starting time.
- Depending on meeting length, schedule breaks at specific times where they will not disrupt important discussions.

Not every meeting requires a formal, written agenda. Often you simply cannot predict where a discussion will lead, or how long it will take. However, focusing your attention on these issues can help you anticipate controversy and be prepared to influence it in a productive manner. Even if you do not prepare a public, written agenda, you should not begin the meeting without having a tentative, private one.

Doing Your Homework.   Your major objective in preparing for the meeting is to collect all the relevant information you can, and to consider its implications. Some of these data may be in written documents, but much of them will probably be in other people's heads. The more important and the more controversial the subject, the more contact you should have with other participants before the actual meeting.

These contacts will help you anticipate issues and disagreements that may arise during the meeting. As you talk with the other participants, try to learn all you can about their personal opinions and objectives concerning the meeting topic. These personal objectives—often called "hidden" agendas—can have as big an impact on what happens during the meeting as your formal, explicit agenda. Thus, the more you can discover about the other participants' goals for the meeting, the better prepared you will be to lead an effective discussion.

These premeeting contacts also give you an opportunity to encourage the other participants to do their homework as well. If there is enough time before the meeting to collect and circulate relevant data or background materials, the meeting itself can proceed much more quickly. Few events are as frustrating as a meeting of people who are unprepared to discuss or decide the issues on the agenda.

As part of your preparation, you may want to brief your boss and other executives who will not be at the meeting, but who have an interest in its outcomes.

Finally, circulate the agenda and relevant background papers a day or two before the meeting if you can. These documents help to clarify your purposes and expectations, and they further encourage the other participants to come to the meeting well prepared. Keep your demands on their time reasonable, however. People are more likely to read and think about brief memos than long, comprehensive reports.

Setting a Time and Place.   The timing and location of your meeting can have a subtle but significant impact on the quality of the discussion. These choices communicate a surprising number of messages about the meeting's importance, style, and possible outcomes.

What time of day is best for your meeting? Often the work flow in the organization will constrain your freedom of choice. For example, you could not meet simultaneously with all of a bank's tellers during the regular business hours, or with all the entry clerks just as the mail arrives. Within these kinds of constraints, however, you often have a wide choice of meeting times. How should you decide?

Early in the day, participants will usually be fresher and will have fewer other problems on their minds. In contrast, late-afternoon meetings can be more leisurely, since there will usually be nothing else on anyone's schedule following your meeting. Perhaps the best question to ask is what the participants will be doing after the meeting. Will they be eager to end the meeting so they can proceed to other commitments, or will they be inclined to prolong the discussion? Which attitude best suits your purposes? There is no "best" time for a meeting, but you should consider explicitly what times would be most suitable for your particular objectives.

Two other factors may also influence when you schedule the meeting. First, try to be sure the time is sheltered so there will be an absolute minimum of interruptions. Second, gear your starting time to the meeting's probable, or desirable, length. For example, if you want the meeting to last only an hour, a good time to schedule it is at 11 A.M.

Try not to plan meetings that last more than ninety minutes. Most people's endurance—or at least their creative capacity—will not last much longer than that. If the subject is so complex or lengthy that it will take longer, be sure to build in coffee and stretching breaks at least every ninety minutes.

Another key decision is where to hold the meeting. The setting in which a discussion takes place can have a marked influence on its tone and content. Just consider the difference between calling three subordinates to your office and meeting them for lunch in a restaurant. Each setting implies a particular level of formality and signals what kind of discussion you expect to have. Similarly, if you are meeting with several peers, a "neutral" conference room creates a very different climate than would any one of your offices. In each case, the appropriate setting depends on your purposes, and you should choose your location accordingly.

The discussion climate will also be affected by the arrangement of the furniture in the meeting room. In your office, you can choose to stay behind your desk and thereby be more authoritative, or to use a chair that puts you on a more equal basis with the other participants. In a conference room, you can choose to sit at the head of the table to symbolize your control, or in the center to be "one of the group."

You should also be certain that you have arranged for any necessary mechanical equipment, such as an overhead or slide projector, an easel, or a blackboard. These vital aids can facilitate both information exchange and problem-solving discussions.

Summary. Each of these suggestions has been intended to help you convene a meeting of people who have a common understanding of why they have come together and are prepared to contribute to the discussion. Of course, this kind of thorough preparation is often simply impossible. Nevertheless, the more preparation you can do, the more smoothly the meeting will go. While you can never anticipate all the issues and hidden agendas, you can clearly identify the major sources of potential disagreement. That anticipation enables you to control the meeting, rather than being caught off guard. Even if you have to schedule a meeting only an hour in advance, you can still benefit from systematic attention to these kinds of details.

Conducting the Meeting

If you have done your homework, you probably have a good idea of where you want the group to be at the end of the meeting. But remember that you called the meeting because you need something from the other participants—either information relevant to the problem, or agreement and commitment to a decision. Your success in achieving those goals now depends not so much on what you know about the problem as on what you and the others can learn during the discussion. Thus, the primary concern as you begin the meeting should be with creating a healthy, problem-solving atmosphere in which participants openly confront their differences and work toward a joint solution.

The following suggestions and meeting leadership techniques should help you achieve that goal.

Beginning the Meeting. If you are well prepared, the chances are that no one else has thought as much about the meeting as you have. Thus, the most productive way to begin is with an explicit review of the agenda and your objectives. This discussion gives everyone an opportunity to ask questions, offer suggestions, and express opinions about why they are there. Beginning with a review of the agenda also signals its importance and gets the meeting going in a task-oriented direction.

Be careful not to simply impose the agenda on the group; others may have useful suggestions that will speed up the meeting or bring the problem into sharper focus. They may even disagree with some of your plans, but you will not learn about that disagreement unless you clearly signal that you consider the agenda open to revision. The more the others participate in defining the meeting, the more committed they will be to fulfilling that definition.

This initial discussion also permits the meeting participants to work out a shared understanding of the problem that brought them together, and of what topics are and are not appropriate to discuss in this meeting.

Encouraging Problem Solving. As the formal leader of the meeting, you can employ a wide variety of techniques to keep the group in a problem-solving mode. Your formal authority as chairman gives you a great deal of power to influence the group's actions. Often a simple comment, a pointed look, or even just a lifted eyebrow is all you need to indicate approval or disapproval of someone's behavior.

Perhaps your best weapon is simply your own style of inquiry; if you focus on facts and on understanding points of disagreement, to the exclusion of personalities, others will generally do the same. As the discussion progresses, try to keep differing points of view in rough balance. Do not let a few individuals dominate; when you sense that participation has become unbalanced, openly ask the quieter members for their opinions and ideas. Never assume that silence means agreement; more often it signals some level of difference with the dominant theme of the discussion.

Effective problem-solving meetings generally pass through several phases. Early in the discussion that group will be seeking to understand the *nature* of the problem. At that point you need to encourage factual, nonevaluative discussion that emphasizes describing symptoms and searching for all possible causes. As understanding is gained, the focus will shift to a search for solutions. Again, you must discourage evaluative comments until all potential alternatives have been throughly explored. Only then should the discussion become evaluative, as the group moves toward a decision.

If you can develop a sensitivity to these stages of problem solving (describing symptoms, searching for alternatives, evaluating alternatives, selecting a solution), you can vary your leadership style to fit the current needs of the group. At all times, however, you want to keep the discussion focused on the problem, not on personalities or on unrelated issues, no matter how important they may be. Make your priorities clear and hold the group to them. Finally, maintain a climate of honest inquiry in which anyone's assumption (including yours) may be questioned and tested.

Keeping the Discussion on Track. When the meeting topic is controversial, with important consequences for the group members, you will have to work hard to keep the discussion focused on the issues.

Controversy makes most of us uncomfortable, and groups often avoid confronting the main issue by finding less important or irrelevant topics to talk about. If the discussion wanders too far from the agenda, you must be willing to exercise your leadership responsibility to swing the group back to the major topic.

Use your judgment in making these interventions, however. If the group is on the verge of splitting up in anger or frustration, a digression to a "safe" topic may be a highly functional way of reuniting. Generally, such digressions are most beneficial when they follow open controversy rather than precede it. If you think the group has reached a decision on the main issue, even if it is only an implicit one, then you may want to let the digression go on for a while. On the other hand, if the discussion is clearly delaying a necessary confrontation, then you will have to intervene to get the discussion back on the main issue.

If you began the meeting with an explicit discussion of the agenda, you will find this focusing task easier to carry out. Often a simple reminder to the group, with a glance at the clock, is enough. Another useful technique for marking progress is to periodically summarize where you think the group has been, and then ask the group to confirm your assessments.

If the discussion seems to bog down, or to wander too far afield, perhaps the group needs to take a short break. Even two minutes of standing and stretching can revitalize people's willingness to concentrate on the problem. And the break also serves to cut off old conversations, making it easier to begin new ones.

Do everything you can to keep the discussion moving on schedule, so you can end on time. The clock can be a very useful taskmaster, and busy managers rarely have the luxury of ignoring it. If you have set a specific ending time, and everyone knows you mean it, there will be far less tendency for the discussion to wander.

Controlling the Discussion. How authoritatively should you exercise control over the discussion? The answer to that question depends so much on specific circumstances that a general response is almost impossible. The level of formality that is appropriate depends on the discussion topic, on which phase of the problem-solving cycle you are in, and on your formal and informal relationships with the other participants. You will normally want to exercise greater control when

- The meeting is oriented more toward information exchange.
- The topic generates strong, potentially disruptive feelings.
- The group is moving toward a decision.
- Time pressures are significant.

There is a whole range of techniques you can use to exert more formal control. For example, if you permit participants to speak only when you call on them, or if you comment on or summarize each statement, there will be very few direct confrontations between other individuals. If you use a flip chart or blackboard to summarize ideas, you will also increase the level of formality and reduce the number of direct exchanges. In some circumstances, you may even want to employ formal parliamentary procedures, such as requiring motions, limiting debate, taking notes, and so on. These procedures might be appropriate, for example, in meetings of a board of directors, in union-management contract negotiations, or in policy-setting sessions involving managers from several different parts of the organization.

Many of these techniques are clearly inappropriate for, and rarely used in, smaller management meetings. Although these techniques can give you a high degree of control, they cannot prevent participants from developing strong feelings about the issues—feelings that often become strong precisely because you have not permitted them to be openly expressed.

Thus, it is entirely possible to control a meeting in a fashion that minimizes conflict within the meeting itself. However, one result of that control may be increased tension and even hostility among the participants, leading to more serious future problems. On the other hand, if tension levels are already so high that a rational discussion will not evolve on its own, then some of these controlling techniques may be absolutely essential.

Reaching a Decision.   Many management groups will fall into decision-making habits without thinking carefully about the consequences of those habits. The two major approaches to reaching a group decision are voting and reaching a consensus. Each strategy has its advantages and disadvantages.

Voting is often resorted to when the decision is important and the group seems deadlocked. The major benefit of taking a vote is that you are guaranteed of getting a decision. However, voting requires public commitment to a position, and it creates a win-lose situation for the group members. Some individuals will be clearly identified as having favored a minority position. Losers on one issue often try to balance their account on the next decision, or they may withdraw their commitment to the total group. Either way, you may have won the battle but lost the war.

Reaching a group consensus is generally a much more effective decision-making procedure. It is often more difficult, however, and is almost always more time-consuming. Working toward a genuine consensus means hearing all points of view and usually results in a better decision—a condition that is especially important when the group members will be responsible for implementing the decision. Even when individuals do not fully agree with the group decision, they are more likely to support it (or less likely to sabotage it) when they believe their positions have had a complete hearing.

Ending the Meeting.   The most important thing to do at the end of the meeting is to clarify what happens next. If the group has made a major decision, be certain you agree on whom is responsible for its implementation, and on when the work will be completed.

If the group has to meet again, you can save a lot of time by scheduling your next meeting then and there. Having everyone check their calendars and mark down the date and time of the next meeting will save you an unbelievable number of telephone calls.

Depending on the discussion topic and the decisions that have been made, either you or someone else should follow the meeting with a brief memo summarizing the discussion, the decisions, and the follow-up commitments that each participant has made. This kind of document serves not only as a record of the meeting, but also as a next-day reminder to the participants of what they decided and what they are committed to doing.

If you can, spend the last five minutes or so of the meeting talking about how well the meeting went. Although most managers are not accustomed to self-critiques, this practice is a useful habit that can contribute significantly to improved group problem solving. The best time to share your reactions to the meeting is right after it has ended. You evaluate the effectiveness of other management techniques all the time; why not apply the same criteria to your meetings?

Summary

Management meetings occur so frequently that most of us fail to recognize how significant an impact they have on organizational productivity. Improving the effectiveness of your meetings is not a difficult task. Apply these simple techniques carefully, with sensitivity to the combination of people and problems you have brought together, and your meetings should become both more effective and more interesting. The important point, however, is that the techniques *are* simple. They require little more than systematic preparation before the meeting and sensitive observation and intervention while it is in progress.

*C*onclusions: Identifying the Desirable Behaviors

This knowledge about running group meetings can be translated into specific behaviors that a manager should demonstrate.

1. Prepare a meeting agenda. A large part of the chairperson's contribution occurs before the meeting begins. You will need to have a clear understanding of what is to be done at the meeting and what, if any, decisions are to be made. You'll have to determine who should attend and the right number of attendees to optimize the group's effectiveness. You'll also need to draw up the planning document that will guide the meeting—the agenda.

As a general rule, keep the number of participants as low as possible. It is unusual for more than a dozen people to do anything important at a meeting. When you get beyond ten or twelve participants, meetings typically get unwieldly. In fact, a meeting of more than a dozen probably exceeds a chairperson's span of control. Evidence indicates that decision-making committees of five are highly effective when all five members possess adequate skills and knowledge (Filley, 1970). As one author noted in assessing the effectiveness of group meetings whose purpose is to make a specific decision, "decision-making is not a spectator sport; onlookers get in the way of what needs to be done" (Grove, 1983, p. 137). So when you're preparing a meeting, include only people who either have the skills and knowledge to contribute or who are important links in the communication network. And keep in mind that effective interaction is less likely when the number of participants exceeds a dozen or so.

The agenda is the planning document that guides what you hope to accomplish at the meeting. This agenda should state the meeting's purpose. Is it only to exchange information or is it to make decisions? Will all relevant parties in the organization be included or merely their representatives? And if decisions are to be made, how are they to be arrived at? Will consensus be sought? If decisions are to be made by voting, what constitutes approval: a simple majority, a two-thirds majority, or . . . ? These issues should be clarified ahead of time in the agenda.

The agenda should also identify who will be in attendance; what, if any, preparation is required of each participant; a detailed list of items to be covered; the specific time and location of the meeting; and a specific finishing time.

2. Distribute the agenda in advance. If you want specific people to attend your meeting, and particularly if participants need to do some homework beforehand, get your agenda out well in advance of the meeting. What's an adequate lead time? That depends on such factors as the amount of preparation necessary, the importance of the meeting, and whether the meeting will be recurring (i.e., every Monday at 8:30 A.M.) or is being called once to deal with an issue that has arisen and will be repeated only under similar circumstances.

3. Consult with participants before the meeting. An unprepared participant can't contribute to his or her full potential. It is your responsibility to ensure that members are prepared. What data will they need ahead of time? Do they have those data? If not, what can you do to help them get them?

4. Get participants to go over the agenda. The first thing you should do at the meeting is to get participants to review the agenda. Do modifications need to be made? If so, make them. Clarify the issues that you plan to discuss. After this review, get participants to approve the final agenda.

5. Establish specific time parameters. Meetings should begin on time and have a specific time for completion (Stoffman, 1986). It is your responsibility to specify these time parameters and to hold to them.

6. Maintain focused discussion. It is the chairperson's responsibility to give direction to the discussion; to keep it focused on the issues; and to minimize interruptions, disruptions, and irrelevant comments (Stoffman, 1986). If participants begin to stray from the issue under consideration, the chairperson should intercede quickly to redirect the discussion. Similarly, one or a few members cannot be allowed to monopolize the discussion or to dominate others. Appropriate preventive action ranges from a subtle stare, a raised eyebrow, or other nonverbal communication, on up to an authoritative command such as ruling someone "out of order" or withdrawing someone's right to continue speaking.

7. Encourage and support participation by all members. Participants were not selected randomly. Each is there for a purpose. To maximize the effectiveness of problem-oriented meetings, each participant must be encouraged to contribute. Quiet or reserved personalities must be drawn out so their ideas can be heard.

8. Maintain an appropriate level of control. The style of leadership can range from authoritative domination to laissez-faire. The effective leader pushes when necessary and is passive when need be.

9. Encourage the clash of ideas. You need to encourage different points of view, critical thinking, and constructive disagreement. Your goals should be to stimulate participants' creativity and to counter the group members' desire to reach an early consensus.

10. Discourage the clash of personalities. An effective meeting is characterized by the critical assessment of ideas, not attacks on people. When running a meeting, you must quickly intercede to stop personal attacks or other forms of verbal insult.

11. Exhibit effective listening skills. If your group meeting is to achieve its objectives, you need to demonstrate the listening skills. Effective listening reduces misunderstandings, improves the focus of discussion, and encourages the critical assessment of ideas. Even if other group members don't exhibit good listening skills, if you do, you can keep the discussion focused on the issues and facilitate critical thinking.

12. Bring proper closure. You should close a meeting by summarizing the group's accomplishments; clarifying what actions, if any, need to follow the meeting; and allocating follow-up assignments (Stoffman, 1986). If any decisions have been made, who will be responsible for communicating and implementing them?

round Rules for Meetings

If the problem-solving session is to accomplish meaningful results, rules and procedures must be established and agreed on in advance by all concerned. Imagine playing a sport in which each participant had his or her own set of rules. Chaos would be a certainty. Most sports need an umpire or referee whose job it is to enforce the rules and prevent infractions. This role is yours to play as the supervisor.

Editor's Note: This is the last work on making meetings successful.

Several essential rules are listed in the subsections that follow. Using this listing as a guide while planning and conducting your meetings should prevent most hazards from occurring—or at least prevent any serious conflicts.

BEFORE THE MEETING

When you have a specific problem to be solved, communicate it to the group members in advance of the meeting. Be as clear as you can be in defining the problem and in specifying the goals you want the meeting to achieve. Be certain that limits such as time, company policy, and the amount of authority the group will have are clear to the group. Are they empowered only to recommend solutions or actually to choose them? In the latter case, you must delegate some of your formal authority to the group. If you alone have the power to decide, tell them so.

Give your members all the relevant data you have accumulated and any boundaries on solutions, such as resource limitations, imposed by management. This information will help the group adopt a realistic point of view. Let them know the order (the agenda) in which the group will consider and the time and duration of the meeting. All who have been chosen to attend should be made aware of their responsibilities to prepare for the meeting. Specifically, each member should make the following preparations:

1. Read the agenda, and prepare a list of questions that he or she should answer before facing the group.

2. Gather the information, materials, visuals, and so on that he or she will be responsible for presenting or disseminating to the group.

3. If a group member should be unable to attend the meeting for any legitimate reason, relay the input expected from that group member to the chairperson.

DURING THE MEETING

Provide name tags and assign seating when necessary. Start the meeting promptly, direct the discussion, stick to the agenda and time limits, draw out each member, list the alternatives, and summarize frequently. Maintain order, and keep the meeting on the subject. Normally, you should make your inputs only after other members in order to avoid inhibiting the group. In some instances you may want to avoid making your opinions known so that the group will take greater ownership of the decision.

During each meeting, the group members have specific responsibilities that should be communicated to them in advance and briefly repeated to them at the start of each session. If the meeting is to be beneficial to all concerned, each member should be prepared to do the following:

1. Be an active participant by listening attentively, taking notes, following the discussions, seeking clarification when confused, and adding input if the group member has the expertise or experience to do so.

2. Promote discussion and input from all members by respecting their right to their opinions and attitudes and by avoiding discourteous or disruptive behavior. (The chairperson should not hesitate to call on quiet members, using specific questions and asking for opinions.)

3. Practice group-serving roles (described in the next section). From the alternatives listed and analyzed, bring the group to one mind about the best alternative or combination of alternatives to endorse. If the solution is to work, the majority must be behind it. Be ready to compromise in order to break any impasse.

Assign tasks to those affected, if need be, and put the solution into operation as quickly as possible. At the close of each meeting, the participants should be made aware of any specific duties or assignments they will have as a result of the meeting. The chairperson should not allow the members to leave until each of them is clear about his or her new tasks. In addition to the specific duties each person may receive, all participants have the following general obligations:

1. When the meeting concerns sensitive matters, preserve the confidentiality of the discussion.

2. Relay decisions and changes to those for whom the group member may be responsible and whom they will affect.

3. Carry out promises made and assignments received as quickly as possible.

AFTER THE MEETING

After a problem-solving meeting, check on the results and on the group reactions. Follow up on individual assignments.

Managing a Team Project

The Project Manager and Management

A project involves many persons in the organization, from senior management to the worker who uses the system or the results of the system daily. These employees must be involved with the development of the project from the onset so their needs and wants can be considered in the design.

Usually, only the project manager is aware that input from employees is essential to the success of the project. This is probably the first experience for most in the organization to be directly involved in a project's development. Therefore, it is the responsibility of the project manager to give all affected employees a role in the development of the project. If he or she fails to do this, then key information remains unknown until the completed project is introduced to the organization.

For example, imagine that a just-in-time inventory system delivers a week's supply of parts to a manufacturing plant. This system involves coordination of the organization's computer systems with those of vendors. In addition, staffing and warehouse construction and other noncomputer systems are components of a just-in-time inventory system.

The project manager and the organization's management assume that demand for the product can be predicted with a degree of accuracy a week in advance. This is a reasonable assumption. However, a few weeks after the

**Editor's Note:
Team leaders are project managers by definition. Basic project management skills are essential to meeting any team's goals.**

Interpersonal Skills for Leadership, Second Edition, by Susan Fritz, F. William Brown, Joyce Poulacs Lunde, and Elizabeth A. Banset. Copyright © 1997 by Simon and Schuster Custom Publishing (now Pearson Custom Publishing).

system is introduced a sales representative asks how the system handles unpredictable heavy demand, since for several weeks during every year major clients are known to require 125% of a manufacturing week's worth of products. These orders are not known seven days in advance, but still must be filled. The current manufacturing method has met this demand because there was always more than a week's supply of parts on hand and the plant was placed on overtime to produce the products.

The bottom line is that the new just-in-time inventory system cannot perform as well as the existing system, and because of this the organization will lose business and possibly major clients. You can imagine the embarrassment of both the project manager and the project's sponsor. After years of planning and development, the "new" technology can't perform as well as the "old" system.

This dilemma could have been avoided if the project manager had consulted with all the stakeholders in the system during its development. Instead, the project manager accepted the approval of the marketing director, assuming he knew everything there was to know about the marketing and sales operations.

THE PROJECT MANAGER'S RESPONSIBILITIES

The project manager's job is to deliver the project on time, within budget, and in perfect working order the first day the project is implemented. This is a broad responsibility that begs questions, such as when is the deadline for the project? How much will the project cost to develop and implement? How will we know if the project is working perfectly?

Try to answer these questions and you'll discover that they are not easily answered. Yet it is your responsibility as project manager to find the answers before the development of the project begins. If you fail to answer these questions, then you allow each manager to devise his or her own answer, which will be used to determine whether your project is successful. This means that if your organization has 30 managers, then there will be 30 definitions of success—none of which might reflect the actual success of the project.

A project manager must take control over every aspect of the project from its inception, and must remain in control until the project is fully implemented. Your job is to manage everyone who is involved in the project, including senior management, the executive committee, the steering committee, stakeholders, and the project team who directly report to you.

Each one has a specific role in the project's development. You must define their role, then make sure they fulfill it. This is not an easy task since most of the participants do not report to you, so you will have to use your influence and political talents to assure that you receive the information you need to complete your assignment.

Here is a checklist that summarizes the steps you must address:

- Develop a consistent definition of the project. Specifically, what is the project to achieve? Be as specific as possible. A broad definition allows for various managers to devise their own interpretations. This could lead to false expectations that can result in the failure of the project.

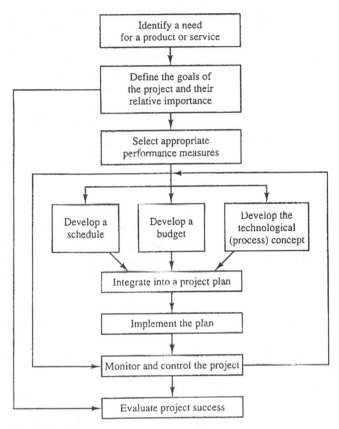

FIGURE 3-2

Major Processes in Project Management

- Identify the scope of the project. What are the constraints imposed on the project by management? What are the realities of the situation? Is there a business reason for an imposed deadline on the project? Does the organization have financial constraints that prohibit the project from meeting management's expectations? Are there technological limitations?

- Identify and develop a rapport with the project sponsor. This is the person who determines whether or not the project is allowed to continue through to implementation. Keep in mind that the project can be stopped at any time if the project sponsor feels doubt that you can deliver the project.

- Identify and develop a rapport with stakeholders. These are the people who will be working either directly or indirectly with the project once it is implemented. They are also the people who know the detailed operations of the organization, information you need to build the project.

- Identify the benefits of the project. How will the organization be better off once the project is completed? The answer to this question provides a concrete purpose for everyone to work towards the same goal.

- Determine what tasks must be performed to complete the project. Even the smallest task must be identified—otherwise cost and time estimates will be inaccurate and a critical component of the project could be overlooked, leading to the failure of the project.

- Develop and maintain a schedule of tasks. Determine when something must be done, by whom, and the dependencies of each task. A *dependency* is a task that must be performed before other tasks can be started.

- Identify milestones. A *milestone* is the completion of a key portion of the development process, such as the *user acceptance* test. The user acceptance test is the time in the development of the project when the users test the system and agree that it meets the original specifications.

- Identify deliverables. A *deliverable* is a piece of the project such as a report, a computer screen, or the foundation of a building that is an indication of progress.

RISK AND UNCERTAINTY

A key role of every project manager is to manage risks and uncertainty. Risk is present in most projects, especially those that use cutting-edge technology where there is little experience using the technology in business. It is prudent to assume that what can go wrong will go wrong. Principal sources of uncertainty include random variations in component and sub-system performance, inaccurate or inadequate data, and the inability to forecast satisfactorily due to lack of prior experience. Specifically, there may be:

1. *Uncertainty in scheduling.* Changes in the environment that are impossible to forecast accurately at the outset of a project are likely to have a critical impact on the length of certain activities. For example, subcontractor performance or the time it takes to obtain a longterm loan are bound to influence the length of various subtasks.

2. *Uncertainty in cost.* Limited information on the duration of activities makes it difficult to predict the amount of resources needed to complete them on schedule. This translates directly into an uncertainty in cost. In addition, the expected hourly rate of resources and the cost of materials used to carry out project tasks may also vary widely.

3. *Technological uncertainty.* Technological uncertainty may affect the schedule, the cost, and the ultimate success of the project. The integration of familiar technologies into one system or product may cause technological uncertainty as well. The same applies to the development of software and its integration with hardware.

4. *Organization and political uncertainty.* New regulations might affect the market for a project, while the turnover of personnel and changes in the policies of one or more of the participating organizations may disrupt the flow of work.

THE PROJECT TEAM

A project is similar to a football game where the project manager is the coach and members of the project team are the players who win or lose the game. The comparison between a project and a football game is probably the best way to fully understand the role of the project team.

The project manager plots a game-winning strategy, then determines the talent required to carry out his or her plan. The type of project determines the kinds of positions that must be fulfilled; for example, a systems project requires different players than a construction project, a distinction that is similar to the difference between a football game and a baseball game.

Each position on the team requires a certain skill set. For example, the customer relations project discussed throughout this section requires a project team member to design the account database. However, the proficiency level can vary among players who have the same skills. For example, a database designer who might be a whiz at getting the most efficiency from a Sybase database may be less than a super star if the database is built using an Oracle system.

It is the job of the project manager to assess the breadth and depth of skills required to play a position on the project team. Then he or she must find the talent to fill the position. And, just as in sports, there are constraints that limit the choice of talented players.

First of all, does such a person exist? The job description for the position might describe a person with an unusual set of skills and there are few players who can meet the requirements. If there is such a person, then how is the project manager going to find him or her? And if the person is found and interested in pursuing the position, will the project manager be able to convince him or her to join the team? Then there is the ultimate limitation— price. Are there sufficient funds in the project budget to compensate the prospective player?

These are many of the same constraints facing a coach of a football team. Talented players demand high compensation. When their price is higher than the amount budgeted for the position, the coach must lower his sights and redefine the job description.

However, before the project manager can start looking for talented players, he or she must determine the skills necessary to complete the project. The project manager should use the zero-based staffing rule to staff the project. *Zero-based staffing* is similar to zero-based budgeting. Each project starts without any staff except for the project manager—every project requires a project manager.

Every position on the project team must be justified based on tasks that need to be performed. In the customer relations project, it can easily be assumed that a database designer is required. However, the decision to create such a position must occur after the project manager determines there is a need for a database.

The project's task list initiates the generation of positions on the project team. Each task requires one or more team members to complete the task. In addition, the project schedule determines the number of positions on the project team.

Let's say five stakeholders must be interviewed for a day to gather details about the existing system. Typically a business analyst handles this kind of job. One business analyst is required if the project schedule allows five days to complete the task. However, five business analysts must be hired if one day is dedicated for the interviews. But if there isn't room in the budget for five business analysts, then the project manager must revise the project plan to coincide with funds available to complete the task.

Staffing a project is a balancing act among constraints that are beyond the control of the project manager. By using tasks and the project schedule as a basis for staffing, the project manager is able to identify players necessary to complete the project.

Once a balance is struck between the requirements of the project and a visible pool of candidates, the project manager must choose players for the project team. This is likely to be one of the most critical decisions that will determine whether the project team wins the game. The game is doomed even before the launch of the project if the project team doesn't gel with personalities, attitude, and technical skills.

A good player must have the desire to work within a team rather than for individual glory. Knowing this principle, a major international Wall Street firm has a policy of requiring candidates to work through several rounds of interviews. Each round requires the interviewer to determine whether the prospective employee has met a requirement of the position.

The question the interviewer has to answer in the first round is whether or not the candidate's personality fits with the organization's culture and with that of the team. The firm doesn't want an ego to get in the way of progress. Each team member is expected to help the others regardless of job assignment. If the candidate doesn't meet the first criterion, he or she is rejected regardless of experience or expertise.

The second round consists of technical interviews where the expertise of staff challenges the candidate's skills. Typically, technicians from various disciplines within the company probe the candidate's depth of knowledge of technology and business as it relates to the project.

No one grades the candidate. Instead, each interviewer subjectively determines the candidate's level of knowledge in each area. The results are submitted to the project manager who determines the proper blend of skills he or she wants on the team.

The remaining rounds of interviews center on whether or not the personality of the candidate clashes with that of the project manager, project sponsor and other managers involved in the project.

The People Skills Component

MANAGING EXPECTATIONS

When is a project successful? This is one of the hardest questions to answer for both project manager and others involved in the project. Each person has his or her own definition of success based upon whatever criteria the person deems important.

TABLE 3.3   A TYPICAL PROJECT TEAM FOR A SYSTEMS PROJECT

Programmer/Analyst

A programmer/analyst defines and analyzes aspects of the project using CASE tools. A CASE tool is used to collect information about a project and to automatically produce specifications and project reports. A programmer/analyst then interprets the specifications into a program.

Systems Analyst

A systems analyst interacts with the business unit and the business analyst to translate the business needs into specifications from which a programmer/analyst can create a component of the application. The systems analyst also creates prototypes of screens, reports and other aspects of the project.

Database Analyst/Administrator

A database analyst/administrator is responsible for the installation and maintenance of the database management system, which stores and retrieves data for the system. In addition, a database analyst/administrator designs and tunes the database used by the system. Designing a database involves organizing the data required by the system. Tuning the database involves taking advantage of all the features of the database management system to obtain the most efficient operation of the database.

Technical Analyst

A technical analyst is responsible for various hardware and software components of the system such as networking, communication, and assuring that components of the system work together. Many technical analysts have in-depth knowledge of a particular technology used in the project, e.g., data communication.

Business Analyst

A business analyst interacts with the business units to define the business requirements of the project. The business requirements are then submitted to the systems analyst, who translates the requirements into the specifications needed for the programmer/analyst to write the application.

Data Analyst

A data analyst extracts the data requirements from the business requirement. The data requirements are submitted to the database analyst/administrator who creates the database for the application.

Think about it. Your success as a project manager is being judged subjectively by the executive committee, steering committee, stakeholders, and your boss. You are bound not to meet someone's definition of success.

Our perception of success is based on our expectations of a result. If a project meets our expectations, then we tend to say the project is successful. Let's say a customer service representative's expectation is to have accurate account information displayed on the screen when a customer call is received. As long as the project meets this expectation, then the customer service representative feels the project is successful.

Likewise, the project sponsor expects the project to increase customer satisfaction. If customer complaints rise, especially when customers are forced to respond to a telephone menu, then the project sponsor feels the project failed.

The project manager has the responsibility to manage the expectations of everyone who is involved with the project so that the project will meet all the expectations. One of the major reasons why projects don't meet expectations is because the expectations are not realistic. For example, there are many factors other than the customer relations system that cause customers to be dissatisfied with an organization. The project manager must point out these factors before the project is launched.

Managing expectations is an ongoing responsibility. Throughout the project, the project manager and the project team must monitor expectations and use reality checks to bring the expectations closer to the true benefits of the project.

The fact that people tend to rely more on their instincts than the word of another poses a dilemma for project managers. Since many managers have little experience with the development of a project, their instincts, uninformed by experience, can cloud their expectations and their judgment of the project's success or failure. It is like a skunk caught on the highway with an 18-wheeler bearing down. The skunk realizes this is a life-threatening situation and instinctively raises its tail.

A project manager must overcome the influence of a manager's instincts by being persuasive. The manager must be convinced that his or her initial impression may not be correct. There are several techniques you can use to persuade a manager. First, gain the manager's trust by being honest, and provide a rational basis for your arguments.

You must be an effective communicator and use terms the manager can easily understand. Let's say the manager expects to have telephone, video, and computer data transferred anywhere in the organization within a fraction of a second. However, you realize the communication infrastructure is unable to meet this expectation because there is insufficient bandwidth.

Bandwidth is a technical concept that is difficult to appreciate unless you are a technician. However, you can easily make an analogy to a highway to illustrate the problem. The organization's communications infrastructure is a four-lane highway. This needs to be increased to a 16-lane highway to meet the manager's expectations.

Another technique to manage expectation is to deliver on a promise. You can pose a rational argument why the manager's expectation isn't reality. However, a little doubt will always remain until you are proven true. Therefore, you must establish achievable goals at the beginning of the project. Those goals must be shared with the manager—and the goals must be achieved.

AVOID THE PITFALLS OF DEALING WITH MANAGERS

The start of every project is predictable. The project sponsor and others involved in the project are confident the project will succeed. Special care is taken to approach the project systematically in an effort to avoid errors of previous projects.

This is called the *honeymoon period* when the project manager, the project sponsor, the steering committee, and the project team form a partnership and define their roles in the project. However, the honeymoon is short lived and soon adversarial relationships develop.

The lack of trust is the basis for the partnership to become unwound. A project manager makes many small and major commitments to management. Fidelity becomes a concern once a commitment is not met. Fail to live up to a commitment, and trust is lost, and is very difficult to regain.

Not every commitment can be met due to factors beyond your control and honest errors in judgment. Managers are supportive only if you are truthful. Support immediately drops once managers discover they are being deceived.

Your role is to deliver bad news to management. You must avoid panic and present the problem objectively. Don't minimize or embellish the situation. Be prepared to explain what you think caused the situation to occur—even if you or a member of the project team made an error.

Explore options to resolve the issue with the manager, and then collectively arrive at a course of action to rectify the situation and prevent it from reoccurring.

BUILDING A RAPPORT WITH MANAGERS

A project manager plays various roles in the project, including coaching the project team, advising management, and making sure a variety of personalities are pleased with the progress of the project. Another key role is to develop a solid rapport with the project sponsor and steering committee members, for these are the people who determine the success or failure of the project.

People tend to become familiar with each other by finding something in common besides working on the project. It is important for the project manager to locate things unrelated to the project that will bring him or her closer to the manager—for example, sports, books, films, family, and education.

Once the relationship is built on common ground, the project manager must be sure not to violate unwritten guidelines of business ethics. For example, appropriate formality and informality can be used depending on the rapport developed between you and the manager. Use comfortable mannerisms and speak in everyday language at all times.

You must be prepared to sell the project sponsor and others involved with the project on various proposals, such as changing the project specifications or hiring another member for the project team.

Trust and respect go a long way to making the sale. However, you must be sure the customer—in this case the manager—doesn't feel rushed into adopting the proposal. Otherwise, the customer may feel you are "putting one over" on him or her. You can avoid this problem by understanding the steps involved in acceptance of a proposal.

Let's use the analogy of selling a car to illustrate this process. First, the customer needs to be aware the car exists. This is called the *awareness step*. Car manufacturers and dealerships tend to accomplish this by showing the benefits of the car in advertisements. The object is to get the customer's attention.

If successful, the customer explores the car further by visiting the show room and asking general questions such as fuel mileage and cost. This is called the *exploration step*. These questions are designed to qualify the car and determine whether the car meets the customer's needs.

If this step is also successful, the customer begins to see the merits of the car and enters the *examination step*. It is here where the customer investigates the details of the car such as the color, CD player, options, and availability.

If the examination step is successful, then the customer is willing to enter the test step. The *test step* is where the customer tries the car, looking for any reason not to make the purchase. If the test step goes well, then a sale is made. This is referred to as the *adoption step*.

TABLE 3.4 STEPS OF ADOPTION

1. Awareness
2. Exploration
3. Examination
4. Test
5. Adoption

HANDLING AN ANGRY MANAGER OR TEAM MEMBER

When a project doesn't proceed as planned, people involved with the project become frustrated, which typically manifests as anger directed at the person responsible for the project—you, the project manager.

You are placed in a difficult situation. There is likely a sensible reason why the project isn't meeting expectations. However, rarely will any reasoning avoid the angry response. Instead, the anger is vented towards you, who are likely helpless to provide immediate satisfaction.

There are steps that can be taken to manage the anger and leave the other person with a positive feeling for the project. You must remain in control at all times and not take the anger personally. The anger is directed at the situation and not you.

Stay calm and let the person know you are sincerely interested in his or her concerns and disappointments. Give the user time to vent the anger, after which he or she will be in a better frame of mind to address the situation rationally.

The objective is to have the person talk about the problem, during which time you can acknowledge facts and defuse myths. Any misperceptions must be resolved. Ask questions that isolate the issues that disturbed the person.

You must remain detached from the situation; otherwise, your emotions will impede your role of being an advisor and manager. This technique is similar to that used by emergency room physicians. No matter the condition of the patient, the physician's job is to identify facts, isolate the problem, explain the reality of the situation to the patient and have the patient agree to a treatment.

An agreed-upon course of action cannot be considered until the person's anger has dissipated. Until then, you must be a good listener and fact-finder. Anger over a project can lead to the break in rapport and damage the bond built between the project manager and others on the project team. You cannot let this happen.

Once the other person is calm, you must rebuild the rapport by showing that both of you are on the same team, working towards the same objective. You must recognize a problem exists and lead the other person towards a solution.

Let's say the project sponsor noticed that critical data are missing from a prototype data entry screen. He anticipates this will cause a month's delay in the project. After the project sponsor has vented his anger, you must provide a reality check and identify the missing data and the effort it will take to revise the screen.

People tend to lose track of the significance of a problem. Small problems take on major proportions in the absence of an understanding of the facts. You must help the person define the magnitude of the problem. Is it really a big problem or a small problem that seems big?

Start by agreeing to what is correct about the situation. This shows that progress has been made. Move on to what is incorrect about the situation, which shows issues that need to be addressed. Next focus attention on a solution. Agree upon how and when the issue will be resolved. It is critical that the solution will work and will be delivered on time. Avoid under- or over-estimating effort required to fix the problem.

THE FEAR FACTOR

A project manager must be aware of apprehensions of managers who are involved in the project. We tend to assume everyone is beginning the project with a "gung-ho" attitude. However, managers are likely to approach the project timidly because a project can be a minefield that can kill a successful career.

Behind the manager's game-face is fear. It is important to recognize this fact and plan to ease any fears. The initial fear is of you. The success or failure of the project—and possibly the manager's career—is in your hands. Will you deliver the project on time and within budget?

There is also the fear of the unknown. No one, including you, knows if the project will be successful. This fear is increased when the fate of the project is out of the manager's hands, as is the case for the project sponsor. For him or her, the experience is like being a passenger on an airliner. The pilot is responsible for getting you to your destination. You and the pilot cannot guarantee that you'll get there—even though the probability is high. You try to recognize problems in flight based on previous bad experiences, but you're never sure if they are serious problems. And you're not sure that the pilot is telling you the truth when he says everything is OK.

Then there is the fear that the project sponsor may lose his or her job. Is the project urgent enough to take such a risk? The sponsor is authorizing expenditure of funds for a project that might fail; he or she is risking making bad decisions and losing face with colleagues and senior management.

It is your job to identify these and other fears and try to minimize their effects on the project.

THE ART OF INTERVIEWING

A substantial amount of project management time is typically spent interviewing executive committee members, the steering committee, project sponsor, and other stakeholders. Interviews can elicit important information needed to complete the project. It is your job and the job of anyone else who conducts interviews to design meetings for the productive exchange of information.

Meetings are usually conducted in one of three ways: *very structured*, such as a town hall meeting with a formal agenda and rules of order to follow; *semistructured*, where there is a known topic and an objective for the meeting; or *ad hoc*, where no planning or control is implemented.

Experienced project managers avoid *ad hoc* meetings, at least to the degree that they depend on the meeting to identify key information for the project. Likewise, a town hall meeting approach rarely is conducive to a free flow of ideas. Most meetings regarding a project are semi-structured. The meeting is called for a particular purpose, such as determining the flow of a process. The meeting also has a clear objective; that is, at the end of the meeting specific information necessary to complete an element of the project is known.

You must carefully plan every meeting to assure it provides for an open exchange of ideas and yet still benefits the project. Below are techniques used by experienced project managers to ensure that project meetings are productive.

First, set an objective each time you meet with someone regarding the project. You should not require a formal agenda, but you must establish the topic before the meeting and share this information with all attendees so they too can prepare to discuss the topic. Limit the meeting to no more than two topics. Meetings are only productive for an hour so you probably won't be able to explore more than two topics.

In addition, only invite to the meeting people who can contribute to the topic. Don't allow anyone to "sit-in" for someone else. For example, a common practice is for a key manager to send a staff member as his or her representative to the meeting. Unfortunately, that staff member is rarely in a position to make decisions or answer questions on behalf of the manager. The meeting is likely to be unproductive.

Begin the meeting or interview by easing into the conversation rather than starting abruptly like a baseball game. It is your meeting, and you set the tone. Make sure everyone is at ease. Your job is to ask questions and keep the meeting focused on the topic. Ask questions respectfully and never sound as if you are interrogating anyone. Let others in the meeting do most of the talking as long as they remain on the topic. Listen carefully, take notes and never dominate the conversation. Give each person time to present his or her thoughts.

Don't be afraid to encourage someone to elaborate on a thought. Likewise, ask test questions to be certain others in the meeting feel the meeting is staying on track. For example, you may ask someone, "How do you feel about what we've discussed? Is there an important issue that you feel we haven't discussed?" If the answer is yes and off the topic of the meeting, then schedule another meeting to explore the issue, and make sure you determine who must make the final decision on the issue.

For example, attendees might be staff employees who have important information and opinions on the topic, but who are not authorized to decide on a course of action. You need to know who are the decisionmakers and what information is required for them to make the decision. Then provide the information and have them make the decision.

Maintain eye contact when someone is responding to your question. Looking away implies disinterest or that what is being said is not important to you. Keep the conversation moving and don't allow anyone to get bogged down in unnecessary details. For example, a conversation discussing a data entry screen should not wander into opinions on a PC monitor or the computer running the screen.

Make sure you clarify each point made by someone. Feedback is the best method to assure you have a firm understanding of what is being said and a way of letting the person know that you are listening. Always try to see the point from the other person's perspective. This helps you to understand their emotions and commitment to the project.

Avoid speaking about politics, religion, or other controversial topics, or allowing negative remarks to be made about anyone during the meeting. These are sensitive areas for most of us and usually have little or nothing to do with a project. They also may cause a difference of opinion that hampers progress.

Always end a meeting on a positive note by having everyone agree on something—even if it is a small item, such as having the notes of the meeting sent to everyone.

Above all, you must maintain your integrity during the meeting—and during the project. Each of us has set our own standards that should not be compromised for the sake of a project. There are two important questions that should be asked before you take any action: Would I want someone to do this to me? Would I be proud to see my actions on the nightly news? If you answer no to either of these questions, then don't do it.

DYNAMICS OF A MEETING

A project manager must be a good facilitator. A facilitator understands the dynamics of people working as a group, and uses this knowledge to assure that the interaction during a meeting results in a consensus.

Let's say you called a meeting to discuss a specification change that will delay the completion date by three months. The appropriate people are invited to attend. Each brings to the meeting expertise, motivation, personality, personal objectives, and opinions. You must manage the meeting so these characteristics don't prevent the group from agreeing to a solution.

Project managers are able to achieve a consensus by using guidelines taken from the study of *group dynamics*. There are three roles that must be managed at every meeting to assure that the group makes a rational decision. These roles are called the *task roles*, the *maintenance roles*, and the *individual-centered roles.* Anyone in the group can take on one or more of these roles during the meeting.

Task Roles

Task roles are those required for the group to make a decision. There are five task roles: initiating, opinion giving/seeking, clarifying, summarizing, and reality testing.

The *initiating role* sets the objective of the meeting and a procedure for reaching the objective, which is inviting appropriate employees to the meeting to determine a course of action. Typically, the project manager fulfills this role, although it is not uncommon for the project sponsor to do the same.

The *opinion giving/seeking role* is demonstrated by someone who expresses his or her feelings on the issue or asks a question. Every attendee can find himself or herself in this role.

The *clarifying role* is fulfilled by someone who explores an issue mentioned during the meeting. The person restates the idea, asks for or offers a definition of terms used to describe the issue, and offers various interpretations of the issue.

The *summarizing role* is taken by someone who assembles the ideas on the table into a course of action. This is an attempt to reach a consensus. Several attempts might be made before there is agreement within the group.

The *reality-testing role* is one where the proposed consensus is critically analyzed. One or more members of the group ask whether or not the proposal is achievable. If the answer is yes, then the group has dealt with the issue; otherwise, the issue is revisited by someone taking on one of the other task roles.

Maintenance Roles

Maintenance roles are those that are performed to continue the decision-making process. Many influences can cause the meeting to go off track and impede movement toward a consensus. Maintenance roles bring the meeting back on track. There are five maintenance roles: harmonizing, gate-keeping, consensus testing, encouraging, and compromising.

The *harmonizing role* reduces tensions and attempts to reconcile disagreements among meeting participants. The person who takes on this role seeks to have differences resolved to the point where they are no longer interfering with the progress of the meeting.

The *gate-keeping role* maintains open communication channels. If the meeting becomes silent, the gatekeeper speaks in order to keep the discussion lively.

The *consensus-testing role* determines whether the group is prepared to reach a decision. The person filling this role might send up a trial proposal and see if there is any agreement. If not, the meeting continues.

The *encouraging role* fosters an environment conducive to exploring an issue. It is this role that seeks to have everyone voice his or her opinion and ideas. For example, some attendees tend to sit silently listening without contributing to the meeting. The person taking on the encouraging role must bring those people into the conversation.

The *compromising role* offers a solution that can be supported by everyone at the meeting. This role is critical whenever conflicts stand in the way of a consensus.

Individual-Centered Roles

Individual-centered roles reflect personal traits that hinder a decision. Each of us at some point assumes most of the individual-centered roles during the meeting. You have the responsibility to recognize these roles as they manifest, and then to try to diminish their effect on the group, even to the point of taking a 10-minute recess. There are five individual-centered roles: aggression, blocking, dominating, out-of-field behavior, and special interest pleading.

The *aggression role* is taken when someone attacks a participant, the group, or the project without providing constructive criticism. Aggression, if out of hand, destroys the decision process and defeats the purpose of the meeting.

The *blocking role* is one in which an unreasonable effort is made to thwart the group's progress. Attendees can and should have a lively discussion that elicits opposing opinions; however, this must not prevent the group from reaching a decision.

The *dominating role* is seen when a person tries to manipulate members of the group by asserting either real or implied authority.

The *out-of-field behavior role* is one in which a person is not relating to the discussion. The person is physically attending the meeting, but is mentally somewhere else.

The *special-interest pleading role* attempts to use the group as a tool to achieve an individual's objective rather than to address the issue related to the project.

TABLE 3.5   STAYING ALIVE

Here is a checklist for keeping a project on track.

1. Keep the project team focused on the mission.
2. Identify managers who make final decisions related to the project.
3. Make sure all plans are approved before work begins.
4. Make sure all changes to the plan are approved before work begins.
5. Manage the expectations of everyone involved with the project.
6. Avoid in-fighting within management groups.
7. Avoid surprising management and the project team.
8. Keep the project proceeding as planned.
9. Don't overemphasize any aspect of the project.
10. Don't allow a personality conflict to overshadow a valuable opinion.
11. Don't allow favoritism to influence objectivity.
12. Don't make judgments based upon preconceived notions.

Making Decisions and Solving Problems as a Team

*D*ecision-making is at the core of team performance. It is often the very reason for the team's existence, and the degree to which the team has an effective decision-making process is the degree to which the team is successful.

In this section we will look at the team decision-making process from several perspectives. First, we will discuss the overall process of decision-making and how it specifically impacts team performance. For each of the key steps in the decision-making process—generating ideas, discussion, and choice of action—we will discuss specific techniques that can improve each aspect of the process. In the section on generating ideas, we will assess three different approaches to brainstorming that teams might use to improve the number of options the team considers. The section on discussion will consider two ways to improve the quality of team decision-making. First, we will look at different kinds of thinking that draw out innovative ideas and resolutions, and then we will describe the verbal behaviors that help the team move effectively through the discussion process. For the third part of decision-making—choice of action—we will look at two very different approaches to deciding—justified decision-making and consensus—and discuss the advantages and disadvantages of each.

That we bring teams together to solve problems itself suggests that the problems the team is charged to address are complex. Otherwise, we would have had an individual make the decision. This is especially true in a culture

Editor's Note: Making decisions and solving problems are not necessarily the same. This section looks at both processes.

131

that prizes individualism and is relatively suspicious of teamwork. Therefore, it is critical to team effectiveness that the team develop a core competency in decision-making. It is not enough that the team understands the process. It is not enough that the team generally applies the principles of effective decision-making. Decision-making is the most critical function of the team, and it needs focused and constant attention to be done well.

Types of Decisions

The first issue that the team needs to address in the decision-making process is which decisions it will make. There are two considerations here. The first is to identify the type of decision so that the appropriate process can be used, and the second is to decide if that decision is within the charter and purpose of the team.

The matrix in Figure 3-3 shows four major categories of decisions the team will face. Decisions will fall on a continuum between minor and major, and their focus will move from task to people. Depending on where the decision falls, the team needs to develop the appropriate decision-making process. In the next section we will look at the common flow of decision-making. The matrix helps the team understand how much time and effort to spend in each of the steps in the matrix and which activities to emphasize.

Teams, like individuals, tend to make all decisions using the same decision criteria and process. The result is that some decisions are made inappropriately. If team decision-making focuses on efficiency, then major task and people decisions tend to be less thoughtful than necessary. If, on the other hand, the team decision-making process tends to be contemplative, minor decisions are overassessed and the team is plagued with analysis paralysis. For today's environment, teams need a decision-making process sophisticated enough to differentiate the requirements of different types of decisions.

The upper lefthand corner of the matrix in Figure 3-3 shows what the team needs to consider in making decisions that are characterized as minor task decisions. These decisions tend to be the daily, operations-driven decisions of the team. Examples might be how to collect data for decision-making, who to invite to a team meeting, the format for presenting team recommendations or decisions, or when to perform a particular part of an overall activity. The critical point with decisions in this quadrant is time frame. This is the quadrant where decisions can get bogged down. These decisions often represent the concrete aspects of the team's charter, that is, issues the team can readily grasp and deal with. As such, there is a great tendency for the team to spend an inordinate amount of time on these issues. However, these issues need to be resolved quickly so that the team can deal with the more substantive, albeit more difficult and ambiguous, issues.

The upper right quadrant of Figure 3-3 also deals with minor issues, but these tend to be more people-based than task-based. These decisions would include sub-group assignments, attendance and tardiness issues, and team recommendations that have an impact on human resource practices. As with minor task decisions, a key to effectiveness is timeliness. The liability in this

Task	*Focus*	People

<table>
<tr><td rowspan="2">M
I
N
O
R</td><td>

Requires decision but has no lasting effect on team or organization.

Time Frame: Fast

Quality: Acceptable

Thinking: Primarily procedural

Process:
1) Identify issue
2) Review facts
3) Consider choices
4) Decide
5) Move on

</td><td>

Important to individual but relatively unimportant to organization/team.

Time Frame: Fast

Quality: Consistent

Thinking: Procedural with some constructed

Process:
1) Identify issue
2) Consider current policy
3) Consider impact on others
4) Decide
5) Communicate decision and rationale

</td></tr>
</table>

Impact is the vertical axis label on the left.

<table>
<tr><td rowspan="2">M
A
J
O
R</td><td>

Has long-term implications for the organization/team.

Time Frame: Moderate

Quality: Accuracy and acceptance

Thinking: Constructed supported by procedural

Process:
1) Identify issue
2) Gather comprehensive information
3) Search for options
4) Evaluate options
   a. consistent with goals
   b. possible side effects
5) Consult those affected
6) Decide
7) Advise those affected
8) Follow up during implementation

</td><td>

Has impact on entire work group.

Time Frame: Long

Quality: Involvement and acceptance

Thinking: Primarily constructed

Process:
1) Involve those affected
2) Gather information on facts and feelings
3) Develop options
4) Consider options carefully
   a. consistent with values/principles
   b. possible side effects
5) Decide
6) Communicate clearly and widely
7) Follow up with learning and development

</td></tr>
</table>

FIGURE 3-3

Team Decision-Making Matrix

decision area is that the team will decide to "reinvent the wheel," redeciding things already covered by policy and practice. While it is true that policy and practice need to be continually challenged, a brief check on the current relevancy of the policy should be sufficient for this level of decision. For this reason, the thinking required in this quadrant is mainly procedural and includes support from constructed thinking since the addition of people into a problem always adds ambiguity. Because these issues involve people, the team needs to consider the impact of the decision on others. Since the decision is at the practice level rather than the policy level, the primary concern for the team rests with consistency; that is, the team needs to be sure that it is applying the same criteria and standards to the decisions that fall in this quadrant.

Major task decisions occupy the lower left corner of the matrix (Figure 3-3). These decisions tend to involve the major goals of the team. Examples of decisions that belong in this category include deciding which options the team should recommend or pursue; making major equipment purchases; and choosing the type of market research to engage in. The implications of these decisions are great, and the decision process is primarily focused on the quality of the decision. Because issues with long-term implications offer the organization an opportunity for innovation, the thinking style for the decision needs to be constructed. However, since the decision is primarily technical, there also needs to be a heavy procedural component to the thinking. Decisions in this quadrant lend themselves to analysis, but the team does not want to use only current mindsets to frame that analysis. Major task decisions offer a true payback for time invested in dialogue and innovation. Being creative is desirable in this quadrant, but being traditional is often the norm.

The final quadrant in the matrix deals with decisions that have major impact on the people of the organization. Mergers, restructuring, philosophy changes such as moving to a team-based organization, and human resource system changes (i.e., compensation, performance management) are all decisions that belong in this quadrant. Like the major task decisions, these issues are often the very reason for bringing the team together. Decisions in this area need to be driven by constructed thinking. The issues are seldom characterized as having right answers, and involvement and acceptance are the keys to effectiveness. Rather than having an internal focus on analysis, these decisions gain value from synthesis and inclusion. Teams that deal with these decisions effectively develop a strong external focus and tolerate many variations around a general resolution. To the extent that the team can discipline itself to clarify first the type of decision it needs to make, the greater likelihood that it can focus on the relevant parts of the decision-making process. Successful teams assess and monitor this critical part of their process on a regular basis, often using outside assessors to provide both insight into the whole process and training for gaining greater decision-making capabilities.

*D*ecision-Making Process

The normal team decision-making process revolves around throwing ideas out on the table during a team discussion period. Relying on a Darwinian effect, the team assumes that the "fittest" of the ideas will survive this process. If the team was not subject to the human liabilities of politics, persuasion, and power, this natural evolution of ideas might work. However, given the nature of organizations and teams, decision-making must have some method to record and develop ideas if it is to be effective.

Figure 3-4 provides an example of a common decision-making process. While most teams are aware of this process, team members often do not follow it in any systematic way. The diagram shows that once the team has accepted the responsibility for the decision, it must gather information to

Developing a Team Process

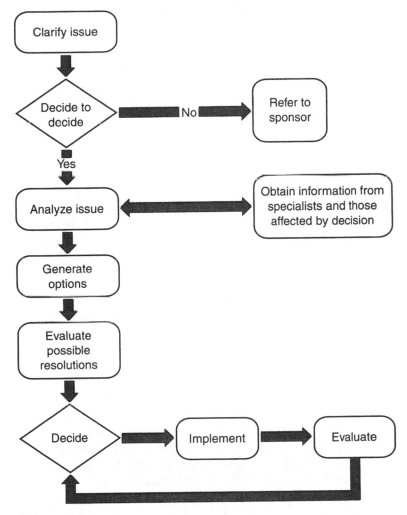

FIGURE 3-4

Team Decision-Making Process

analyze the nature of the issue. Referring back to the decision matrix at the beginning of the section, the team needs to monitor the time it spends on this step. The information sought must be sufficient to assure a quality decision, but gathering information cannot become an end unto itself. It often helps the team to define its purpose and set parameters on the information needed before the search begins. That way, team members know what to look for and when to stop gathering data.

Once the team has appropriate information, it can move on to generating options. If the team is deciding a major issue, gathering background information may be the most important part of the decision-making process. The more ideas and options the team can generate, the more possibilities for resolution, especially given that major issues are by definition complex and defy a "one right answer" approach. Once generated, options are developed and evaluated. The use of quality thinking and inquiring verbal behaviors enhance these discussion steps in the decision-making process. The conversation skills of both dialogue and discussion are necessary for this step to lead to enlightened decisions.

When the issue is understood and the options are articulated, the team needs to select one or more pathways to resolution. Coming to a clear and agreed upon decision often eludes the team. Team members frequently complain that issues are discussed and discussed but not resolved. To make progress, the team needs to make choices and move on to the next issue. Selecting the appropriate choice mechanism can help the team decide.

There are, then, three parts to the decision-making process, in particular, that teams need to manage carefully: (1) generating ideas; (2) exploring ideas; and (3) deciding on a course of action. In the following sections we will discuss each of the three parts. However, the success or failure of the decision is often in its implementation. In successful teams, the work is not done with the decision. Mutual accountability demands that the team manage the implementation of the decision and then evaluate its impact.

Generating Ideas and Options

Over the years researchers in the area of decision-making have been aware that if a quality decision is to be made, quality ideas must first come from the group. In addition to generating ideas, the group needs a way to capture those ideas so that they can be explored. Without some sort of recording structure or method, most ideas will not be considered. In addition, given the political nature of the group, the ideas that are most likely to be considered are based on the position power of the suggestor. Not only does this approach discourage members of the team, it is also very detrimental to the organization because it generates few new ideas. People with high position power in the organization are generally most interested in preserving the current system that supports their position. It is unlikely that such a person will suggest an idea that will radically change the way business is done. This undermines the whole reason for the team, which is to bring in new ideas and consider new ways of doing things. Therefore, generating quality ideas is vital to the effectiveness of the team.

Brainstorming

A common method teams use to generate ideas is brainstorming. Brainstorming is characterized by an intensive period of spawning as many ideas as possible without critique. The purpose of brainstorming is driven by the principle that if you want to end up with some good ideas, it is best to start off with many ideas. For a team to use brainstorming effectively, it must capture all the ideas, prioritize them, discuss the key ideas at length, and then decide on a course of action. To simply throw out several ideas at the beginning of the meeting is not brainstorming. In Figure 3-5 we describe three

Technique	Advantages	Disadvantages
Nominal Group Technique	• Controls for power • Makes efficient use of time • Establishes priorities • Can build on ideas • Preserves all ideas • Builds acceptance • Openness	• Very structured • No time for elaboration • Needs strong and objective leader • Restlessness with large group
Affinity	• Builds acceptance • Provides for small-group discussion • Shows scope and support for ideas • Controls for power • Makes efficient use of time • Preserves ideas	• Little synergism of ideas in first phase • No accommodation for second round of ideas • Requires writing skills • Requires most time
Delphi	• Does not require bringing people together • Can determine the strength of support for a given idea • Can preserve all ideas	• No synergism of ideas • People afraid of being identified • No chance for elaboration on idea • People suspicious that process has been manipulated

FIGURE 3-5

Brainstorming Techniques

general examples of brainstorming and the advantages and disadvantages associated with each.

NOMINAL GROUP TECHNIQUE

Historically, one of the most effective methods of brainstorming has been the Nominal Group Technique (NGT). The technique, developed by Andrew Delbecq, greatly formalized the idea-generation process. The process begins with a facilitator clearly defining the problem or opportunity to be addressed. Then, in round-robin fashion, members of the group put forth ideas in short simple phrases. As is common in brainstorming, there is to be no advocacy or criticism during the idea-generation phase. The group continues to go around the table until all ideas have been expressed. All ideas are recorded and numbered on flip charts and posted around the room.

The group then spends a short time clarifying the ideas presented. The purpose here is twofold: (1) to be sure everyone understands (even if they do not agree with) the ideas listed; and (2) to eliminate duplication of ideas. Again, there is no advocacy nor criticism allowed during clarification. Once the ideas have been clarified, each member individually prioritizes the ideas recorded. This is usually done by having group members vote, in rank order, for the three to five ideas she or he thinks would be most valuable to pursue. The facilitator records each person's selections and then presents the results of the voting to the group in the form of the ideas that received the most support.

The Nominal Group Technique is very efficient. A group of 20 people can usually generate more than a hundred ideas in 15 minutes. Voting identifies those issues most acceptable to the group, and if each member in a group of 20 selects and ranks three issues, five or six will surface as the most important to pursue. Recording preserves all the ideas. Therefore, even if an issue is not substantive enough to reach the final list, it can be separately pursued as an individual "good idea."

The Nominal Group Technique also minimizes position power, because all ideas are listed in the same way, regardless of who suggested them, and the voting is done privately. Thus, a first-level employee's idea has the same opportunity for acceptance as the president's. Because of the openness of the process, the results of the voting are easily accepted by the groups as a good place to begin the exploration process.

AFFINITY

Total quality management initiatives in the early 1990s promoted a variation on the NGT called an affinity diagram. The process is similar to the NGT except that people write down their ideas and then post them on a board rather than verbally going round robin. The group then collectively sorts the ideas into general categories; that is, they group things that have an "affinity" for one another. Each category is then labeled and given to a group to decipher. The group is to combine the ideas, preserving intent and language, into a set of suggestions.

Affinity is somewhat easier to use than the NGT, though it takes more overall time. It allows everyone to generate ideas at the same time and thus reduces the restlessness that often occurs at the end of the NGT idea-generating portion when all but a few people are ready to move on. The evaluation of ideas is done in small groups, which provides for expansion and understanding. However, Affinity loses some of the power of suggestion that comes with the Nominal Group Technique. When one member of the group hears the idea of another, it may spark a new idea. In Affinity, ideas are confined initially to the mind of each member, and so the suggestions that the small teams have to work with can be fairly narrow. Both the Nominal Group Technique and Affinity gather a wealth of information from a group of people in a short period of time. The NGT is more specific in its recording and prioritizing, but Affinity gets a sense of intensity for an idea and generally has more information from which to work.

DELPHI

When a team needs to gather information from members outside the team, Delphi can be an attractive brainstorming technique. In the Delphi process, the key issue is defined and then members are polled for their suggestions. Once the suggestions are collected, the common or unusual ones are culled from the group. These suggestions then become the agenda for further discussion. Delphi allows the team to gather information from widely separated groups and to get a feeling for the support for given suggestions. The process can be repeated to gain additional information or to refine the list of suggestions. The team can also keep track of the sources of suggestions, so it would be able, for example, to separate issues and ideas associated with field offices from those associated with headquarters.

The advantages of Delphi are also its weaknesses. Like Affinity, the generation of ideas, at least in the first round, does not benefit from having heard the ideas of others. This drawback can be offset somewhat by using follow-up rounds, but some of the dynamic of the NGT is lost. The ability in Delphi to identify sources of suggestions is a tradeoff to the anonymity of both the NGT and Affinity. Depending on the sensitivity of the issue, the existence of trust in the organization, and the importance of position power, this is a more or less serious tradeoff.

Delphi, then, is most appropriately used to gain information from large, widely dispersed groups or to narrow the focus of a larger issue. All three brainstorming techniques have value to the team, and as with the decision-making process in general, the team needs to choose a technique that is well suited to the dynamics and type of decision required.

All of the brainstorming processes described above suffer from three shortcomings: originality of ideas, the size of group, and follow-through. Unless the process of brainstorming is unusually intense, the ideas generated tend to be rather ordinary. Also, the ideas presented will not necessarily give you multiple perspectives on an issue. If the group is highly homogeneous or is composed of long-term members of the organization, brainstorming will probably generate variations of ideas or practices already in use in the organization. Since brainstorming does not challenge the thinking process itself, the results tend to be shades of the familiar rather than new ideas.

One way to improve brainstorming is to require the group to go through the process several times. Edward DeBono, the corporate guru for creativity and the author of *Serious Creativity*, suggests that a group must go through at least three iterations of any brainstorming activity before it begins to generate any truly new ideas. In his approach, effective brainstorming requires the group to come up with all the ideas it can and then discard them—both literally and figuratively. Then the group starts over. By the third iteration, the group is really stretching for new responses and is most likely to be creative. As you can imagine, this type of brainstorming can be a much more time-consuming and difficult process than just a single swipe at new ideas. However, if the team is working on a major issue, the investment in time and energy is likely worthwhile.

Two final issues that determine the effectiveness of the team's use of brainstorming are group size and follow-through. It is important to take the size of the group into account when choosing a brainstorming process. If the group consists of more than 24 people, it is probably better to use Affinity than the Nominal Group Technique. As the group increases in size, it takes longer and longer for the round robin discussion to reach each person. Group members will become restless and may lose interest in the process. The larger the group, the more important it is for the facilitator to keep the process moving. With Affinity, each person works on his or her own and then gathers in small groups. There is no period of time when the individual is not immersed in the process. It is therefore easier to keep a large group involved and focused.

Brainstorming generates many ideas, some of them worth pursuing. It is important that the team identify a range of ideas to follow through on after the session and be persistent in acting on those ideas. If in the end, the process is just a list of ideas with no action having been taken, participants will become cynical and unwilling to participate in future brainstorming activities.

Exploring Ideas and Options

Once ideas come to the table, they must be explored and enriched. In the exploration phase of decision-making, dialogue is the most effective conversation style. Understanding rather than judging will draw out the best insights from the team and allow people to bring forth innovative ideas.

Below we describe two important elements of effective exploration. First, we consider the need for good thinking by the team. No matter how open the group, if the thinking is not clear and disciplined, the decisions will be flawed. Next, we look at verbal behaviors that are especially important to the exploration step in decision-making.

Thinking

Thinking skills, like other human capacities, grow and develop over time. Like other skills, they are enhanced through learning and practice. Figure 3-6 is a continuum that sets forth a general evolution of thinking skills used within the organization. The least sophisticated skills are found at the left end of the scale. Received thinking skills tend to be limited and cautious, and to look for others to solve the team's problems. As such, they contribute little to team thinking, especially if the team has been called together for problem solving or opportunity pursuit. Moving up the scale, subjective thinking allows the team itself to address problems, but it tends to be very conservative and traditional in approach. Only if the team has firsthand experience with the specific issues presented will subjective thinking lend insight to the discussion. Procedural thinking is the most common form of team thinking. Teams use procedural thinking in both discussion and decision-making.

Received	Subjective	Procedural	Constructed
• Authoritative	• Experiential	• Anwers given	• Questions raised
• Dualistic	• Owns its own authority	• Analysis made	• Synthesis sought
• Quantitative	• Goes on "gut feeling"	• Argumentative	• Exploration pursued

FIGURE 3-6

Development of Our Thinking Processes

Unlike received and subjective thinking, procedural thinking adds greatly to the teaming process. Constructed thinking represents the most sophisticated level of team interaction. Dialogue requires constructed thinking. Teams that can blend procedural and constructed thinking have the best chance for innovative thinking and quality decisions.

Received thinking depends heavily on authority for opinions and conclusions. If the boss, the union, the manual, or for that matter the newspaper or TV says something is so, then that ends the discussion. Therefore, received thinking tends to operate from a dualistic perspective—good/bad, right/wrong, smart/stupid—and has a great deal of trouble working well in an ambiguous environment. In received thinking, a paradox is simply not possible.

There was a time when organizations valued received thinking. People who did what they were told and did not question authority were valued; the company manual was right; competitors were evil. In today's teams, received thinking can bring discussion to a halt. It offers little capacity to deal with complexity, and risk taking is undesirable. Fear of reprisal and overvaluing tradition causes the team to fear to do anything without permission.

When a team finds its conversation studded with statements like the ones in the list below, it has fallen into received thinking and needs to challenge its discussion process:

> "The boss said . . ."
>
> "According to the report, we cannot do that."
>
> "We have always done it that way."
>
> "If they cannot tell us exactly what will happen, I am not buying in."
>
> "He's wrong about that."

Subjective thinking is more developed than reactive in that it allows the team to form its own opinions. Subjective thinking fosters more willingness to consider new approaches. The drawback in subjective thinking is that opinions and conclusions tend to be based only on emotion. When the team relies on subjective thinking, it does not seek out facts and does not value other points of view. These teams are likely to ignore policies that they think are "stupid" or information deemed "irrelevant" in favor of the experience of team members. It is not easy for teams engaged in subjective thinking to imagine; if a team member has not seen something work, it simply will not work.

Teams are likely to slip into subjective thinking when issues become complex and information hard to understand. Frustrated by facts and figures, the conversation reverts to statements like:

> "I just know it will work."
>
> "Maybe they are right, but I am not going along."
>
> "I have never seen it work before."
>
> "That's what the manual says, but I know better."
>
> "If you haven't been here 20 years, you just can't understand."

The "gut feeling" that comes from subjective thinking can be valuable to the decision process. However, it cannot be confused with fact. Unlike received thinking, subjective thinking can be brought forward along the thinking continuum as part of developing more complex thinking skills.

PROCEDURAL THINKING

Procedural thinking is where most teams operate. Most managerial training and administrative systems are based on procedural thinking. The value of procedural thinking is in its method. Procedural thinking breaks things apart for analysis and is reliant on information. It can deal with complexity and create strategy. The shortcoming of procedural thinking lies in its search for "the" answer, its dependence on objectivity, and its overuse of critique. Procedural thinking is useful for dealing with bounded problems for which there are right answers (numbers-based problems) and for assessing past situations. It is necessary for choosing options, candidates, and proposals. It is not useful for innovation, negotiation, or for solving problems for which there are no "right" answers (i.e., customer satisfaction).

Teams know they are engaged in procedural thinking when they hear statements such as:

"Let's vote."

"We need to control . . ."

"What's wrong with this approach is . . ."

"There are 3 ways we could solve this."

"Let's divide it up."

"They all agreed, so it must be the right thing to do."

Procedural thinking is best suited for the choosing part of the decision-making process. Constructed thinking is much more valuable for the exploration step.

CONSTRUCTED THINKING

Constructed thinking requires the use of both subjective and procedural thinking plus an ability to imagine and a willingness to consider multiple pathways for resolution. Constructed thinking focuses more on understanding than knowing; on asking the right questions rather than having the right answers. When the team engages in constructed thinking, it is willing and able to blend intuitive and factual information and to value both subjective and objective information. Both experience and abstract information have a place in deciding, and outside information is seen as an asset, not a challenge. Since the team recognizes that there is more than one way to do things, suggestions from others do not result in defensiveness. Two of the most useful aspects of constructed thinking are its ability to deal with ambiguity and its willingness to challenge the status quo. Not fearing ambiguity allows the team to embrace change. Rather than frustrating the team, new ideas and information invigorate it. Constructed thinking encourages the team to challenge its mindsets; to look at things differently; and to value multiple perspectives.

A team knows it is engaging in constructed thinking when it hears:

"No one has ever tried this before."

"How will this affect others?"

"What other ways could we do it?"

"These numbers support the feeling I have that . . ."

"What if they didn't react that way?"

"What will the whole thing look like?"

"These changes offer us many opportunities."

Constructed thinking does not encourage all team members to agree. In fact, differences in opinion are valued. Complex problems do not lend themselves to single solutions. Differences in opinion should lead to different methods for addressing specific issues. With the demands for speed in today's work environment, there is no time for proceeding in a sequential manner. Yet many decision-making practices demand just that. The team agrees on one path of action and pursues that until all team members are convinced that it is not working or has become obsolete, and only then does the team look for another way. Constructed thinking encourages the use of multiple pathways for action. If we work on ideas in parallel, not only have we increased our likelihood of finding methods that work, but we have made synergy possible. Doing things in sequence does not allow for synergy, because there is no interaction between activities. The best one can hope for is a good memory so that you do not repeat the same mistakes. Multiple paths for action allow team members to learn from each other and to come together or continue on their separate ways depending on the need.

Constructed thinking is not "better" than procedural thinking; it is simply different. Because team members tend to be much more familiar with and skilled in procedural thinking, the team uses it for everything. Successful teams learn the skills of constructed thinking and use them when appropriate and especially in the exploration activities of the team. Procedural and constructed thinking support the discussion and dialogue dimensions of conversation respectively. Figure 3-7 shows the movement from procedural to constructed thinking.

CHALLENGE ASSUMPTIONS

Another useful way to improve team thinking is through a process that challenges the current assumptions of the group. A team conversation with this focus begins by clarifying the assumptions that the group holds about the problem or issue presented. Once those assumptions are listed, the group is asked to challenge or reverse them and then to use these new assumptions as the basis for brainstorming activity. An example will help clarify this process.

Imagine yourself as the city manager for a small city. You are under increasing pressure to provide more services to your citizens; to provide them in a faster time frame; and at the same time to contain costs. You have brought together a cross-functional process improvement team to find ways to improve the way the administrative services of the city operate.

Procedural Thinking		Constructed Thinking
Bounded issues	➡	Complex issues
Answers	➡	Questions
Analysis	➡	Synthesis
Argue; defend	➡	Explore
Relies on method	➡	Challenges assumptions
Vertical; sequential	➡	Lateral; parallel
Reduce; separate	➡	Expand; holistic
Judgmental	➡	Accepting
Controlling	➡	Self-organizing
Objective; impersonal	➡	Intuitive and factual
Multiple realities	➡	Multiple perspectives
Knowing; one right answer	➡	Understanding; no absolute truth

FIGURE 3-7

Thinking Styles for Effective Decision-Making

This is a very typical quality-management team scenario. Under normal discussion processes, the team would begin to come up with ways to be more efficient. The team would likely talk about how to improve the process of issuing licenses, holding hearings, dealing with complaints, and so forth. The focus would be on how we can better do what we do. This is a laudable task but will probably not result in any truly new ideas.

Now, if the group first begins by challenging assumptions, the course the team follows could be much different. For example, the process improvement team described above might come up with the following assumptions:

- You need to have a license to do business with the city.
- People need to come to this office to get licenses.
- The city needs to issue the licenses.
- Our customers are not smart enough to understand the licensing process.
- The office is open from 8 to 5, Monday through Friday.
- Exception hearings must be held in our hearings rooms.

Take the first assumption. If the team challenges this assumption, they would say that you do not need a license to do business with the city. The team could then discuss what would happen if business licenses were eliminated and how the impact would be different for different types of licenses. The results might be that the team recommends that several licensing processes simply be abolished. Under the old brainstorming method the team would likely consider ways to do the licensing process faster rather than eliminate it altogether.

As the team challenges its current assumptions, it begins to look for new ways to do things that are outside those assumptions. Just because the team challenges an assumption does not mean that it cannot, in the end, validate that assumption. However, in the exploration part of decision-making, it is important for the team to be able to "turn things upside down" and explore options outside the normal mindset of the team.

How the team explores ideas, therefore, has a great impact on the effectiveness of its decision-making. Unless teams change the way they traditionally make decisions, they will not be able to reap the benefit of the new thinking and new ideas that organizations expect from teams.

Successful teams focus on skill development within the decision-making process. Thinking is a discipline that is gaining recognition as a critical part of the team and of the decision-making process. Teams that include thinking skills as part of their development and evaluation process are well on their way to enhancing their decision-making competencies.

*V*erbal Behaviors

To take advantage of methods like dialogue and to improve its way of thinking, the team must also change its language. In this section we will look at the verbal behaviors that impact decision-making. The language the team uses greatly influences the quality of ideas generated and the willingness of team members to share those ideas. There are five interactive behaviors that impact the team's ability to engage in effective decision-making:

- proposing
- building
- clarification
- ridicule
- arguing

PROPOSE: SUGGEST A COURSE OF ACTION

Meetings are often characterized by lots of talk and little action. The primary reason for this is that people prefer to share their opinions more than they like to take the risk of making suggestions. As a result, opinions abound but without direction. In order for discussion to move the group forward, team members must suggest alternatives for action. Effective teams continually move from general talk to recommended action. Proposing is the verbal behavior that causes this shift. In the spirit of dialogue, these recommendations need to be enriched and preserved for use when the team moves to a final decision.

Proposing is a suggestion for a course of action. Proposals can come in the form of either a statement or a question. "Let's change the specifications to require follow-up service" is a proposal statement. "Should we recommend the downtown convention center to the executive committee?" is a question-based proposal. They both suggest action. However, the question-based proposal is softer and encourages continuing discussion. Team members who have strong position power relative to the rest of the group should consider using question-based proposals. Team members who are quiet or who are trying to establish their role in the team might do better to use the stronger proposal statement.

Another type of proposal that is very helpful to the team is a process proposal. This type of proposal suggests process action. Process proposals would include suggestions such as:

> "Let's spend the first half of the meeting just generating ideas and then after a break we can come back and make our decision."

> "Let's gather information from our key customers before we make the final decision."

Process proposals suggest "how" the team should accomplish something, not the specifics of "what" it should do. Many people are reluctant to discuss substantive issues until they understand the process rules of the game.

Process proposals are particularly important because they can get a reluctant team started or a stuck team moving. To get the team moving, a team member might propose:

> "Let's just go around the table and get an initial reaction to the new legislation."

> "Let's use an Affinity process before we begin our discussion so we get all the problems out on the table."

To get a team through a discussion log jam, a team member might suggest:

> "We have been going in circles on this for over an hour. Let's assign it to a subcommittee for recommended action."

> "Let's put the cost issue aside for awhile and discuss desired outcomes."

Verbal behaviors that propose action keep the team moving. Without proposals, both the process and substantive kind, the team treads water and often loses its energy. If the team discussion seems to be stagnant and repetitive, team members need to see how many suggestions for action have been made recently. Such a search will probably reveal that the team has just been giving information and opinions and not making proposals. The team can then focus on recommended actions and make progress.

BUILDING: EXPANDING AND DEVELOPING THE PROPOSAL OF ANOTHER

Another interaction behavior that helps the team with discussion is building. Building refers to the process of expanding and enriching a proposal made by another.

Ideas are seldom presented in complete form. They are frequently just snippets of information, and in their initial form they often seem unworkable. The verbal behavior of building allows the team to add to initial ideas to create a complete recommendation or plan:

> "If we replace the old computers we could then donate them to the 'adopt a school' program we are supporting."

> "In addition to presentations at the sales conference we could bring some prototypes to demonstrate the improvements we expect in the new product line."

Both are building statements. They take the original idea of another and expand on it.

Another powerful dimension of the verbal behavior of building is its ability to let a team member change direction without rejecting the ideas of others. As emphasized before, a key condition for dialogue is nonjudgment. Say that during the exploration part of decision-making, team members reject ideas they have prematurely moved to the deciding phase of the decision-making process. Instead of focusing on rejection, team members can refocus the discussion and preserve the option. For example, a team member might say:

> "I agree that we need to provide these inspections for our customers, but I think we should open several substations around the city rather than require people to come to the main office."

> "We should be able to manage the project in the timeframe you suggest, but what if we brought in some contract people just to be sure?"

Building is one of the most important verbal behaviors team members can master. It provides for well-thought-out proposals for action, a feeling among team members that each has been listened to, and a way to disagree without being disagreeable. This is a huge return for an investment in a single verbal behavior. The drawback is that building is hard to do. First, it requires that the team member listen carefully to the ideas expressed by others. Listening requires attention and a focus on the speaker rather than on oneself.

The second requirement for the team to develop the verbal behavior of building is that team members forego their reliance on debate. Debate encourages arguing and counterproposals, and stresses using one's own idea rather than considering the other person's idea. Building encourages the integration of several concepts to develop a complete idea. Building is an essential skill for constructed thinking.

CLARIFY: ASK QUESTIONS TO ASSURE THAT THE IDEA IS CLEARLY UNDERSTOOD BY THE ENTIRE TEAM

Communication is an imprecise art. The differences in meaning between what the sender intends and what the receiver understands are often vast. Disagreements in decision-making are as often based on misunderstanding as on true differences in opinion. If the team is going to understand issues and ideas, it must learn to ask clarifying questions regularly. Clarifying questions include:

> "Tell me again how this will work."

> "Did you say the proposal would be ready by the end of the week?"

> "Can you give me an example so I can understand?"

Occasionally, a team member will feel that she or he could benefit from a misunderstanding. For example, the team is about to agree to a course of action but does not understand all of the implications from such an action. If the team member is likely to benefit from the action, it is hard for that person to raise the clarifying questions to be sure that the team understands exactly what it is getting into. However, if the team decides on the basis of misinformation, the results are seldom positive. The best case response is that when the team gets correct information, it will need to go back and discuss and decide the issue again. Those who supported the initial decision may be reluctant to go through the process again. The worst-case response is that the team members who should have sought clarification are seen as deceptive, and team trust is damaged.

To be effective, the team needs to operate from good, clear information and ideas. Because misunderstanding is so easy in a group of 8 to 12 people who all filter information according to their own perspectives, the team needs to consciously use clarifying verbal behaviors to keep misunderstanding from being the norm.

RIDICULE: CRITICISM FOCUSED ON THE PRESENTER

Teams often tie the value of an idea to the person who presents it. Support or criticism of the idea then becomes personal rather than based on the idea itself. The result is that the proposer becomes defensive if the idea is criticized and indebted if the idea is supported. Either way, it becomes difficult to accept or amend the idea. Ridicule is a verbal behavior that focuses criticism on the proposer of the idea rather than on the idea itself. The use of ridicule is a very common problem in team decision-making, and team members must make a special effort to control this behavior. One indicator that the team discussion has slipped into ridicule is if you hear people using the word "you." When the word "you" is the focus, then the idea has lost focus. For example, if a team member responds to an idea about a way to keep costs down with

"You always have to think of the bottom line,"

the discussion has shifted away from costs and on to the person.

Another indicator that the discussion has shifted to the personal is the use of judgment words. An example would be a team-member response to a suggestion that the team run its recommendation past the other divisions such as:

"You are always so political. I don't care if the other divisions don't like this. It is the right thing to do."

Phrases like "you are always so political" cast judgment on the person rather than the idea being discussed. Judgment words are fighting words. The person is likely to take umbrage with the remark and get defensive and perhaps hostile. The result is that the team discussion is damaged and the issue is lost.

It is very difficult for the team to move focus back to the issue once a personal attribution has been made. People can differ on issues and still maintain respect and trust. Once the focus is personal, however, both are often lost. Teams can minimize the use of ridicule in team discussion through the use of ground rules designed to emphasize how to make things work rather than what is wrong with an idea. The team can also develop good questioning skills. Drawing out information on the idea and allowing it to ripen will help the group determine its value and avoid personal attacks.

ARGUE: CHALLENGE ANOTHER'S POSITION; LECTURE

As discussed earlier, the real value gained from working with teams is bringing multiple perspectives together to address an issue. In order to realize that value, the team must accept those differing ideas of team members. While the team usually agrees that this is desirable, and even makes ground rules to reinforce the desire for multiple perspectives, the verbal behavior of arguing often undoes that intent.

Arguing is challenging and cutting off the ideas and suggestions of another. It is usually characterized by quick reaction to an initial statement. Typical arguing behaviors include:

> "That will not work because . . ."
>
> "You are wrong about . . ."
>
> "I think two weeks is enough."

We talked about the pervasiveness of debate as a model for our verbal interactions. Arguing behaviors are very much a part of the debate process, and their primary intent is to cut off discussion of the other person's ideas.

Within the decision-making process, arguing interferes with the team's ability to explore and fully develop alternatives. Arguing also makes it very difficult for the team to consider multiple options because argument is fundamentally driven by a concept of a right-and-wrong approach. One of the ways that successful teams minimize arguing is by separating the options-generating part of decision-making from the deciding part. This separation encourages nonjudgment and allows the team to enforce brainstorming rules. Even in the deciding part of the process, the successful team tries to encourage questioning behaviors to clarify options rather than arguing behaviors that cut off disclosure.

As in participation, it does matter what and how you say things in decision-making. Words and tone are not neutral. They greatly influence the climate of team interaction and the quality of results. Talking is so natural to people that they often forget to monitor its effectiveness. Successful teams work to develop sophisticated, verbal behaviors and to monitor the quality of team conversation on a regular basis.

*D*eciding on Action

Once the team has discussed options thoroughly, and understanding of context and content is clear, it is time to make a choice. Choice does not mean a focus on one and only one answer, but it invariably means narrowing the paths to follow.

The team can employ a variety of methods for making choices that go from a general sense of agreement to a mathematically based prioritizing process. Depending on the maturity and trust level of the team and on the complexity of the task, the team may choose from one or a combination of methods.

Figure 3-8 describes methods that fall at different points along the choice continuum. Justified decision-making represents a process that is driven by the weight of fact and logic. By their nature, these decisions are largely procedural, relying as they do structure and calculation to bring forth a "correct" decision. The process of Rational Decision-Making developed by Kepner and Tregoe in the 1960s is perhaps the best articulated and most widely used of the justified decision-making methods, but other techniques such as decision trees are a common part of a logic-based decision-making process.

At the other end of the choice continuum is consensus, an agreement-based choice process. That it is agreement-based does not mean that consensus is void of logic. However, in consensus, it is the drive to agreement that validates the logic. That is, if we all agree, then this option must be the right course of action. Compare this belief with the one that drives justified decision-making: If we can justify a course of action through evidence and logic, it follows that everyone will agree. It is just logical!

In the middle of the continuum is a process that draws from both ends of the continuum. Teams need to use facts to clarify and understand the complexity of an issue.

Without good information, team thinking is incomplete. The team must also deal with member feelings and the emotional issue of commitment to the decision. The team does not need to reach consensus, but it does need a level of agreement. Mindful decision-making, the midpoint on the continuum, draws from information and emotion to attain the minimal amount of agreement that will allow for differences but still engender commitment to an overall direction.

JUSTIFIED DECISION-MAKING

Justified decision-making attempts to take emotion and bias out of decision-making, or at least to bring it to a manageable level. This approach asks team members first to identify the criteria for making a good decision. These might be price, features, schedule, and so forth. Once the criteria are set, each alternative can be objectively weighed against the criteria. The option that receives the highest score is the first choice.

FIGURE 3-8

Decision-Making, Choice Continuum

A common example for justified decision-making is buying a car. The criteria might include the price of the car, the standard equipment included, the repair record for that make and model car, expected miles per gallon, availability of financing, and so forth. The person using a justified decision-making model first has to decide which of the criteria represent requirements and which represent desirables. For our example, let's say the most the person can afford to pay for a car is $20,000. Therefore, a price of $20,000 or less is a requirement, and any car that is presented as an alternative MUST satisfy this criterion to receive further consideration. Having a radio, air conditioning, or antilock brakes are likely desirables, and each is rated in terms of importance to the person buying the car. Once requirements are identified and desirables are ranked, the person looks at car choices. Each model of car considered receives a numerical rating (from 1 to 10) based on the degree to which it satisfies the person's desires. The model is not considered if it does not meet the requirements—in this case a price of less than $20,000. Figure 3-9 depicts the justified decision-making process for buying a car as described above.

While this process may seem contrived, justified decision-making is the basis of many decisions made in business. Sometimes the use of justified decision-making is very clear, as when a company requests proposals for a project. Proposal evaluators often use strict justified decision-making approaches to evaluate bids. In other instances, the method is more oblique, but the fundamental assumptions of justified decision-making still prevail; that is, each alternative is given a value, and the alternative with the highest value is chosen.

REQUIREMENTS: Price less than $20,000

DESIRABLES:

	Weight
Air conditioning	7
CD player	5
ABS brakes	2
Good repair record	8
Good gas mileage	6

Alternatives	*Air*	*CD*	*ABS*	*Repair*	*Gas*	*Total*
Car 1	6 ×7	2 ×5	6 ×2	5 ×8	7 ×6	146
Car 2	6 ×7	10 ×5	10 ×2	8 ×8	8 ×6	224
Car 3	2 ×7	5 ×5	0 ×2	5 ×8	7 ×6	121
Car 4	10 ×7	8 ×5	10 ×2	9 ×8	6 ×6	238

CHOICE: Car 4

FIGURE 3-9

Jusitified Decision-Making: Choosing a Car

Sometimes the value is numeric and clearly stated, as when a company calculates expected return from a new product or selects a new piece of equipment. Sometimes the value is more emotional, as when an alternative is chosen on the basis of the sponsor's personal ability to persuade or as in the selection process used to bring new people into the organization. Whichever the type of calculation, the result is the same. All alternatives are compared, and a single "best" choice is made based on the weight of the evidence.

Teams that use justified decision-making usually find it quite efficient, if not always effective. Some criteria are hard to articulate, and team members often withhold their true preferences for fear of ridicule from the rest of the group. For example, drawing on the example of choosing a car, Car 4, which received the most points, turns out to be a conservative four-door sedan. The car satisfies the price constraint, gets good gas mileage, has a good repair record and the desired equipment. While this might be a "right" and practical decision, it can leave the buyer disappointed. Perhaps the buyer wanted a car with some style that would impress his or her friends. It may not seem logical or practical to include this criteria in the decision-making matrix. The more emotional issues of "pizzazz" and status can easily be left out of the justified decision-making process, resulting in practical but common decisions. Thus, decisions made with this method seldom engender outright rebellion, because the process is outwardly unbiased, but indifference is a common response. The process is logical, the decision is logical, and the commitment is logical. Unfortunately, logical commitment often does not generate much energy and enthusiasm.

Justified decision-making can provide a useful decision-making process to teams, and it is particularly valuable for new teams or teams faced with very complex issues, because it provides a step-by-step way to proceed toward decision-making. Justified decision-making is commonly used for making major task decisions. The weakness of justified decision-making lies in its illusion of and dependence on objectivity. If the team gets caught up in the mechanics of the process and fails to allow for the feelings of team members, the decision-making becomes hollow.

Consensus

A more emotional and less structured approach to decision-making is consensus. When a team uses consensus as its guide for decision-making, everyone must agree and fully accept the decision of the team. There is an expectation in consensus that the level of acceptance be both equal and enthusiastic.

However, anyone who has ever been involved in team decision-making knows how difficult it is for every member of the team to agree to a decision with equal commitment. The energy and time needed for every member to reach consensus is enormous. And there is always the possibility that one or more persons simply will not or cannot go along. The decision-making process then comes to a halt and often deteriorates into finger pointing and argument.

The biggest problem with consensus, however, is its assumption that agreement indicates a quality decision. That is, we have confidence in the decision because we all agree. There is no real basis for such a conclusion. Agreement has little to do with the quality of the decision we are making. In fact, agreement is probably a more common indicator of poor quality than disagreement would be. An overemphasis on consensus can lead to group-think, a group behavior that favors agreement over quality.

Team members need to determine the value of consensus for a decision before they begin discussion. The more the decision represents a core value or principle, the more consensus is important. In these situations, the team needs to be of common mind, and it is worthwhile for the team to take the time to reach a consensus level of agreement.

MINDFUL DECISION-MAKING

Teams in today's organizations will usually be most effective if they choose a decision-making process between the two ends of the continuum (see Figure 3-9). Reflecting on the various demands placed on teams, the choice process needs to be more considered than prescribed; that is, as the team reaches the choice phase of the decisionmaking process, it needs to consciously define the choice method it will use.

If the choice is a bounded one, the team will move toward a justified decision-making method. Bounded decisions are characterized by clear-cut parameters (boundaries) and a relatively narrow definition for a right answer. Team decisions that fall into this category might include a site for a new building, choice of a vendor to provide a product, or choice of a major piece of equipment. For these decisions the emphasis is primarily technical. The decisions are major and the implications may be great, but they tend to be technical in nature.

When the team decision is primarily concerned with commitment, the choice process needs to focus on consensus. Defining a shared vision for the organization, changes in organizational structure, and customer satisfaction initiatives are examples of this type of decision-making.

*C*onclusion

Developing a team process maximizes efficiency. There are three phases an efficient team must go through: formation, development, and renewal. These phases are evolutionary in progress and require team commitment and communication to pass the breakpoints between the phases. The formation phase deals with more than just the makeup of the team. It includes adjustment within the team, which is where team ground rules, roles, and responsibilities are solidified. The development phase includes cohesion and reinforcement, which enables teams to focus on tasks. Development deals with how teams perceive themselves and their tasks. The renewal phase encompasses learning and transformation, and for the teams that work through the breakpoints, serves as a reward for improved formation and development. Key learnings from previous processes are evaluated and applied to restructuring for the next level of team work.

Problem Solving

The problem-solving process applies to managing the internal and external influences on the team. Remember that part of good politics is the art of solving problems and communicating recommendations in a way that meets each constituent's needs. The problem-solving process is closely tied to goal setting and is one of the key purposes for teams. Figure 3-10 represents the science of problem solving, or the steps for achieving a solution. The way in which these steps are achieved, through sensitivity and political awareness, represents the art of "positive politicking."

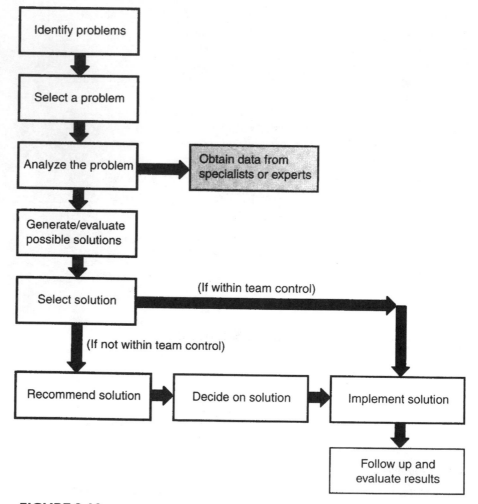

FIGURE 3-10

Problem-Solving Process

Teams: Structure, Process, Culture, and Politics, by Eileen K. Aranda, Luis Aranda, with Kristi Conlon. Copyright © 1998 by Prentice Hall, Inc.

IDENTIFY THE PROBLEMS

This may be the easiest step, because team members, organization members, or community influences are often quick to identify problems for the team. Teams are often formed after a problem has been identified and then given the task of solving that problem. The team must look, however, at the issues that have been identified and then break those issues down to their most fundamental elements. Some questions are: Do the issues identified have a common theme? Are they symptoms of a different, smaller, or bigger problem? The goal of this step is to identify true problems that can be solved.

SELECT A PROBLEM

Because more than one problem can usually be identified, it is important to deal with a single problem at a time. (The process becomes muddled when teams attempt to solve many problems at once.) In prioritizing problems, the team needs to look at resources like time, money, and energy, and then select the most important problem that can be solved given the resources of the team. The team must ask itself, "What are the risks if this problem is not solved?"

ANALYZE THE PROBLEM

Once the problem has been identified and selected, what information is needed to learn more about the whats, whys, wheres, and whens of it? Teams are often so focused on generating possible solutions that they skip the important, yet often time-consuming, step—obtaining data that flushes out the problem so that it can be analyzed. The quality of information analyzed will determine the quality of the solution and implementation. Teams do not want to be "caught with their pants down" from not doing the homework on the problem. A suggested tool is the "Team Decision-Making Summary Sheet."

GENERATE/EVALUATE POSSIBLE SOLUTIONS

Brainstorming is an effective way to generate possible solutions, because it is creative and places no restrictions/conditions on the ideas. The goal of brainstorming is to generate as many solutions as possible. Only after ideas have been generated can they be evaluated. Remember: There are many roads to the same destination. Teams should have more than one viable solution.

SELECT A SOLUTION

The next task of the team is to select the solutions that are best, then determine whether or not each is within the team's control. The tendency at this stage is to entertain only the solutions that can be implemented by the teams. Teams should determine criteria for the best solution. Examples of criteria include the least expensive solution; the ease of implementing the solution quickly; the degree of solving the problem; and the likelihood of creating new problems. Values may also be placed on the criteria to weight them for a more scientific process.

After selecting a solution, the team should decide whether or not implementation is within their control. If it is, the team should plan and execute the solution, then follow up and evaluate results. If it is not within the team's control, a recommendation of how to implement the solution should be prepared and delivered to decision makers. This recommendation should include the appropriate level of participation for the team in the implementation and evaluation processes.

RECOMMEND SOLUTION

The recommendation may be in the form of a written report and/or presentation to one or more decision makers. This is the stage in which teams draw on their positive politicking skills. The degree to which teams determine and meet needs/agendas directly impacts the extent to which the solution and implementation plan will be well received. A common mistake is for a team to fail to explain how it arrived at a recommended solution. Guiding the stakeholders and decision makers through the team's process often eliminates objections before they arise.

DECIDE ON SOLUTION

Those who are in control of selecting and implementing a solution will be accountable for the success or failure of the solution. This accountability can cause individuals and teams to be cautious in their decisions. Decisions may be made immediately, or they may be delayed, avoided, or referred to a committee, depending on the level of risk and accountability decision makers feel. There are many factors at work in making decisions: acquired information and facts, feelings, and even intuition. Individuals rely on unique combinations of these and other factors to make decisions. Every decision process is different.

IMPLEMENT SOLUTION

Many solutions fail because a robust implementation plan is not designed as part of the solution, or because the implementation plan is not executed in a way that minimizes risk to the environment. For example, if a solution is to change software that is essential to business operations at multiple sites, the implementation might be staged by site so that operations do not suffer from the change. Ongoing evaluation should occur while changes are being made. Checks should include questions such as: Are the changes occurring smoothly, on schedule, within budget?

FOLLOW UP AND EVALUATE RESULTS

At this stage the problem has been identified, selected, and analyzed, and a solution evaluated, selected, and implemented. After an appropriate period of time, a final evaluation should include these questions:

Did we solve the problem?

Are there signs that the problem could reoccur?

Why was the solution successful/unsuccessful?

Do we have any unfinished business regarding this specific problem/solution?

If so, how and to whom do we wish to communicate it?

$\mathcal{O}$bstacles to the Problem-Solving and Decision-Making Processes

In the decision-making process, teams often encounter issues that challenge both the quality of a decision and its acceptance. Particularly problematic to the process are:

Loss of focus

Rush to accomplishment

Rigid mindsets

Intimidating environment

Unwillingness to deal with difficult issues

Domineering and reluctant participants

Process disruptions

LOSS OF FOCUS

Teams often find themselves treading water in the decision-making process. They rehash the same ideas or issues over and over again but have difficulty coming to a resolution. Meetings are characterized by hours of conversation with little progress.

This problem of focus can be addressed in two ways. The first way is to follow the decision-making process consciously, that is, clearly identify the problem or opportunity and reduce it to writing. If necessary, post it in a well-trafficked area so that everyone can see it. Then, deliberately move to the exploration stage and track the ideas and suggestions that come up. Once again, make a deliberate shift to the next stage where alternatives are clear and visible. This logging of specific information and actions is particularly helpful for issues that become complex. Team members need to see how issues are related to each other, what to do next, and what has been accomplished.

The second method of assuring focus is to record in writing the minutes of meetings, highlighting the key issues and decisions made by team members. An ongoing action plan format that lists responsibilities accepted by individual team members is useful to track progress from meeting to meeting. Teams may also find the mindmap helpful. Use it both for taking minutes and tracking the decision-making process. The mindmap can be a living document that the team can add to and amend as the decision-making process evolves.

RUSH TO ACCOMPLISHMENT

Teams are often keenly aware of the pressure for them to make timely decisions. Unfortunately, the pressure to act quickly often results in the team engaging in superficial and limiting discussions where fewer alternatives are explored and the quality of decisions is compromised.

The specific liability that a team incurs when it rushes to accomplishment is that of *satisficing*, a coined term derived from the words "satisfied" and "sacrifice," because when a team "satisfices," it stops exploration when the first acceptable alternative comes to the table. As ideas are being discussed, a team member says, "That will work," and if the rest of the team agrees, the decision is made. Perhaps better ideas are "sacrificed" at the expense of quickly "satisfying" the issue with a decision.

Again, by deliberately following the problem-solving process, the team is building in a reminder to explore more than one idea. There are several other methods a team can use to prolong and improve the exploration part of decision-making. One is the skilled use of dialogue. By continually asking questions around a topic without accepting or rejecting any ideas, the team extends its time to make a decision and is likely to generate more alternatives.

RIGID MINDSETS

Teams are comprised of individuals who have outlooks based upon their past experiences. Team members through self-assessment must check their paradigms for sets of beliefs which are very strong. If a member has experiences and attitudes that create a rigid mindset, others in the team can participate in exercises that challenge assumptions.

INTIMIDATING ENVIRONMENT

Intimidating environments create a climate where team members are reluctant to speak for fear of being verbally attacked. Verbal attacks are characterized by two elements: the use of the word "you" and the presence of negative judgment. Examples of statements that create intimidating environments would include:

> "You never listen."
>
> "You only care about your own department."
>
> "Money is all you ever talk about."
>
> "You never come to meetings prepared."
>
> "You are always afraid to try something new."
>
> "You talk just like an accountant."
>
> "You just don't see the big picture."

Statements like these have a negative impact not only on the person speaking but on all members of the team, who usually conclude it is better to remain silent than to risk ridicule.

Ground rules that discourage personal "put downs" and ongoing process assessments of how team members communicate with each other can keep this problem under control. If the person in power is creating the negative environment, it might be useful to bring in an outsider to do a process assessment. If the growth and development of the team is valued, the team should address issues from a team perspective rather than assess individual blame. The truth is that when a team experiences a negative environment, everyone has played a role in creating it and must play a role in repairing the damage.

An exercise that can be used regularly to help every member improve the team process is completing a "Contributor Feedback Worksheet," such as the one following:

Team member name: _____

You make the team more effective when you: _____

_____

_____

_____

_____

The team process would improve if you would do the following:

_____

_____

_____

There are many variations for this exercise. The keys to making it effective are:

1. Do the exercise regularly as part of an ongoing improvement process rather than just in response to a problem. Doing the exercise as expected and routine allows people to be less defensive in receiving the feedback.

2. Focus on how to improve the future work of the team so that the feedback does not degenerate into blame.

3. Teach participants to give helpful feedback that focuses on behaviors rather than personalities. Such a focus allows people to be able to use the information and adjust their behavior without feeling attacked. It is easier to change behaviors than personalities.

UNWILLINGNESS TO DEAL WITH DIFFICULT ISSUES

Many teams have sacred cows—issues they are unwilling to discuss. Often these issues are critical to addressing problems at hand. Avoiding discussion of these issues frequently results in the team's rehashing nonsignificant aspects of the problem, thereby never being able to move forward.

Difficult issues need to be addressed in a straightforward but nonthreatening manner. For example, as a regular part of dealing with a new or chronic issue, the team can draw out underlying causes, politics, and emotions that could keep the team from resolving the issues at hand. This information could be gathered either in an open forum, or, if the difficulties are threatening, by using the following feedback form:

Issue:_____

What uncomfortable things do we need to discuss and resolve about this issue before we can begin to address it seriously?

Current mindsets _____

Personal politics _____

Organization history _____

Other _____

Each person completes the form. All forms are collected, and common issues are identified. One by one the team deals with these issues either in an open session or in subgroups that present their recommendations to the entire team.

DOMINEERING AND RELUCTANT PARTICIPANTS

Teams bring together people with many different styles of interaction. At the extreme ends of the interaction continuum you have domineering and reluctant participants. Both are quite common in team situations, and both cause special communication problems for the team.

Domineering participants affect two important resources for teams: time and ideas. When the domineering member monopolizes air time, other members, especially less assertive ones, often conclude that participating is just not worth the effort. The impact of the decision not to participate goes beyond simply not communicating at the meeting. Deprived of input, the team member loses interest in the team and its task and becomes a member in name only.

This leads to the second loss to the team—ideas. Domineering team members prevent other ideas from coming to the table. The team is frustrated and becomes less effective than it could be. It is unlikely that the domineering member has the best ideas all of the time, but even if that person's ideas are good, those ideas represent only one approach. The choice of multiple perspectives is lost.

There are two kinds of domineering team members—positive and negative. If the domineering person is simply talkative and enthusiastic, coaching the person to change his or her verbal behaviors tends to be most effective. Perhaps the most valuable behavior change is to get the person to move from giving information to asking questions of others. Given that the person is generally positive, it is not desirable for the person just to keep quiet, which is probably not possible anyway. Allowing a positive domineering person to play the role of facilitator can be effective as the person focuses his or her energy on getting ideas from others.

The negatively domineering person poses a different sort of problem. This person drives others out, not only by monopolizing airtime but through negative and critical remarks. Tightening up the team's process structure is the best way to handle this person. The team must establish and enforce ground rules on supportive verbal behaviors. These ground rules can be formally enforced by structuring the conversations around the issue, if necessary. A good method for formal structuring for the facilitator is to use a "T" account for recording information on issues. On a white board or flip chart the facilitator makes two columns, representing the positive and negative sides of the issues or recommendation. The facilitator systematically addresses each team member, asking for information to go on both sides of the chart. By collecting information in such a manner, the team gets a holistic view of the issues, and the impact of the domineering person is minimized.

Depending on the culture of the team, there are other informal approaches that can be used to monitor negative verbal behaviors. Some teams give each member a soft sponge ball, and when a team member starts to get negative, someone tosses a ball at him or her. At the end of the meeting, team members discuss the level of negativity in the discussion and how to minimize it. On occasion, a team will assess a fine or punishment (e.g., bring treats to the next meeting) for collecting too many sponge balls. This exercise is best used intermittently to remind teams to keep their discussions on the "can do" track. It is also more effective with a team that is mature enough to use humor effectively. The newer or stressed team is better off using a formal structure such as the "T" account to balance the discussion in the face of domineering participants.

Reluctant participants create a less visible but no less damaging obstacle to effective team participation. A basic tenet of successful teams is that people are members because they have an interest in the team task and something to offer in accomplishing that task. If the participant is not contributing, the underlying cause is usually one of two things: commitment or intimidation. If the person is unprepared or does not seem to care, it is time for the team to discuss team purpose and commitment. Perhaps the team has gotten off track; or maybe the organization politics have changed to make the team task less valuable. It is important for the team not to jump prematurely to the conclusion that it is the team member who is at fault. This is particularly true if the reluctance is a new behavior for the member or if the team as a whole is becoming less participative.

If the reluctance is an individual team member issue, discussion of the roles and responsibilities of team members may help. Team member interest and outside demands often shift over time. The team needs to assess that members and their roles are still appropriate to the task. Successful teams make it possible for a team member to change commitment level or to leave the team without hassle or disgrace. A sign of team maturity is the ability for members to address the internal changes that accompany team evolution.

If the reluctance to participate is caused by intimidation, the team first must look at its process. Is it easy for people to have an opportunity to speak? Is it safe for team members to throw out suggestions? A good evaluation of the team style of participation will help explain why any team member is reluctant to participate. The team can then encourage more participation. Examples of appropriate encouragement might include organized opportunities for input, increased use of supportive verbal behaviors, or action that reduces the importance and influence of power in the group.

PROCESS DISRUPTIONS

It is easy for people to slip into unsupportive verbal habits. Interrupting and engaging in side conversations are two behaviors that frequently occur in team meetings and have a negative impact on the team process. Teams usually use ground rules to prevent these disruptions, but because these habits are so commonplace, the team often has to monitor and reinforce its ground rules.

Interruptions signal an unwillingness on a team member's part to listen to what another team member is saying. Not listening often contributes to an intimidating team environment. Interruptions can be driven by ego, power, or just poor manners, but for the team to be effective, conversation must be relatively free of interruptions.

Increasing awareness is the first step in changing interrupting behavior. Using silence following the interruption, or making a statement recognizing the interruption often makes the speaker aware of his or her actions. From a team perspective, an effective tool to identify and modify this and other verbal behaviors is to videotape or audiotape a meeting. When the video or audiotape is played back, the team can see and hear itself in action. Video is particularly effective because team members can see not only their own behavior, but they can also witness their impact on others.

Team members will be reluctant to use and view the video if it is a source of embarrassment or blame. The key to using video as a feedback tool is to focus on finding examples of useful verbal behaviors. A focus of understanding how the team interacts and of learning new skills will go a long way toward making this highly useful tool a part of the team's continuous improvement effort.

Side conversations are a plague to many meetings. While one person is trying to address the group, two or three other members are engaged in another conversation. Team size can encourage side conversations. As the team grows past ten or twelve members, it becomes difficult for everyone to have adequate airtime. While most people have an interest in what others think, they also have a need for input. Without the opportunity to contribute, the team member may become indifferent or bored. The resulting behavior is often a side conversation.

To avoid side conversations the team first needs a ground rule that sets the expectation for attention to the speaker. After that foundation, effective teams provide means for every member to contribute on a regular basis. Using the verbal behaviors of seeking information and asking questions can assure that everyone has a chance to contribute to the conversation.

Team members should be encouraged to write down the ideas, questions, and related issues that they want to contribute during presentations. Teams may even create their own forms for note taking. This practice encourages organized discussions and provides an expectation that side conversations and interruptions are not valued or necessary.

REFLECTION

Reflect on a past team that you have observed for some time. Complete the process assessment below to identify the strengths and weaknesses of the team's participation. Note that this assessment may be used in the current team as well.

PROCESS ASSESSMENT		
	Strength	**Weakness**
Focus		
Mindsets		
Pace of progress		
Environment		
Participants		
Process disruptions		
Willingness to deal with difficult issues		

*H*andling Conflict within the Team

While there are a number of things we can do to minimize conflict, there are times when conflict surfaces and must be addressed. Conflict is usually emotionally driven and often involves anger. Whether the conflict is one-on-one or among more than two team members, we can learn to deal positively with our own angry feelings by understanding that their source is almost always a perceived threat.

We can effectively attempt to control ourselves by:

- *Putting the situation in its proper perspective:* Ask ourselves questions such as, Will this matter in a month, a year, ten years? Would this situation seem as important if other people were involved? Must I learn to accept the circumstances, or can they be changed?

- *Examining the best and worst case scenarios:* Often, visualizing the extreme outcomes and realizing that the end result will be better than the worst case scenario keep speculations in check.

- *Examining personal attachment to the outcome:* Ask ourselves questions such as, Will I be embarrassed if the situation doesn't go as I want? Why do I feel so strongly about this?

We can effectively confront the anger of others by:

- *Not allowing it to hook us into conflicts that are none of our business:* Realizing when conflicts are not about us and our positions enable us to pick only the important battles.

- *Recognizing the futility of attempting to dissolve anger through logic:* When there is frustration, it only adds to the conflict. Avoid frustration by remembering that logic may not dissolve the anger.

- *Stating what we feel and want as clearly and pleasantly as possible:* We can do this by focusing on "I" statements rather than "You" statements.

- *Being reasonable but sticking to our principles:* There are times when we do not want to compromise if it will compromise integrity.

- *Ignoring abuse and responding only to reasonable statements:* By communicating in this fashion, we send the message that we are not going to get hooked into an argument or into making negative responses.

We can use the following strategies for communication that involves conflict:

- *Avoid being judgmental:* We can do this by dealing only with present behavior rather than past or potential injustices.

- *Pay attention to the nonverbal content of communication:* Are statements made with open or positive body language?

- *Avoid interpreting motives of others:* Interpretation may more accurately be projection or speculation.

- *Use questions of clarification:* This practice prevents statements from being taken the wrong way.

- *Refrain from giving advice:* "If I were you" statements cause people to become defensive.

- *Summarize points of agreement and disagreement:* This shows a more balanced picture of a situation and avoids focusing only on areas of disagreement.

Occasionally, conflict may escalate to a level where it is appropriate to leave the scene. When disagreements become very emotional, it is important to draw from the following techniques.

- *Attempt to maintain nonthreatening body posture:* This must become a conscious self-check.

- *Never touch a person in an attempt to calm them down:* Touching to some people is a way of communicating power or control.

- *Use distracting questions:* This may help to lessen the escalation temporarily.

- *Speak calmly, firmly, and soothingly:* If we are not sincere, this tone will come across as being patronizing.

*T*eam Decision-Making: Conformity, Pitfalls and Solutions

"I . . . grabbed the photographic evidence showing the hot gas blow-by comparisons from previous flights and placed it on the table in view of the managers and somewhat angered, admonished them to look at the photos and not ignore what they were telling us; namely, that low temperature indeed caused significantly more hot gas blow-by to occur in the joints. I received cold stares. . . . with looks as if to say, 'Go away and don't bother us with the facts.' No one in management wanted to discuss the

*facts; they just would not respond verbally to . . . me. I felt totally
helpless at that moment and that further argument was fruitless,
so I, too, stopped pressing my case" (Boisjoly, 1987, p. 7).*

We all know that decisions made by committees can be of the worst caliber.
It might seem, because the downside potential is so great, that team decisions are not worth the risk. However, good team decisions can be outstanding—far better than those attainable by any individual. The key, of
course, is doing it right, and doing it right is the topic of this section.

The space shuttle *Challenger* disaster may have resulted, in part, from a
poor team decision process. The opening quote from Roger Boisjoly, an engineer who tried to halt the flight in 1986, led the Presidential Commission to
conclude that the disaster was, indeed, the result of a "flawed decision-
making process."[1] Another example from the business world is the American
Medical Association's decision to allow Sunbeam to use the AMA name as a
product endorsement. Because bad team decisions can have disastrous consequences, it is important to understand the particular kinds of faults that lead
to faulty decision-making, specifically in teams.

DECISION-MAKING IN TEAMS

Decision-making is an integrated sequence of activities that includes gathering, interpreting, and exchanging information; creating and identifying
alternative courses of action; choosing among alternatives by integrating the
often differing perspectives and opinions of team members; and implementing a choice and monitoring its consequences (Guzzo, Salas, & Associ-
ates, 1995). Decision-making is a key activity that teams must do, no matter
what their governance structure—self-managing, manager-led, or self-directing. This is true for tactical, problem-solving, and creative teams. In teams,
information is often distributed unequally among members and must be
integrated, and the integration process may be complicated by uncertainty,
status differences among members, failure of members to appreciate the significance of the information they hold or of the information not held by others, and so on.

This section focuses on four decision-making pitfalls that teams often
encounter. For each, we describe the problem and then provide preventative
measures. The first problem that we focus on is groupthink, the tendency to
conform to the consensus viewpoint in group decision-making. We then discuss escalation of commitment and the Abilene paradox. Finally, we discuss
group polarization.

The quality of group decision-making is impacted by conformity, and
conformity can lead to any of the four main pitfalls of group decision-
making. We begin the chapter with an analysis of conformity and then discuss the four main group decision-making pitfalls.

---

[1]Committee on Science and Technology, House of Representatives, House Report 99–1016,
   "Investigation of the Challenger Accident," October 29, 1986.

CONFORMITY: WHY IT OCCURS AND HOW IT WORKS IN TEAMS

Suppose that you are meeting with your team. The question facing your team is a simple one: Which of the three lines in panel 2 is equal in length to the line in panel 1? (See Figure 3-11.)

The team leader seeks a group consensus. She begins by asking the colleague sitting to your left for his opinion. To your shock, your colleague chooses line 1; then, each of the other four team members selects line 1—even though line 2 is clearly correct. You begin to wonder whether you are losing your mind. Finally, it's your turn to decide. What do you do?

Most people who read this example find it nearly impossible to imagine that they would choose line 1, even if everyone else had. Yet 76 percent make an erroneous, conforming judgment (e.g., choose line 1) on at least one question; on average, people conform one-third of the time when others give the obviously incorrect answer (Asch, 1956).

The line experiment is a dramatic illustration of the power of conformity pressure. **Conformity** occurs when people bring their behavior into alignment with a group's expectations and beliefs. In this example, the people who give the wrong answer know that the answer is wrong; nevertheless, they feel compelled to provide an answer that will be acceptable to the group.

Although many people think their beliefs and behavior are based on their own free will, social behavior is strongly influenced by others. Why do people conform? There are two main reasons: They want to do the "right" thing and they want to be liked.

The Need to Be Right

Groups are presumed to have access to a broader range of decision-making resources and, hence, to be better equipped to make high-quality decisions than any person can alone. By pooling their different backgrounds, training, and experience, group members have at least the potential for working in a

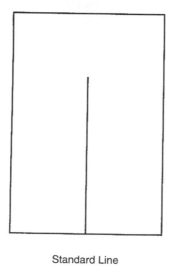

Standard Line

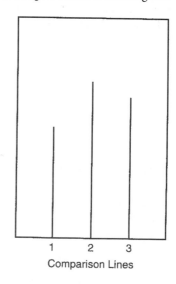

1   2   3
Comparison Lines

FIGURE 3-11

Conformity Pressure

more informed fashion than would be the case were the decision left to any single individual. The implication of these two assertions is that individuals are **information dependent**—that is, they often lack information that another member has. Consequently, individuals look to the team to provide information that they do not know. On the one hand, this is an adaptive response. However, it can lead to problems when people treat others' opinions as facts and fail to question their validity. The need to be right, therefore, is the tendency to look to the group to define what reality is—and the more people who hold a particular opinion, the more right an answer appears to be. Whereas this information-seeking tendency would seem to be contradictory to the common information effect, the two processes are not inconsistent. The common information effect (and all of its undesirable consequences) are driven by a biased search for information. Conformity, or the adoption of group-level beliefs, is strongest when individuals feel unsure about their own position.

The Need to Be Liked

Most people have a fundamental need to be accepted and approved of by others. Conformity is often a ticket to group acceptance. There is good reason for this: Teams provide valuable resources. One of the most straightforward ways to gain immediate acceptance in a group is to express attitudes consistent with those of the group members. Stated another way, most people like others who conform to their own beliefs. This means that people in groups will become more extreme in the direction of the group's general opinion, because attitudes that are sympathetic toward the group are most likely to be positively rewarded. The need to be liked refers to the tendency for people to agree with a group so that they can feel more like a part of that group.

Conformity is greater when the judgment or opinion issue is difficult and when people are uncertain. People are especially likely to conform if they face an otherwise unanimous group consensus (Asch, 1956; Wilder & Allen, 1977). Conformity is greater when people value and admire their team—rejection from a desirable group is very threatening (Back, 1951). However, we do not want to paint the picture that managers lack integrity. People are more willing to take a stand when they feel confident about their expertise, have high social status (Harvey & Consalvi, 1960), are strongly committed to their initial view (Deutsch & Gerard, 1955), and do not like or respect the people trying to influence them (Hogg & Turner, 1987).

Coupled with the need to be liked is the desire not to be ostracized from one's team. There is good reason for concern, because individuals who deviate from their team's opinion are more harshly evaluated than are those who conform (Levine, 1989). A group may reject a deviant person even when they are not under pressure to reach complete consensus (Miller, Jackson, Mueller, & Scherisching, 1987). Apparently, holding a different opinion is enough to trigger dislike even when it does not directly block the group's goals. For this reason, people are more likely to conform to the majority when they respond publicly (e.g., Deutsch & Gerard, 1955), anticipate future interaction with other group members (e.g., Lewis, Langan, & Hollander, 1972), are less confident (Allen, 1965), find the question under consideration to be ambiguous or difficult (Tajfel, 1978), and are interdependent concerning rewards (e.g., Deutsch & Gerard, 1955).

Most managers dramatically underestimate the conformity pressures that operate in groups. Perhaps this is because people like to think of themselves as individualists who are not afraid to speak their own minds. However, conformity pressures in groups are real and they affect the quality of team decision-making. The key message for the manager is to anticipate conformity pressures in groups, to understand what drives it (i.e., the need to be liked and the desire to be right), and then to put into place group structures that will not allow conformity pressures to endanger the quality of group decision-making. This leads us to the first of the decision-making problems that teams may encounter.

DECISION-MAKING PITFALL I: GROUPTHINK

Groupthink occurs when team members place consensus above all other priorities—including using good judgment when the consensus reflects poor judgment, improper or immoral actions, and so on. Groupthink, at its core, involves a deterioration of mental efficiency, reality testing, and moral judgments as a result of group pressures toward conformity of opinion. For a list of groupthink decisions in the political and corporate world, see the box titled: Instances of Groupthink in Politics and the Corporate World. The desire to agree can become so dominant that it can override the realistic appraisal of alternative courses of action (Janis, 1972, 1982). The reasons for groupthink may range from group pressures to conform to a sincere desire to incorporate and reflect the views of all team members. Such pressure may also come from management if the directive is to reach a decision that all can agree to, such as in cross-functional teams.

Conformity pressures can lead decision makers to censor their misgivings, ignore outside information, feel too confident, and adopt an attitude of invulnerability. The pressure for unanimity is thought to be a recipe for ineffective group decision-making and explains how a group of otherwise intelligent and thoughtful people can make serious miscalculations that result in disastrous outcomes.

Symptoms of groupthink cannot be easily assessed by outside observers. Rather, most groupthink symptoms represent private feelings or beliefs held by group members or behaviors performed in private. There are three key symptoms of groupthink that take root and blossom in groups that succumb to pressures of reaching unanimity:

- **Overestimation of the group:** Members of the group regard themselves as invulnerable and, at the same time, morally correct. This lethal combination can lead decision makers to believe they are above, and exempt from, standards.

- **Closemindedness:** Members of the group engage in collective rationalization, often accompanied by stereotyping outgroup members.

- **Pressures toward uniformity:** There is a strong intolerance in a groupthink situation for diversity of opinion. Dissenters are subject to enormous social pressure. This often leads group members to suppress their reservations. Thus, the group perceives itself to be unanimous.

INSTANCES OF GROUPTHINK IN POLITICS AND THE CORPORATE WORLD

Examples from Politics

- Neville Chamberlain's inner circle, whose members supported the policy of appeasement of Hitler during 1937 and 1938, despite repeated warnings and events that indicated it would have adverse consequences (Janis & Mann, 1977).

- President Truman's advisory group, whose members supported the decision to escalate the war in North Korea, despite firm warnings by the Chinese Communist government that U.S. entry into North Korea would be met with armed resistance from the Chinese (Janis & Mann, 1977).

- President Kennedy's inner circle, whose members supported the decision to launch the Bay of Pigs invasion of Cuba, despite the availability of information indicating that it would be an unsuccessful venture and would damage U.S. relations with other countries (Janis & Mann, 1977).

- President Johnson's close advisors, who supported the decision to escalate the war in Vietnam, despite intelligence reports and information indicating that this course of action would not defeat the Viet Cong or the North Vietnamese, and would generate unfavorable political consequences within the United States (Janis & Mann, 1977).

- The decision of the Reagan administration to exchange arms for hostages with Iran and to continue commitment to the Nicaraguan Contras in the face of several congressional amendments limiting or banning aid.

Examples from the Corporate World

- Gruenenthal Chemie's decision to market the drug thalidomide (Raven & Rubin, 1976).

- The price-fixing conspiracy involving the electrical manufacturing industry during the 1950s.

- The decision by Ford Motor Company to produce the Edsel (Huseman & Driver, 1979).

- The selling of millions of jars of "phony" apple juice by BeechNut, the second largest baby food producer in the United States.

- The involvement of E. F. Hutton in "check kiting," wherein a money manager at a Hutton branch office would write a check on an account in Bank A for more money than Hutton had in the account. Because of the time lag in the check-collection system, these overdrafts sometimes went undetected, and Hutton could deposit funds to cover the overdraft the following day. The deposited money would start earning interest immediately. The scheme allowed Hutton to earn a day's interest on Bank A's account without having to pay anything for it—resulting in $250 million in free loans every day (ABA *Banking Journal,* 1985; Goleman, 1988).

- The illegal purchases by Salomon Brothers at U.S. Treasury auctions in the early 1990s (Sims, 1992).

Deficits arising from groupthink can lead to many shortcomings in the decision-making process. Consider, for example, the following lapses that often accompany groupthink:

- Incomplete survey of alternatives
- Incomplete survey of objectives
- Failure to re-examine alternatives
- Failure to examine preferred choices
- Selection bias
- Poor information search
- Failure to create contingency plans

Each of these behaviors thwarts the rational decision-making process we outlined at the beginning of this chapter.

Learning from History

Consider two decisions made by the same United States presidential cabinet—the Kennedy administration. The Kennedy cabinet was responsible for the Bay of Pigs operation and the Cuban Missile Crisis. The Bay of Pigs was a military operation concocted by the United States in an attempt to overthrow Fidel Castro, the leader of Cuba. The Bay of Pigs is often seen as one of the worst foreign policy mistakes in U.S. history. The operation was regarded as a disaster of epic proportions, resulting in the loss of lives and the disruption of foreign policy. It is also a kind of puzzle because the invasion, in retrospect, seems to have been so poorly planned and so poorly implemented—yet it was led by people whose individual talents seemed to make them eminently qualified to carry out an operation of this sort. What led capable people who should have known better to proceed with such a disastrous plan? In contrast, Kennedy's response to the Cuban Missile Crisis was regarded as a great foreign policy success. These examples, from the same organizational context and team, make an important point: Even smart and highly motivated people can make disastrous decisions under certain conditions. Kennedy's cabinet fell prey to groupthink in the Bay of Pigs decision, but not in the Cuban Missile Crisis. Why was the same cabinet so successful in one instance, but such a miserable failure in another?

A number of detailed historical analyses have been performed (Kramer, 1999; Peterson, Owens, Tetlock, Fan, & Martorana,1998) comparing these two historical examples, as well as several others. Some sharp differences distinguish between groupthink and effective groups.

Table 3.6 summarizes three kinds of critical evidence: (1) factors that may lead to groupthink; (2) factors that may promote sound decision-making; and (3) factors that do not seem to induce groupthink. We focus on two types of behavior: That of the leader and that of the rest of the group.

A number of factors may lead to groupthink. Leader behavior that is associated with too much concern for political ramifications, or the analysis of alternatives in terms of their political repercussions, is a key determinant of groupthink. The same is also true for group behavior; when groups are overly concerned with their political image, they may not make sound decisions.

TABLE 3.6	PRECIPITATING AND PREVENTATIVE CONDITIONS FOR THE DEVELOPMENT OF GROUPTHINK	
Conditions	**Leader Behavior and Cognition**	**Team Behavior and Cognition**
Precipitous conditions (likely to lead to groupthink)	• Narrow, defective appraisal of options • Analysis of options in terms of political repercussions • Concern about image and reputation • Loss-avoidance strategy	• Rigidity • Conformity • View roles in political terms (protecting political capital and status) • Large team size • High sense of collective efficacy • Perceived threat to social identity
Preventative conditions (likely to engender effective decision-making)	• Being explicit and direct about policy preferences allows the team to know immediately where the leader stands	• Task orientation • Intellectual flexibility • Less consciousness of crisis • Less consciousness of crisis • Less pessimism • Less corruption (i.e., more concerned with observing correct rules and procedures) • Less centralization • Openness and candidness • Adjustment to failing policies in timely fashion • Genuine commitment to solving problems • Encouraging dissent • Acting decisively in emergencies • Attuned to changes in environment • Focus on shared goals • Realization that trade-offs are necessary • Ability to improvise solutions to unexpected events
Inconclusive conditions (unlikely to make much of a difference)	• Strong, opinionated leadership	• Risk taking • Cohesion • Internal debate

In terms of preventative conditions, the behavior of the team has a greater impact on the development of groupthink than does leader behavior. Sound group decision-making can be achieved through task orientation, flexibility, less centralization, norms of openness, encouraging dissent, focus on shared goals, and realizing that trade-offs are necessary.

How to Avoid Groupthink

In this section, we identify some specific steps managers can take to prevent groupthink. Prevention is predicated on two broad goals: The stimulation of constructive, intellectual conflict and the reduction of concerns about how the group is viewed by others—a kind of conformity pressure. We focus primarily on team design factors because those are the ones managers have the greatest control over. None of these can guarantee success, but they can be effective in encouraging vigilant decision-making.

Monitor Team Size Team size is positively correlated with groupthink, with larger teams more likely to fall prey to groupthink (McCauley, 1998). People grow more intimidated and hesitant as team size increases. This is related to the principle of performance anxiety. There is no magic number for team size, but with teams larger than 10, individual members may feel less personal responsibility for team outcomes and their behaviors may be too risky.

Get Buy-In from Organizational Authorities Teams whose members are preoccupied with their political image are less effective than are teams whose members do not get caught up in their self-image. This should not be construed to mean that teams should be completely oblivious to organizational issues. It is obvious that teams, like individuals, are sensitive to how they are viewed by the organization and relevant organizational authorities. When teams believe that their decisions are important to organizational authorities, they are more likely to make sound decisions than if they believe that their decisions are unimportant (Thompson, Kray, & Lind, 1998).

Provide a Face-Saving Mechanism for Teams A small team who has the respect and support of their organization would seem to be in an ideal position to make effective decisions. Yet often, they fail to do so. One reason is that they are concerned with how their decision, and its fallout, will be viewed by others. Many teams are afraid of being blamed for poor decisions—even decisions for which it would have been impossible to predict the outcome. Often, face-saving concerns keep people from changing course, even when the current course is clearly doubtful. For this reason, it can be useful to provide teams with a face-saving mechanism or a reason for why outcomes might appear to be poor. This basically amounts to giving teams an external attribution for poor performance. Indeed, teams that are given an excuse for poor performance before knowing the outcome of their decision are less likely to succumb to groupthink than teams that do not have an excuse (Turner, Probasco, Pratkanis, & Leve, 1992).

The Risk Technique The risk technique is a structured discussion situation designed to reduce group members' fears about making decisions (Maier, 1952). The discussion is structured so that team members talk about the dangers or risks involved in a decision and delay discussion of any potential gains. Following this is a discussion of controls or mechanisms for dealing with the risks or dangers. This strategy may sound touchy-feely, but it basically amounts to creating an atmosphere in which team members can express doubts and raise criticisms without fear of rejection or hostility from the team. There are many ways to create such an atmosphere. One way is to have a facilitator play the role of devil's advocate for a particular decision. The mere expression of doubt about an idea or plan by one person may liberate others to raise doubts and concerns. A second method may be to have members privately convey their concerns or doubts and then post this information in an unidentifiable manner. Again, this liberates members to talk about their doubts.

Adopt Different Perspectives In this technique, team members assume the perspective of other constituencies with a stake in the decision (Turner & Pratkanis, 1998). For example, in the *Challenger* incident, group members might have been asked to assume the roles of the federal government, local citizens, space crew families, astronomers, and so on. Although the *Challenger* disaster happened in large part because of a disastrously poor understanding of how to interpret statistical data, the key point of adopting different perspectives is to create a mechanism that will instigate thinking more carefully about problems, which could prompt these groups to reconsider evidence.

Debias Training Techniques The goal of debiasing training techniques is to expose how human decision-making can be faulty and based on limited information. For this reason, it is often helpful to have a decision expert work with a team and elaborate upon key decision biases, ideally through simulations and exercises. It is usually unhelpful to simply inform teams about biases, because they appear to be absurdly obvious after the fact. Rather, it is best to actively challenge teams with a realistic decision scenario and then use the team context to discuss the process of decision-making and methods for improving its quality.

Structure Discussion Principles The goal of structured discussion principles is to delay solution selection and to increase the problem-solving phase. This prevents premature closure on a solution and extends problem analysis and evaluation. For example, teams may be given guidelines that emphasize continued solicitations of solutions, protection of individuals from criticism, keeping the discussion problem-centered, and listing all solutions before evaluating them (Maier, 1952).

Establish Procedures for Protecting Alternative Viewpoints Although teams can generate high-quality decision alternatives, they frequently fail to adopt them as preferred solutions (Janis, 1982; Turner et al., 1992). This means that most problems that teams face are not simple, "eureka" types of decisions, in which the correct answer is obvious once it is put on the table. Rather, team members must convince others about the correctness of their views. This is a difficult task when things like conformity pressure are operating and especially after individual team members have publicly committed to a particular course of action. For these reasons, it can be useful to instruct members to keep a log of all alternatives suggested during each meeting.

Second Solution This technique requires teams to identify a second solution or decision recommendation as an alternative to their first choice. This enhances the problem-solving and idea generation phases as well as performance quality (Hoffman & Maier, 1966).

Beware of Time Pressure Decisions involve idealistic considerations, such as moral principles and ideals, as well as practical considerations, such as difficulty, cost, or situational pressures. Therefore, it is undeniable that decision makers often make trade-offs. Moral principles are more likely to guide decisions for the distant future than for the immediate future, whereas difficulty, cost, and situational pressures are more likely to be important in near future decisions. In other words, managers are more likely to compromise their principles in decisions regarding near future actions compared with distant future actions (Liberman & Trope, 1998).

DECISION-MAKING PITFALL 2: ESCALATION OF COMMITMENT

It would seem that one remedy for groupthink would be clear feedback as to the effectiveness of the decision-making process. For example, the Coca-Cola Company's decision to introduce New Coke was eventually recognized as a mistake and reversed. Do such clear failures prompt teams to revisit their decision-making process and improve upon it? Not necessarily. In fact, under some conditions, teams will persist with a losing course of action, even in the face of clear evidence to the contrary. This type of situation is known as the **escalation of commitment** phenomenon.

Consider the decision-making problem in the box titled: New Product Investment Decision.

Next, consider the following decision situations.

- A senior marketing manager at a major pet food corporation continues to promote a specific brand, despite clear evidence that the brand is losing market share to its competitors.

NEW-PRODUCT INVESTMENT DECISION

As the president of an airline company, you have invested $10 million of the company's money into a research project. The purpose was to build a plane that would not be detected by conventional radar, in other words, a radar-blank plane. When the project is 90 percent completed, another firm begins marketing a plane that cannot be detected by radar. Also, it is apparent that their plane is much faster and far more economical than the plan your company is building. The question is: Should you invest the last 10 percent of the research funds to finish your radar-blank plane?

☐   Yes, invest the money.
☐   No, drop the project.

- A company continues to invest in a manager who is known to have handled many situations poorly and receives consistently subpar 360-degree evaluations.

- Quaker Oats continued to push Snapple, even though its market share dropped staggeringly.

- When the stock market tide is running, wildly enthusiastic investors will bid up companies' stock prices to levels known to be too high, in the certainty that they can "only go up." Two years later, they dump these companies at any price, believing with equal certainty that they are becoming worthless (Train, 1995).

- A company continues to drill for oil, despite being unable to turn a profit on drilling efforts in the past 3 years.

- John R. Silber, previous president of Boston University, decided to invest in Seragen, a biotechnology company with a promising cancer drug. After investing $1.7 million over 6 years, the value is now $43,000 (Barboza, 1998).

In all of these situations, individuals and teams committed further resources to what eventually proved to be a failing course of action. This leads to the decision bias known as the escalation of commitment. In most cases, the situation does not turn into a problem for a while. The situation becomes an escalation dilemma when the persons involved in the decision would make a different decision if they had not been involved up until that point, or when other objective persons would not choose that course of action. Often, in escalation situations, a decision is made to commit further resources to "turn the situation around." This process may repeat and escalate several times as additional resources are invested. The bigger the investment and the more severe the possible loss, the more prone people are to try to turn things around. Consider the situation faced by Lyndon Johnson during the early stage of the Vietnam War. Johnson received the following memo from George Ball, then undersecretary of state:

> The decision you face now is crucial. Once large numbers of U.S. troops are committed to direct combat, they will begin to take heavy casualties in a war they are ill-equipped to fight in a noncooperative if not downright hostile countryside. Once we suffer large casualties, we will have started a well-nigh irreversible process. Our involvement will be so great that we cannot—without national humiliation—stop short of achieving our complete objectives. Of the two possibilities I think humiliation will be more likely than the achievement of our objectives—even after we have paid terrible costs. (Sheehan et al., 1971, p. 450).

The escalation of commitment process is illustrated in Figure 3-12. In the first stage of the escalation of commitment, a decision-making team is confronted with questionable or negative outcomes (e.g., a price drop, decreasing market share, poor performance evaluations, or a malfunction). This external event prompts a reexamination of the team's current course of action, in which the utility of continuing is weighed against the utility of withdrawing or changing course. This decision determines the team's commitment to

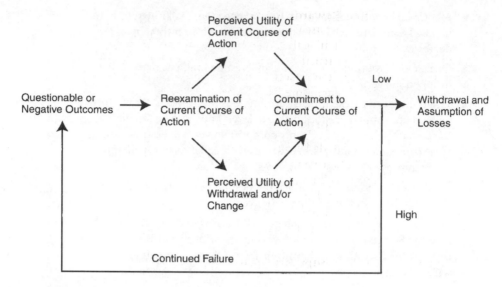

FIGURE 3-12

Escalation of Commitment

Source: Adapted from Ross, J., & Staw, B. M. 1993, August. "Organizational Escalation and Exit: Lessons from the Shoreham Nuclear Power Plant." *Academy of Management Journal*, 701–732.

its current course of action. If this commitment is low, the team may withdraw from the project and assume its losses. If this commitment is high, however, the team will continue commitment and continue to cycle through the decision stages. There are four key processes involved in the escalation of commitment cycle: Project-related determinants, psychological determinants, social determinants, and structural determinants (Ross & Staw, 1993).

Project Determinants

Project determinants are the objective features of the situation. Upon receiving negative feedback, team members ask whether the perceived setback is permanent or temporary (e.g., is reduced market share a meaningful trend or a simple perturbation in a noisy system?). If it is perceived to be temporary, there may appear to be little reason to reverse course. Then, when addressing questions like whether to increase investment in the project or to commit more time and energy to it, the team is essentially asking whether it wishes to escalate its commitment. Of course, this may often be the right choice, but it should be clear that such decisions also make it harder for the team to terminate that course of action if results continue to be poor.

Psychological Determinants

Psychological determinants refer to the cognitive and motivational factors that propel people to continue with a chosen course of action. When managers or teams receive indication that the outcomes of a project may be negative, they should ask themselves the following questions regarding their own involvement in the process:

What Are the Personal Rewards for Me in This Project?   In many cases, the *process* of the project itself, rather than the *outcome* of the project, becomes the reason for continuing the project. This leads to a self-perpetuating reinforcement trap, wherein the rewards for continuing are not aligned with the actual objectives of the project. Ironically, people who have high, rather than low, self-esteem are more likely to become victimized by psychological forces—people with high self-esteem have much more invested in their ego and its maintenance than do those with low self-esteem.

This advice may seem rather odd because it appears to be inconsistent with self-interest. That is, it would seem to be in a project manager's best interest to invest in the product, rather than to benefit the company as a whole. However, managers or teams who fall prey to escalation of commitment will ultimately end up losing because their product won't be successful, and they will have suffered more than if they simply cut off the project earlier on.

Is My Ego and the Team's Reputation on the Line?   "If I pull out of this project, would I feel stupid? Do I worry that other people would judge me to be stupid?" Ego protection often becomes a higher priority than the success of the project. When managers feel personally responsible for a decision, monetary allocations to the project increase at a much higher rate than when managers do not feel responsible for the initial decision (Staw, 1976).

In some sense, it does not seem too surprising that when managers personally oversee a project, they attempt to ensure that the project has every chance of success (e.g., by allocating more resources to it). After all, that is their job. A manager who works on a project through from beginning to end is going to know more about it and may be in a better position to judge it. Furthermore, personal commitment is essential for the success of many projects. Whereas it is certainly good to nurture projects so that they have their best chance of survival, it is nearly impossible for most managers to be completely objective about it. This is where it is important to have clear, unbiased criteria by which to evaluate the success of a project.

Are We Evaluating All of the Facts in an Unbiased Fashion?   The confirmation bias is the tendency for people to only see what they already believe to be true. When people are ego-invested in a project, the confirmation bias will even be stronger. It is striking how even upon the receipt of what appears to be unsupportive data, people who have fallen prey to the confirmation bias will maintain, and in some cases increase, their resolve. For example, the confirmation bias is related to the costly protraction of strike activity—a form of escalation of commitment. As a quick demonstration of the confirmation bias, take the test in the box titled: Card Test.

Is the Glass Half-Empty or Half-Full?   If decision makers see themselves as trying to recover from a losing position, chances are they will engage in greater risk than if they see themselves as starting with a clean slate. Like the gambler in Las Vegas, decision makers who wait for their luck to turn around have fallen into the trap. For these reasons, decision makers who were initially responsible for the decision are likely to feel more compelled to continue to pursue the same course of action as compared to the successors of such man-

CARD TEST

Imagine that the following four cards are placed in front of you and are printed with the following symbols on one side:

Card 1	Card 2	Card 3	Card 4
E	K	4	7

Now, imagine you are told that a letter appears on one side of each card and a number on the other. Your task is to judge the validity of the following rule, which refers only to these four cards: "If a card has a vowel on one side, then it has an even number on the other side." Your task is to turn over only those cards that have to be turned over for the correctness of the rule to be judged. Which cards do you want to turn over? *(Stop here and decide which cards to turn over before reading on.)*

Averaging over a large number of investigations (Oaksford & Chater, 1994), 89 percent of people select E, which is a logically correct choice because an odd number on the other side would disconfirm the rule. However, 62 percent also choose to turn over the 4, which is not logically informative because neither a vowel nor a consonant on the other side would falsify the rule. Only 25 percent of people elect to turn over the 7, which is a logically informative choice because a vowel behind the 7 would falsify the rule. Only 16 percent elect to turn over K, which would not be an informative choice.

Thus, people display two types of logical errors in the task. First, they often turn over the 4, an example of the confirmation bias. However, even more striking is the failure to take the step of attempting to disconfirm what they believe is true—in other words, turning over the 7 (Wason & Johnson-Laird, 1972).

agers. Escalation of commitment is partially responsible for some of the worst financial losses experienced by organizations. For example, from 1966 to 1989, the Long Island Lighting Company's investment in the Shoreham Nuclear Power Plant escalated from $65 million to $5 billion, despite a steady flow of negative feedback. The plant was never opened (Ross & Staw, 1993).

Social Determinants

Most people want others to approve of them, accept them, and respect them. Consequently, they engage in actions and behaviors that they think will please most of the people most of the time, perhaps at the expense of doing the right thing, which may not be popular.

The need for approval and liking may be especially heightened among groups composed of friends. Indeed, groups of longtime friends are more likely to continue to invest in a losing course of action (41 percent) than groups composed of unacquainted persons (16 percent) when groups do not have buy-in from relevant organizational authorities. In contrast, when they are respected by their organization, groups of friends are extremely deft at extracting themselves from failing courses of action (Lind, Kray, & Thompson, 1998).

Structural Determinants

The same determinants that create groupthink on a team level also exist at the level of the institution. For instance, a project can itself become institutionalized, thereby removing it from critical evaluation. Instead, old-timers and newcomers learn to perceive the project as an integral part of the culture. It becomes impossible for these teams to consider removal or extinction of the project.

Often in organizations, political pressure can kill an otherwise viable project. Similarly, political support can keep a project alive that should be terminated. The escalation of commitment phenomenon implies that more often than not, teams will persevere with a losing course of action because of the psychological, social, and structural reinforcements in the situation. Teams become entrenched and committed to their positions and reluctant to move away from them.

Avoiding the Escalation of Commitment Problem

Most teams do not realize that they are in an escalation dilemma until it is too late. Complicating matters is the fact that, in most escalation dilemmas, the team might have some early "wins" or good signs that reinforce the initial decision. How can a team best get out of an escalation dilemma?

Unfortunately, there is no magical, overnight cure. The best advice is to adopt a policy of risk management: Be aware of the risks involved in the decision; learn how to best manage these risks; and set limits, effectively capping losses at a tolerable level. It is also important to find ways to get information and feedback on the project from a different perspective. More specifically:

Set Limits Ideally, a team should determine at the outset what criteria and performance standards will be necessary to continue to invest in the project or program in question. These should be spelled out and distributed to all relevant personnel.

Avoid the Bystander Effect In many situations, especially ambiguous ones, people quite frankly are not sure how to behave and, therefore, do nothing out of fear of acting foolishly. This dynamic explains the bystander effect, or the tendency to not help others who obviously need help in emergency situations (Latane & Darley, 1970). If team members have well-defined, predetermined limits, they need not try to interpret others' behavior; they can refer to their own judgment and act upon it.

Avoid Tunnel Vision Get several perspectives on the problem. Ask people who are not personally involved in the situation for their appraisal. Be careful not to bias their evaluation with your own views, hopes, expectations, or other details, such as the cost of extricating the team from the situation, because that will only predispose them toward the team's point of view. This is not what you want—you want an honest, critical assessment.

Recognize Sunk Costs   Probably the most powerful way to escape escalation of commitment is to simply recognize and accept sunk costs. Sunk costs are basically water under the bridge: Money (or other commitments) previously spent that cannot be recovered. It is often helpful for teams to have built into their agenda a period in which they consider removal of the project, product, or program. In this way, the situation is redefined as one in which a decision will be made immediately about whether to invest or not; that is, if you were making the initial decision today, would you make the investment currently under consideration (as a continuing investment), or would you choose another course of action? If the decision is not one that you would choose anew, you might want to start thinking about how to terminate the project and move on to the next one.

External Review   In some cases, it is necessary to remove or replace the original decision makers from deliberations precisely because they are biased. One way to do this is with an external review of departments.

DECISION-MAKING PITFALL 3: THE ABILENE PARADOX

In the case of groupthink and escalation of commitment, teams pursue a course of action largely because they are personally involved; a decision to discontinue might involve admission of a poor earlier choice. There is another kind of behavior that can lead teams to make undesirable choices—choices, in fact, that none of the individuals would have made on their own. Known as the **Abilene paradox** (Harvey, 1974), it is a kind of consensus seeking that has its roots in the avoidance of conflict. The Abilene paradox is basically a form of **pluralistic ignorance**: Group members adopt a position because they feel other members desire it; team members don't challenge one another because they want to avoid conflict or achieve consensus. Although this is a kind of "expectational bubble"—a set of expectations about other people's expectations that could be burst if even one person expressed a contrary view—it can have a dramatic impact on the actual decision-making behavior of the team. The story in the box titled: The Abilene Paradox, illustrates the dilemma.

To the extent that team members are more interested in consensus than debate, they may end up in Abilene. Indeed, the mismanagement of agreement can be more problematic than the management of disagreement (Harvey, 1974). This may seem counterintuitive, but the consequences are very real.

It may seem strange to think that intelligent people who are in private agreement may somehow fail to realize the commonality of their beliefs and end up in Abilene. However, it is easy to see how this can happen if members fail to communicate their beliefs to each other.

Quandaries like the Abilene paradox may seem absurd, but they are easy to fall into. Strategies to avoid the situation include playing devil's advocate, careful questioning, and a commitment on the part of all team members to both fully air their opinions as well as respectfully listen to others. Note that none of these requires team members to abandon consensus seeking as a goal—if that is indeed their goal. However, it does require that consensus actually reflect the true beliefs of the team.

THE ABILENE PARADOX

The July afternoon in Coleman, Texas (population 5,607), was particularly hot—104 degrees as measured by the Walgreen's Rexall Ex-Lax temperature gauge. In addition, the wind was blowing fine-grained West Texas topsoil through the house. But the afternoon was still tolerable—even potentially enjoyable. There was a fan going on the back porch; there was cold lemonade; and finally, there was entertainment. Dominoes. Perfect for the conditions. The game required little more physical exertion than an occasional mumbled comment, "Shuffle 'em," and an unhurried movement of the arm to place the spots in the appropriate perspective on the table. All in all, it had the markings of an agreeable Sunday afternoon in Coleman—that is, it was until my father-in-law suddenly said, "Let's get in the car and go to Abilene and have dinner at the cafeteria."

I thought, "What, go to Abilene? Fifty-three miles? In this dust storm and heat? And in an unairconditioned 1958 Buick?"

But my wife chimed in with "Sounds like a great idea. I'd like to go. How about you, Jerry?" Since my own preferences were obviously out of step with the rest I replied, "Sounds good to me," and added, "I just hope your mother wants to go."

"Of course I want to go," said my mother-in-law. "I haven't been to Abilene in a long time."

So into the car and off to Abilene we went. My predictions were fulfilled. The heat was brutal. We were coated with a fine layer of dust that was cemented with perspiration by the time we arrived. The food at the cafeteria provided first-rate testimonial material for antacid commercials.

Some four hours and 106 miles later we returned to Coleman, hot and exhausted. We sat in front of the fan for a long time in silence. Then, both to be sociable and to break the silence, I said, "It was a great trip, wasn't it?"

No one spoke. Finally my mother-in-law said, with some irritation, "Well, to tell the truth, I really didn't enjoy it much and would rather have stayed here. I just went along because the three of you were so enthusiastic about going. I wouldn't have gone if you all hadn't pressured me into it."

I couldn't believe it. "What do you mean 'you all'?" I said. "Don't put me in the 'you all' group. I was delighted to be doing what we were doing. I didn't want to go. I only went to satisfy the rest of you. You're the culprits."

My wife looked shocked. "Don't call me a culprit. You and Daddy and Mama were the ones who wanted to go. I just went along to be sociable and to keep you happy. I would have had to be crazy to want to go out in heat like that."

Her father entered the conversation abruptly. "Hell!" he said.

He proceeded to expand on what was already absolutely clear. "Listen, I never wanted to go to Abilene. I just thought you might be bored. You visit so seldom I wanted to be sure you enjoyed it. I would have preferred to play another game of dominoes and eat the leftovers in the icebox."

After the outburst of recrimination we all sat back in silence. Here we were, four reasonably sensible people who, of our own volition, had just taken a 106-mile trip across a god-forsaken desert in a furnace-like temperature through a cloud-like dust storm to eat unpalatable food at a hole-in-the-wall cafeteria in Abilene, when none of us had really wanted to go. In fact, to be more accurate, we'd done just the opposite of what we wanted to do. The whole situation simply didn't make sense (Harvey, 1974).

What factors lead to problems like the Abilene paradox? In general, if individual team members are intimidated or feel that their efforts will not be worthwhile, then they are less likely to air or defend their viewpoints. This is called *self-limiting behavior*.

According to a survey of 569 managers by Mulvey, Veiga, & Elsass (1996), there are six key causes of self-limiting behavior in teams:

- **The presence of someone with expertise:** When team members perceive that another member of the team has expertise or is highly qualified to make a decision, they will self-limit. Members' perceptions of other teammates' competence play a key role, and these evaluations are formed quickly—often before a team meets for the first time.

- **The presentation of a compelling argument:** Frequently, the timing of a coherent argument influences decision-making—such as when the decision is made after a lot of fruitless discussion.

- **A lack of confidence in one's ability to contribute:** If team members feel unsure about their ability to meaningfully contribute to the decision, they will be inclined to self-limit.

- **An unimportant or meaningless decision:** Unless the decision is seen as vital or important to the individual's well-being, there is a powerful tendency to adopt a "who cares" attitude.

- **Pressure from others to conform to the team's decision:** Roger Boisjoly reported that he felt incredible pressures to conform exerted by the management team.

- **A dysfunctional decision-making climate:** When team members believe that others are frustrated, indifferent, disorganized, or generally unwilling to commit themselves to making an effective decision, they are likely to self-limit. Such a climate can be created in the early stages of a decision by inadvertent remarks such as, "this is a ridiculous task," "nothing's going to change, so why bother," and so on.

How to Avoid the Abilene Paradox

The following suggestions are taken from Harvey (1974) and Mulvey et al. (1996).

Confront the Issue in a Team Setting The most straightforward approach involves meeting with the organization members who are key figures in the problem and its solution. The first step is for the individual who proposes a solution to state it and then be open to any and all feedback. For example:

> I want to talk with you about the research project. Although I have previously said things to the contrary, I frankly don't think it will work and I am very anxious about it. I suspect that others may feel the same, but I don't know. Anyway, I am concerned that we may end up misleading one another, and if we aren't careful, we may continue to work on a problem that none of us wants and that might even bankrupt us. That's why I need to know where the rest of you stand. I would

appreciate any of your thoughts about the project. Do you think it can succeed? (Harvey, 1974, p. 32).

Conduct a Private Vote People often go along with what they think the team wants to do. Dissenting opinions are easier to express privately—pass out blank cards and ask team members to privately write their opinions. Guarantee them anonymity and then share the overall outcomes with the team.

Minimize Status Differences High-status members are often at the center of communication, and lower status members are likely to feel pressures to conform more quickly. Although this can be difficult to avoid, reassurances by senior members about the importance of frank and honest discussion reinforced by the elimination of status symbols, like dress, meeting place, title, and so on, may be helpful.

Minimize the Size of the Team As we have seen, teams that are too large often experience social loafing, free riding, and a diffusion of responsibility—all of which can contribute to making a trip to Abilene.

Frame the Task as a Decision to Be Made Framing the task as a decision to be made, rather than a judgment (which suggests personal opinion), helps cast a tone of somber decision-making, absent of the trappings of power or personal prestige. When team members are given a decision-making responsibility, they fundamentally approach the problem differently when the decision that needs to be made is framed as a problem to be solved. The typical approach is to view decisions as judgments, not problems. People typically view a problem as needing more analysis, such as pros and cons, and less opinion. Telling your team that you believe in "fact-based decision-making" is a potentially helpful way of framing the decision.

Provide a Formal Forum for Controversial Views This may be achieved by segmenting the discussion into pros and cons. Debate must be legitimized. Members should not have to worry about whether it is appropriate to bring up contrary views; it should be expected and encouraged.

Take Responsibility for Failure It is important to create a climate where teams can make mistakes, own up to them, and then move on without fear of recrimination. Consider what happened to a three-man forge team, called the "Grumpy Old Men," at Eaton Corporation in the Forge Division plant. Through an assumption at the start of their shift, they made an error that resulted in about 1,200 pieces of scrap. It was not an inexpensive mistake, but it was not one that would close the plant. The team had jeopardized the plant's output to customers. The team came forward to the plant leadership, admitted their error, described its potential impact, and demanded to be allowed to take corrective action so that the problem could never occur again. They even took it a step further and demanded to be allowed to go before the entire workforce at the start of each of the three shifts and admit their error and describe what they were doing to make sure it would not happen again (Bergstrom, 1997).

DECISION-MAKING PITFALL 4: GROUP POLARIZATION

Consider the case in the box titled: Advice Question. Most people independently evaluating the problem state that the new company would need to have nearly a two-thirds probability of success before they would advise Mr. A. to leave his current job and accept a new position (Stoner, 1961). What do you think happens when the same people discuss Mr. A.'s situation and are instructed to reach consensus?

You might expect the outcome of the team to be the same as the average of the individuals considered separately. However, this is not what happens. The group advises Mr. A. to take the new job, even if it only has slightly better than a 50–50 chance of success! In other words, groups show a **risky shift**.

Now consider a situation in which a company is deciding the highest odds of an engine malfunction that could be tolerated on the release of a new vehicle. In this case, individual advisors are cautious, but when the same people are in a group, they collectively insist on even lower odds. Thus, they exhibit a **cautious shift**.

Why are teams both more risky and more cautious than are individuals, considering the identical situation? The reason for this apparent disparity has to do with some of the peculiarities of group dynamics. Teams are not inherently more risky or cautious than individuals; rather they are more *extreme* than individuals. **Group polarization** is the tendency for group discussion to intensify group opinion, producing more extreme judgment than might be obtained by pooling the individuals' views separately (see Figure 3-13).

Group polarization is not simply a case of social compliance or a bandwagon effect. The same individuals display the polarization effect when queried privately after group discussion. This means that people really believe the group's decision—they have conformed inwardly! The polarization effect does not happen in nominal groups. The polarization effect grows stronger

---

ADVICE QUESTION

Mr. A., an electrical engineer who is married and has one child, has been working for a large electronics corporation since graduating from college 5 years ago. He is assured of a lifetime job with a modest, though adequate, salary and liberal pension benefits upon retirement. On the other hand, it is very unlikely that his salary will increase much before he retires. While attending a convention, Mr. A. is offered a job with a small, newly founded company that has a highly uncertain future. The new job would pay more to start and would offer the possibility of a share in the ownership if the company survived the competition with larger firms.

Imagine that you are advising Mr. A. What is the lowest probability or odds of the new company proving financially sound that you would consider acceptable to make it worthwhile for Mr. A. to take the new job? Before reading on, indicate your response on a probability scale from zero to 100 percent.

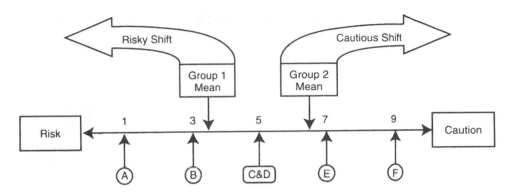

FIGURE 3-13

Group Polarization Processes. Imagine that Group 1 includes Person A (who chose 1), Person B (who chose 3), and Persons C and D (who both chose 5); the average of pregroup choices would be (1 + 3 + 5 + 5)/4, or 3.5. Because this mean is less than 5, a risky shift would probably occur in Group 1. If, in contrast, Group 2 contained persons C, D, E, and F, their pregroup average would be (5 + 5 + 7 + 9)/4 or 6.5. Because this mean is closer to the caution pole, a conservative shift would probably occur in the group.

Source: Adapted from Janis, I. L. 1982. *Victims of Groupthink* (2nd ed.). Boston: Houghton Mifflin.

with time, meaning that the same person who was in a group discussion 2 weeks earlier will be even more extreme in his or her judgment.

Two explanations for group polarization hearken back to our discussion of conformity at the beginning of the section: The need to be right and the need to be liked. Simply stated, people want to make the right decision and they want to be approved of by their team. Take the case concerning Mr. A., the electrical engineer. Most people are positively inclined when they agree to recommend to Mr. A. that he seriously consider a job change. However, they vary greatly in their reasons for why Mr. A. should change jobs. Someone in the group may feel that Mr. A. should leave the secure job because it does not represent a sufficient challenge; others may think that Mr. A. should leave the company because he should increase his standard of living. Thus, people feel that Mr. A. should consider a move, but they have different (yet complementary) reasons supporting their belief. This is the rational type of conformity we discussed earlier. At the same time, members of the team want to be accepted—part of the socialization process.

CONCLUSIONS

Teams make important decisions and some of them will not be good ones, despite the very best of intentions. It is unrealistic to suggest that poor decision-making, or for that matter even disastrous decision-making, is avoidable. The key message hearkens back to creating an organization that can optimally learn from failure. Learning from failure is difficult when people suffer—especially innocent ones. As a case in point, consider the steps that were taken by NASA following the space shuttle *Challenger* accident, including the redesign of the joints and solid rocket booster, which went through hundreds of modifications; the institution of full hazard analysis for thousands of parts; certification of flight readiness, which includes verbal and video-recorded affirmation from a variety of NASA officials; the institution of a veto policy, in which anyone at any level can stop the process—a policy that has been exercised by NASA members; and creation of launch criteria, which occurs in the cool of the morning, rather than in the heat of the afternoon. Is there a downside to the creation and use of decision-making procedures and criteria that err on the side of safety? As Don McMonagle, manager of launch integration at NASA puts it: If every one of the hundreds of thousands of components on space vehicles were required to work perfectly, no one could ever launch and this would effectively paralyze the U.S. space program (personal communication, July 1998). The key for NASA and other decision-making teams within organizations is to develop and use decision-making procedures, such as veto policies and preestablished criteria to guide decision-making. All of these decisions involve a certain level of risk, but that risk can be minimized.

Errors in Team Decisions

Editor's Note:
A much simpler, but nonetheless valuable perspective on avoiding decision errors.

Unfortunately groups and teams are prone to a number of decision-making errors of which supervisors, team-leaders, and team members need to be aware. One error, called the Abilene paradox, results from failures of team members to communicate their real wants. Because of members' desires to get along with the group, they sometimes make decisions to pursue alternatives that no members really want. Thus a group might make a decision to take an automobile trip to Abilene although no one really wants to go, as was the case with the original paradox (Mulvey, Veiga, and Elsass, 1996). One of the authors has an insightful colleague who has helped his department avoid bad group decisions by making timely announcements that "It looks like we're on our way to Abilene." A similar error is called *self-censorship*. This error occurs in cohesive groups in which individuals do not critically examine various alternatives because they do not want to rock the boat (Mulvey, Veiga, and Elsass, 1996).

Another error caused by pressures for group conformity is called *groupthink*. Conditions leading to groupthink include high pressure for conformity, strong desire to remain in the group, punishment of individuals who offer deviant input, and the presence of individuals within the group who are perceived to have extraordinary expertise. Groupthink among presidential advisors has been cited as the cause of the escalation of the Vietnam War and the disastrous Bay of Pigs invasion of Cuba. In these examples the groups were comprised of intellectual super stars who did not want to be excluded from their high-powered groups. As a result, they did not vigorously challenge the group even when they disagreed. This form of "collective dumbness by

Supervision: Diversity and Teams in the Workplace, Ninth Edition, by Charles R. Greer and W. Richard Plunkett. Copyright © 2000, 1996, 1994, 1992, 1989, 1986, 1983, 1979, 1975 by Prentice Hall, Inc.

smart people" (Feinberg and Tarrant, 1995, p. 155) also is practiced in business. For example groups of smart people made the decision to produce the Cadillac Allanté, a beautiful and expensive car that turned out to be a commercial failure. Such groups also approved NBC's rigging of crash tests for a sensational exposé about explosions of General Motors trucks in collisions (Feinberg and Tarrant, 1995).

Several conditions cause group members to avoid critical thinking or self-limit their own input when it deviates from the developing position of the group. Professors Paul Mulvey, John Veiga, and Priscilla Elsass have found that the following conditions make groupthink more likely (1996):

1. Perceptions of great expertise among one or more individuals
2. A compelling argument is made
3. Individuals lack confidence in their potential contributions
4. Decisions to be made are perceived as unimportant
5. Pressures for conformity
6. Disorganized and unproductive meetings

In order to offset such conditions, these researchers make a number of suggestions for reducing pressures for conformity. These include using smaller decision-making groups, minimizing status differentials among group members, clarifying the purpose of the group, emphasizing the importance of the decision, and describing the procedures to be used in the decision-making process (Mulvey, Veiga, and Elsass, 1996).

Using Technology to Team

"The VeriFone sales rep knew his big sale of the quarter was unraveling when he left the offices of an Athens bank at 4:30 P.M. A competitor had raised doubts about whether VeriFone could deliver a new payment-service technology, one that had not been used extensively in Greece. In fact, VeriFone was the main supplier of that technology in the United States and many other countries, with more than half a million installations and many satisfied customers. But the rep didn't have any particulars about those users to be able to make a rebuttal. He scouted out the nearest phone and hooked up his laptop to it. Then he sent an S. O. S. email to all VeriFone sales, marketing, and technical-support staff worldwide. That e-mail launched a process that would create a virtual team to gather customers' testimonials and other data to make his case while he slept. In San Francisco, an international marketing staffer who was on duty to monitor such S.O.S calls got the message at home when he checked his email at 6:30 A.M. He organized a conference call with two other marketing staffers, one in Atlanta and one in Hong Kong, where it was 9:30 A.M. and 10:30 P.M., respectively. Together, they decided how to handle the data coming in from everyone who'd received the post. A few hours later, the two U.S. team members spoke on the phone again while they used the company's wide area network to fine-tune a sales presentation that the San Fran-

cisco team leader had drafted. Before leaving for the day, the leader passed the presentation on to the Hong Kong team member so he could add Asian information to the detailed account of experiences and references when he arrived at work. The Greek sales rep awakened a few hours later. He retrieved the presentation from the network, got to the bank by 8 A.M., and showed the customer the data on his laptop. Impressed by the speedy response to get business, the customer reasoned that VeriFone would also respond as fast to keep business. He placed the order" (Pape, 1997, p. 29).

A group of top managers at a progressive Silicon Valley company hated their weekly meetings, but enjoyed e-mail because it is quick, direct, and to the point. They thought meetings were "gassy, bloated, and a waste of time." So they decided to cancel their regular meetings and meet only when confronted with problems just too tough to handle over the network. Three months later, the same people resumed their regularly scheduled face-to-face meetings. They discovered that they had created a "morale-busting, network-generated nightmare." When the managers did get together, the meetings were unpleasant and unproductive. Precisely because they could use e-mail to reach consensus on easy issues, arguing the thorny issues face-to-face turned their "big problem" meetings into combat zones. E-mail interaction had eliminated the opportunity for casual agreement and social niceties that make meetings enjoyable. Even the e-mail communication became most hostile as participants maneuvered themselves in anticipation of the big-problem meetings (Schrage, 1995).

In some cases, technology works, whereas in others, it doesn't—as illustrated in the previous examples. In the rush to go global, corporations are requiring their managers to be effective across distances and cultures never before mastered. Teams of managers armed with laptop computers, fax modems, e-mail, voice mail, video conferencing, interactive databases, and frequent-flyer memberships are being charged with conducting business in the global arena. Virtual teams can efficiently harness the knowledge of company employees regardless of their location, thereby enabling the company to respond faster to increased competition. The VeriFone example is a testament to the power of information technology to bring together teams of people who would otherwise not be able to interact. As we saw in our analysis of group brainstorming, information technology offers the potential for improving information access and information-processing capability. Furthermore, information technology, in transcending time and place, offers the potential for members to participate without regard to temporal and spatial impediments.

However, as the Silicon Valley company example illustrates, not all virtual teamwork proceeds seamlessly. Managers responsible for leading virtual teams have found that distance is a formidable obstacle, despite electronic media and jet travel. A decision made in one country elicits an unexpected reaction from team members in another country. Remote offices fight for influence with the head office. Telephone conferences find distant members struggling to get onto the same page, literally and figuratively, in terms of shared viewpoint or strategy. Conflicts escalate strangely between distributed groups. Group members at sites separated by even a few kilometers begin to talk in the language of "us" and "them" (Armstrong & Cole, 1995). Thus, there is considerable debate among managers as to whether technology fosters or hinders teamwork in the workplace at the global, and even local, level.

This chapter examines the impact of information technology on teamwork at the global and local levels. We begin by describing a simple model of social interaction called the place-time model. This model will give us a framework through which we can evaluate the various forms of information technology and how they apply to team interaction. The model focuses on teams whose members either work in the same or different physical *location* and at the same or different *time*. For each of these cases, we describe what to expect and ways to deal with the limitations of that communication mode. Then, we move to a discussion of virtual teams, making the point that whenever teams must work together in a non-face-to-face fashion, this constitutes a virtual team. We describe strategies to help virtual teams do their work better. We then discuss transnational teams; we describe what transnational teams do and what it takes to get there. Obviously, transnational teams and global teamwork involve diversity issues. We follow this discussion with a section on how information technology affects human behavior. We do not attempt to provide a state-of-the-art review on types of information technology; our purpose is to identify the considerations that managers must wrestle with when attempting to bring together groups of people who are not in the same place.

*P*lace-Time Model of Social Interaction

The **placetime model** is based on the options that teams have when working across different locations and times. It is useful to conceptualize teams in terms of their geographic location (together versus separated) and in terms of their temporal relationship (interacting in real time versus asynchronously). For any team meeting, there are four possibilities as depicted in the place-time model in Table 3.7. As might be suspected, communication and teamwork unfold differently face-to-face than they do via electronic media.

TABLE 3.7   PLACE-TIME MODEL OF INTERACTION

	Same Place	Different Place
Same Time	Face-to-face	Telephone Videoconference
Different Time	Single text editing Shift work	E-mail Voice mail

Source: Thompson, L. 1998. *The Mind and Heart of the Negotiator.* Upper Saddle River, N. J.: Prentice Hall.

Richness is the potential information-carrying capacity of the communications medium. Communication media may be ordered on a continuum of richness, with face-to-face communication being at the relatively "rich" end, and formal written messages, such as memos, being at the relatively "lean" or modality-constricted end (Daft & Lengel, 1984; Daft, Lengel, & Trevino, 1987; see Figure 3-14). Face-to-face communication conveys the richest information because it allows the simultaneous observation of multiple cues, including body language, facial expression, and tone of voice, providing people with a greater awareness of context. In contrast, formal, numerical documentation conveys the least rich information, providing few clues about the context. Depending upon the space and time relationships that characterize a team, groups are often constrained in their choice of communication medium.

Let's consider each of the four types of communication in the place-time model.

FACE-TO-FACE COMMUNICATION

Face-to-face interaction is the clear preference of most managers and executives; and rightly so. Face-to-face contact is crucial in the initiation of relationships and collaborations, and people are more cooperative when interacting face-to-face than via other forms of communication. Personal, face-to-face contact is the lubricant of the business engine. Without it, things don't move very well and relationships between business persons are often strained and contentious.

Face-to-face meetings are ideal when teams must wrestle with complex problems. For example, researchers need regular face-to-face contact to be confident that they accurately understand each other's work, particularly if it involves innovative ideas. The half-life of confidence decays over time as

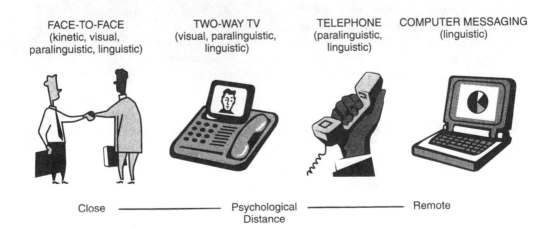

FACE-TO-FACE (kinetic, visual, paralinguistic, linguistic)   TWO-WAY TV (visual, paralinguistic, linguistic)   TELEPHONE (paralinguistic, linguistic)   COMPUTER MESSAGING (linguistic)

Close ——————— Psychological ——————— Remote
Distance

FIGURE 3-14

Psychological Distancing Model

Source: Adapted from Wellens, A. R. 1989, September. "Effects of Telecommunication Media upon Information Sharing and Team Performance: Some Theoretical and Empirical Findings." *IEEE AES Magazine*, 14.

researchers communicate through telephone and computer conferences; facetoface contact is required to renew trust in their mutual comprehension (DeMeyer, 1991, 1993). Face-to-face team meetings are particularly important when a group forms, when commitments to key decisions are needed, and when major conflicts among members must be resolved (DeMeyer, 1991; Galegher, Kraut, & Egido, 1990; Sproull & Keisler, 1991). Work groups form more slowly, and perhaps never fully, when they don't have face-to-face contact (DeMeyer, 1991; Galegher et al., 1990).

In most companies, the incidence and frequency of face-to-face communication is almost perfectly predicted by how closely people are located to one another: Employees who work in the same office or on the same floor communicate much more frequently than those located on different floors or in different buildings. The incidence of communication literally comes down to feet—even a few steps can have a huge impact. For example, communication frequency between R&D researchers drops off logarithmically after only 5 to 10 meters of distance between offices (Allen, 1977). In a study of molecular biologists, MacKenzie, Cambrosio, and Keating (1988) found that critical techniques for producing monoclonal antibodies were not reported in journals, but were passed from scientist to scientist at the lab bench. Workers in adjacent offices communicate twice as often as those in offices on the same floor, including via e-mail and telephone transmissions (Galegher et al., 1990).

Just what cues do people get out of face-to-face contact that makes it so important for interaction and productivity? Primarily, two things: First, *face-to-face communication is easier and, therefore, more likely to occur* than are other forms of communication. Simply stated, most people need a reason to walk up the stairs or to make a phone call. They underestimate how much information they get from chance encounters—which never happen in any mode but face-to-face because of this perceived effort. Second, although it is seldom consciously realized, *people primarily rely on nonverbal signals to help them conduct social interactions.* One estimate is that 93 percent of the meaning of messages is contained in the nonverbal part of communication, such as voice intonation (Meherabian, 1971). Perhaps this is why business executives will endure the inconveniences of travel across thousands of miles and several time zones so that they can have face-to-face contact with others, even if it is only for a short period of time.

The emphasis on the human factor is not just old-fashioned business superstition. Important behavioral, cognitive, and emotional processes are set into motion when people meet face-to-face. However, unless people are specially trained, they don't know what exactly it is about face-to-face interaction that facilitates teamwork—they just know that things go smoother.

Face-to-face interaction allows people to develop rapport—the feeling of being "in sync" or "on the same wavelength" with another person. Whether or not people feel rapport is a powerful determinant of whether they develop trust. The degree of rapport determines the efficiency and the quality of progress toward goal achievement, and whether the goal is ever achieved (Tickle, Degnen & Rosenthal, 1987).

Nonverbal (body orientation, gesture, eye contact, headnodding) and paraverbal behavior (speech fluency, use of "uh-huhs," etc.) is the key to building rapport. When the person we are interacting with sits at a greater distance, with an indirect body orientation, backward lean, crossed arms, and low eye contact, we feel less rapport than when the same person sits with a forward lean, an open body posture, nods, and maintains steady eye contact. These nonverbal and paraverbal cues affect the way people work and the quality of their work as a team.

However, face-to-face communication is not the best modality for all teamwork. As a clear case in point, we saw in our discussion of creativity and brainstorming that face-to-face brainstorming is less productive compared to other, less rich forms of interaction.

SAME TIME, DIFFERENT PLACE

The same-time, different-place mode, in which people communicate in real time but are not physically in the same place, is often the alternative to face-to-face teamwork. The most common means is via telephone; video conferencing is another example. Team members often rely on the telephone, but they do not always reach their party; up to 70 percent of initial telephone attempts fail to reach the intended party (Philip & Young, 1987). In telephone conversations, people lack facial cues; in video conferencing, they lack real-time social cues, such as pauses, mutual gaze, and another person's immediate nonverbal response to what is being said (e.g., looking away or down). Yet at the same time, electronic interaction, such as in brainstorming groups, can greatly increase team productivity.

When technology tries to replace the dynamics of face-to-face interaction, it often falls short. The technology designed to make groups feel as though they are face-to-face does not lead to more and better communication. As a case in point, consider an engineering work group, located in two offices 1,000 kilometers apart, that experimented with an omnipresent video wall and cameras in all offices to link the sites together (Abel, 1990). Generally, the engineers interacted across the distance as one cohesive group, but there were some key exceptions: Video links were not very effective in generating new relationships or in resolving divisive differences, and miscommunication was treated as rudeness. Members of a design team were unable to listen to each other's ideas until they met face-to-face for 3 days, where they reached effective consensus.

What are the major ways in which group members who are physically distant from one another suffer because of their physical separation? There are several effects of physical separation of the team, some of which might not be immediately obvious (Armstrong & Cole, 1995).

Loss of Informal Communication

Probably the most-felt impact is the inability to chat informally in the hall, inside offices, and so on. The impromptu and casual conversations that employees have by the water cooler and the coffee machine are often where the most difficult problems are solved, and the most important interpersonal issues are addressed. Beyond a very short distance, people miss out on spontaneous exchanges that occur outside of formal meetings. Remote group members feel cut off from key conversations that occur over lunch and in the hall. Vince Anderson, director of environmental programs for Whirlpool Corp.'s North American Appliance Group in Evansville, Indiana, oversaw a

2-year project using a virtual team that developed a chlorofluorocarbon-free refrigerator, involving the United States, Brazil, and Italy. The team met approximately every 4 months to discuss the project and it was these informal meetings—a backyard cookout and a volleyball game—that were the most valuable for the project (Geber, 1995).

Separation of Feedback

Another negative impact of physical separation is feedback; greater distance tends to block the corrective feedback loops provided by chance encounters. One manager contrasted how employees who worked in his home office related to his decisions, compared with employees 15 kilometers away (Armstrong & Cole, 1995). Engineers in the home office would drop by and catch him in the hall or at lunch. "I heard you were planning to change project X," they would say. "Let me tell you why that would be stupid." The manager would listen to their points, clarify some details, and all would part better informed. In contrast, employees at the remote site would greet his weekly visits with formally prepared group objections, which took much longer to discuss and were rarely resolved as completely as the more informal hallway discussions. In short, groups working remotely do not get the coincidental chances to detect and correct problems on a casual basis. Managers tend to think of their home group as the people they sit beside at work. Geographic sites promote an informal, spontaneous group identity, reinforced by close physical proximity and the dense communication it promotes. Those working in an office all tend to have friends in nearby companies or groups, hear the same industry rumors, and share similar beliefs about technological trends. Thus, any distance—whether it be 15 miles or 15,000 miles—is problematic in this regard.

Loss of Informal Modeling

Another impact is the loss of informal modeling and observational learning. Distance tends to block casual observation, which is often invaluable to monitoring and mentoring performance, especially for one-on-one team coaching. The inability of remote employees to watch successful project managers enact their roles, along with the inability to observe the learned employee, is a barrier to effective coaching of task and interpersonal-related skills.

Out-of-the-Loop Employees

Another problem is that distant employees tend to be left out of discussions or forgotten. In a sense, they are "out of sight, out of mind." The default behavior is to ignore the person on the speakerphone. This is especially magnified when the person or group with less status is on the phone.

Time differences amplify the effects of physical distance. Distributed group members face the challenge of finding each other at the same time while they are living in different time zones. Furthermore, time differences sometimes highlight cultural differences. However, teams can try to overcome these cultural barriers. One group based in the United States and in Italy celebrated a project milestone in their weekly video conference by sharing foods on the video screen and fax. The East Coast U.S. team, at 9 A.M., sent images of bagels and coffee. The Italian team, at 3 P.M. in their time zone, sent images of champagne and cookies.

Conflicts are expressed, recognized, and addressed more quickly if group members work in close proximity. A manager can spot a problem, "nip it in the bud," and solve the problem quickly. In geographically separated groups, the issues are more likely to just get dropped and go unresolved, contributing to a slow buildup in aggravation. People complain to their coworkers, reinforcing local perceptions of events, but do not complain to the distant leaders until feelings reach extremely high levels.

Although there are many disadvantages of distance, it is not always a liability for teams. The formality of a scheduled phone meeting can compel each party to better prepare for the meeting and to address the issues more efficiently. In addition, distance can reduce micromanagement. Some managers hinder their employees' performance by monitoring them too closely and demanding frequent updates. Distance can mitigate this problem. Most notably, groups can often be much more creative when interacting via information technology.

DIFFERENT TIME, SAME PLACE

In the different-time, same-place mode, team members interact asynchronously, but share the same work space. An example might be shift workers who pick up the task left for them by the previous shift or collaborators working on the same electronic document. After one partner finishes working on the document, it goes to the other partner, who will further edit and develop it.

Although people may not realize it, they rely a lot on their physical environments for important information and cues. The concept of transactive memory systems. People often supplement their own memories and information-processing systems—which are fallible—with systems located in the environment. How people use other team members as information storage, retrieval, and processing devices. The same is true for the physical environment. A Post-it note on the back of a chair, or a report placed in a certain bin can symbolize an entire procedural system (e.g., how to make a long-distance conference call). Just as people become information dependent on other people, they also can become information dependent upon aspects of the physical environment in order to do their work. At the extreme, this type of dependence can be a limitation for groups that find it impossible to work outside the idiosyncratic confines of their workspace. Information and work-space dependence can negatively affect the productivity and motivation of a team.

The productivity of any team, and organizational effectiveness in general, is a joint function of the technical and the social system (Emery & Trist, 1973). The structure of a group, both internally and externally, and the technology the group works with are products of an active adaptation process, in which the technology is shaped by the organization or its subunits, as well as being a factor in shaping the organization. For example, consider the introduction of a new technology, CT scanners, in two hospitals (Barley, 1996). The introduction of the CT scanners increased uncertainty and upset the distribution of expertise and the division of labor in the hospital units. Both hospital units became more decentralized with the introduction of the CT scanners and the associated increase in uncertainty.

DIFFERENT PLACE, DIFFERENT TIME

In the different-place, different-time model, interactants communicate asynchronously in different places. The most pervasive means is e-mail. Asynchronous, distributed communication seems to be growing at a faster rate of popularity than are other forms of communication, such as the telephone and videoconferencing. The telephone has been around for 120 years, but less than half of the people on the planet have ever made a phone call. In contrast, the Internet is only about 30 years old, and it is expected that by the year 2000, there will be anywhere between 200 million to 1 billion Internet users.

Yet e-mail changes the nature of behavior and team dynamics. Because it is easy to send a message, and social norms are not present when sending e-mail, people often are more risk taking. Furthermore, there is virtually no competition to attain and hold the floor, so people are at liberty to send frequent and long messages. Some people receive several hundred electronic messages each day.

There is an etiquette to sending e-mail. You can check your e-mail savvy by reviewing the box titled: Keys to Successful E-Mail Collaboration, which indicates keys to successful e-mail collaboration.

Is e-mail effective for learning? In the fall of 1996, an experiment was carried out in which 33 students enrolled in a social statistics course at California State University at Northridge. The students were randomly divided into two groups—one taught in a traditional classroom and the other taught virtually on the World Wide Web (Schutte, 1996). Text, lectures, and exams were standardized for both classes; the virtual class scored an average of 20 percent higher than the traditional class on examinations. Furthermore, the virtual class had significantly higher peer contact, more time spent on class work, a perception of more flexibility, better understanding of the material, and a greater liking for math than the traditional class. The virtual students seemed more frustrated, but not from the technology. Instead, their inability to ask questions of the professor in a face-to-face environment led paradoxically to greater involvement among classmates, who formed study groups to "pick up the slack of not having a real classroom." Thus, the key performance differences here are most likely attributable to the collaboration among students instigated by the technology. It appears that the lack of rich communication in the virtual class led to the improved performance of students, who were sparked by the inadequacies of the virtual medium.

Information technology (in particular, the World Wide Web and the Internet) has led to the formation of new groups of people and communities. With over 40 million people on the Web, up from 1 million in December of 1994, these communities have been called the "colonizing of cyberspace." According to Andrew Busey, chairman and chief technology officer of ichat Inc., an Internet startup organization in Austin, Texas, that makes software for on-line chats, "Community and communications is the next big wave on the internet" (Hof, Browder, & Elstrom, 1997). The Web is not just a meeting place for young people; 67 percent are 30 years of age or older, including 19 percent over age 50. Women account for a bigger portion of the Internet population than ever before—41 percent, up from 21 percent a year and a half ago.

KEYS TO SUCCESSFUL E-MAIL COLLABORATION

Given that you've got an international team that must communicate via information technology, how can you best achieve group goals? The following prescriptions are important (Thompson, 1998):

Make your messages concise and clear. Most people overestimate the ability of others to make sense out of what they mean (Keysar, 1994). People have a hard enough time deciphering our messages in face-to-face interactions; accuracy decreases dramatically in e-mail exchanges. Many people assume that longer means clearer. It doesn't. People have a short attention span and often dislike long e-mail messages, or perhaps even stop reading them if they begin to fall off of the screen. Most people are capable of only retaining seven, plus-or-minus two, ideas in their head at any one time. As a general rule of thumb, most e-mail messages should fit on a single screen. **Screen loading,** or the tendency to write very long messages, can annoy the recipients, especially if they are busy. Teams perform better when they exchange a greater number of shorter e-mails, rather than fewer but longer e-mails. Increasing the rate of e-mail exchange prevents misunderstanding because misperceptions can be quickly rectified. This also builds reciprocity in exchange.

Responding to e-mail. The asynchronous nature of e-mail provides people with the dubious luxury of not having to immediately receive or respond to e-mail messages. However, the sender of e-mail messages often expects a timely response. Not responding to e-mail may be perceived as rejection or disinterest. Newer forms of software allow senders to ascertain whether recipients have read their e-mail. Failure to provide a timely response to e-mail is akin to giving the "silent treatment" to someone. Suspicion and hostility increase as the communication between parties diminishes.

Metacommunication. **Metacommunication** is communication about communication. This boils down to people talking about how they should communicate. This is of critical importance in electronic interaction because the norms of turn-taking and conversation are not clear. In any electronic communication, it is important to let team members know how often you check your e-mail, whether you or someone else reads and responds to your e-mail, and whether you forward your e-mail to others.

Light of day test. The golden rule of e-mail is the **light of day test**—is what you're saying in the e-mail suitable to be read by your mother, supervisor, or jury? Could it appear on the front page of the newspaper? If not, it's probably not a good idea to send it.

Watch your temper. **Flaming** refers to the insults, criticisms, and character assassinations that people hurl over e-mail. Flaming remarks make fun of grammar, are patronizing (e.g., "I would recommend that you more closely read my first transmission prior to responding"), and include labeling and accusations (e.g., "That is completely ridiculous"; "Your idea is ludicrous"), character attacks, backhanded compliments ("I'm glad to see that you've come around to my point of view"), and blunt statements (e.g., "Why don't we stop treating each other as fools and start talking seriously?"). Flaming and other negative interpersonal behaviors that are found among computer-mediated communication system users stem from feelings of isolation (Keisler, Zubrow, Moses, & Gellar, 1985). In contrast, face-to-face groups have mechanisms and norms, such as conformity pressure, that largely prevent flaming (Rhoades & O'Connor, 1996).

People react to each other with less politeness, empathy, or inhibition if they cannot sense the other's social presence (Short, Williams, & Christie, 1976). People are much more likely to issue threats when communicating via information technology.

There is more uncertainty, doubt, and ambiguity in electronic mail exchanges. This stems from the asynchronous nature of communication. As a consequence, people become frustrated and seek to control the exchange by issuing threats (e.g., "I am not going to read my e-mail again"; "if I don't hear from you by 5 P.M., I will assume that the specifications are acceptable"). Along these lines, don't chastise or deliver negative feedback via e-mail; face-to-face (or telephone) communication is more appropriate.

Some even argue that these technologies are redefining individuals' identities as they explore the boundaries of their personalities, adopt multiple selves, and form on-line relationships that can be more intense than real ones (Turkle, 1995). Internet communities such as Women's Wire, Talk City, Parent Soup, Geocities, and Tripod are composed of various "netizens" who find they are spending more and more of their existence communicating in a virtual, as opposed to real, fashion (Hof et al., 1997).

It might seem that this type of community interaction is a far cry from the business world of information technology, but that is just the point: It is becoming harder to separate the personal lives of people and the communities to which they belong from their professional or business lives. The Internet does not make the clear distinction between work and home; the traditional distinction arises from physical separation, which is not the case on the Internet.

*I*nformation Technology and Social Behavior

Information technology has extremely powerful effects on social behavior (Keisler & Sproull, 1992). Many people are surprised at how they behave when communicating via e-mail. What are the key things to expect when interacting with teammates via information technology?

STATUS AND POWER: THE "WEAK GET STRONG" EFFECT

In face-to-face interactions, people do not contribute to conversation equally. One person or one clique usually dominates the discussion. In general, those with the higher status tend to talk more, even if they are not experts on the subject. Not surprisingly, managers speak more than subordinates and men speak more than women.

However, an odd thing happens on the way to the information technology forum: The traditional static cues are missing and the dynamic cues are distinctly less impactive. This has a dramatic effect on social behavior: Power and status differences are weakened. Decision-making occurs on the basis of task expertise, rather than status (Eveland & Bikson, 1989). People who are in weak positions in face-to-face encounters become more powerful because status cues are harder to read in non-face-to-face interaction (Sproull & Keisler, 1991). Traditional, static cues, like position and title, are not as obvious on e-mail. It is often impossible to tell whether you are communicating with a president or clerk because traditional e-mail simply lists the person's name, not a title. In most networks, when people send e-mail, the only signs of position and personal attributes are names and addresses. Addresses are often shortened and may be difficult to comprehend. Even when they can be deciphered, addresses identify the organization, but not the subunit, job title, social importance, or level in the organization of the sender. Dynamic status cues, such as dress, mannerisms, age, and gender, are also missing in email. In this sense, email acts as an equalizer because it is difficult for high-status people to dominate discussions (see the box titled: Technology Can Be Empowering for Women).

TECHNOLOGY CAN BE EMPOWERING FOR WOMEN

When a group of executives meet face-to-face, the men in these groups are five times more likely than the women to make the first decision proposal: When the same groups meet via computer, women make the first proposal as often as do men (McGuire, Keisler, & Siegel, 1987).

Additionally, when interacting via e-mail, an interesting dynamic happens: People respond more openly and conform less to social norms and other people. They focus more on the content of the task and less on the direction of high-status opinion leaders. E-mail and other forms of computer-mediated communication (CMC) are becoming increasingly prevalent. CMC is more democratic and less hierarchical in this way, with bad news conveyed upward to superiors with less delay (Sproull & Keisler, 1991). At the same time, there is less awareness of the needs of the group or its members (McGrath, 1990). With more rudeness and less inhibition, conflicts in CMC are sharper and escalate more quickly. Consensus on complex, nontechnical issues is more difficult to reach (Hiltz, Johnson, & Turoff, 1986).

THE IMPACT OF TECHNOLOGY ON SOCIAL NETWORKS

Social networks are the circulatory system of an organization. We also saw that people with entrepreneurial networks are more likely to advance in their organizations than those with clique networks. The types of networks that characterize and shape organizational life change dramatically when information technology enters the picture as a form of communication.

Technology Can Lead to Face-to-Face Meetings

An important value of information technology may come from the ability to generate face-to-face meetings that simply would not have occurred otherwise. For example, Boeing used a high-level computer-aided engineering network to manage the development of its new 777 passenger jet. This software network has the ability to alert Boeing engineers whenever their proposed modifications in subassemblies interfere with other subassemblies—for example, when a hydraulic system modification might interfere with an electrical system. Boeing management discovered that its engineers were deliberately making modifications in the plans that interfered with other systems. What appeared to be a form of software sabotage was actually Boeing engineers taking advantage of the network to find out who was working on the other systems. That way, they could get together to talk about their designs. In other words, the network created the opportunity for productive collaboration around the 777 that Boeing's own management structure could not (Schrage, 1995).

Increased Speed of Information Exchange

E-mail networks, or connections between people who communicate via electronic mail, increase the information resources of low-network people. When people need assistance (e.g., information or resources), they often turn to their immediate social network. When such help is not available, they use weak ties, such as relationships with acquaintances or strangers, to seek help that is unavailable from friends or colleagues. However, there is a problem: In the absence of personal relationships or the expectation of direct reciprocity, help from weak ties might not be forthcoming or could be of low quality.

Some companies, particularly global companies and those in the fields of information technology and communications, need to rely on e-mail and employees within the company forming connections with each other on the basis of no physical contact. The incentives for taking the time to assist someone who is dealing with a problem and is located in a different part of the world are pretty minuscule.

Tandem Corporation is a global computer manufacturer that has a highly geographically dispersed organization (Sproull & Keisler, 1991). Managers in the Tandem Corporation need technical advice to solve problems, but they cannot always get useful advice from their local colleagues. Simply stated, the local networks are often not sufficient to solve problems. What can be done?

One possibility is to catalogue or store information in some easily accessible database. In a technical company, this would mean published reports and scientific manuals. However, engineers and managers do not like to consult technical reports to obtain needed information; most of the information they use to solve their problems is obtained through face-to-face discussions. People in organizations usually prefer to exchange help through strong collegial ties, which develop through physical proximity, similarity, and familiarity.

An investigation of Tandem's e-mail revealed some startling and encouraging findings (Sproull & Keisler, 1991): Managers who put out a request for technical assistance received an average of 7.8 replies per request. All of the replies were serious and respondents spent 9 minutes per reply. The replies solved the problem 50 percent of the time. Information providers gave useful advice and solved the problems of information seekers, despite their lack of a personal connection with the person requesting information.

Risk Taking

People intuitively perform cost-benefit analyses when considering different courses of action and, consequently, do not treat gains commensurately with losses. However, electronic interaction has an effect on risk-taking behavior. Consider the following choices:

A. Return of $20,000 over 2 years

B. 50 percent chance of gaining $40,000; 50 percent of gaining nothing

Option A is the safer investment; option B is riskier. However, these two options are mathematically identical, meaning that in an objective sense, people should not favor one option over the other. When posed with these choices, most managers are risk averse, meaning that they select the option that has the sure payoff as opposed to holding out for the chance to win big (or, equally as likely, not win at all). However, consider what happens when the following choice is proposed:

C. Sure loss of $20,000 over 2 years

D. 50 percent chance of losing $40,000; 50 percent of losing nothing

Most managers are risk seeking and choose option D. Why? According to the **framing effect** (Kahneman & Tversky, 1979), people are risk averse for gains and risk seeking for losses. This can lead to self-contradictory, quirky behavior. By manipulating the reference point, a person's fiscal policy choices can change.

Groups tend to make riskier decisions than do individuals in the same situation. Thus, risk seeking is greatly exaggerated in groups that meet face-to-face. Paradoxically, groups that make decisions via electronic communication are risk seeking for both gains and losses (McGuire, Keisler, & Siegel, 1987). Furthermore, executives are just as confident of their decisions whether they are made through electronic communication or face-to-face communication.

SOCIAL NORMS

As mentioned previously, when social context cues are missing or weak, people feel distant from others and somewhat anonymous. They are less concerned about making a good appearance, and humor tends to fall apart or to be misinterpreted. Additionally, the expression of negative emotion is no longer minimized because factors that keep people from acting out negative emotions are not in place when they communicate via information technology. Simply, in the absence of social norms that prescribe the expression of positive emotion, people are more likely to express negative emotion. When people communicate via e-mail, they are more likely to negatively confront others. Conventional behavior, such as politeness rituals and acknowledgment of others' views, decreases; rude, impulsive behavior, such as flaming, increases. People are eight times more likely to flame in electronic discussions than in face-to-face discussions (Dubrovsky, Keisler, & Sethna, 1991).

TASK PERFORMANCE

Are people more effective when they communicate via information technology? We saw that in terms of brainstorming and generating new ideas, face-to-face interaction is less effective than are some other forms of mediated communication.

It takes longer to write than it does to speak; hence, communicating via information technology is slower. It takes four times as long for a three-person group to make a decision in a realtime computer conference as in a face-to-face meeting (Siegel, Dubrovsky, Keisler, & McGuire, 1986). It takes as much as 10 times as long in a four-person computer-conference group that lacks time restrictions (Dubrovsky et al., 1991). This is especially true when the technology is new.

All of the team configurations discussed in this section, with the exception of the same-time, same-place teams, are virtual teams, and as such, face special challenges. In the sections that follow, we consider strategies for enhancing rapport and teamwork in local teams and in remotely distributed teams.

*E*nhancing Local Teamwork: Redesigning the Workplace

Telecommuting, or working from home, was the popular mantra of the late twentieth century. However, this is rapidly being replaced by a new work concept: Work anywhere, anytime—in your car, your home, your office, even your client's office. It means a radical disaggregation of work, going beyond the walls and confines of the traditional office (O'Hamilton, Baker, & Vlasic, 1996). For example, Jarlath MacNamara, founder of the Dublin, Ireland-based Cabs-on-Line, fitted a Ford Galaxy taxi with a laptop with e-mail and a browser, a cell phone, and a wireless modem and fax (Lyons, 1998). The traditional corporation exemplified by private offices, elevators, and cubicled workspaces is giving way to informal gatherings and chatting among employees in community spaces, such as lunchrooms and lounges. Corporate America is changing and the walls of the corporation are falling down and being replaced by mobile office systems that conform to the needs of the team, not the other way around.

For example, at the Alcoa Aluminum Company of America, senior executives work in open cubicles and gather around "communications centers" replete with televisions, fax machines, newspapers, and tables that encourage impromptu meetings. CEO Paul H. O'Neill's favorite hangout is the kitchen, where he and his staff heat up take-out food and talk work (O'Hamilton, Baker, & Vlasic, 1996). This type of change is radical and it is at the heart of team redesign. By redesigning the environment that they work in, teams work more efficiently and effectively.

Indeed, technology that can boost employee efficiency and mobility is surpassing facilities and real estate as the second biggest corporate operating expense, after salaries and benefits (O'Hamilton et al., 1996). Increasingly, architects, interior designers, facilities managers, and furniture companies are assuming the new role of strategic design consultants not only with blueprints, but also with human behavior in the organization. This means that many of the old perks, such as large, private paneled offices and private lunchrooms, are disappearing. Instead, employees of every rank are out in the open. According to a 1995 survey by the International Facility Management Association, 83 percent of companies are embracing alternative office strategies. The following are some of the most promising options for maximizing team productivity in the new office space.

VIRTUAL OR FLEXIBLE SPACE

Virtual or flexible space is physical space that is used on a temporary and changing basis to meet different needs. Instead of physical space setting limits on managerial behavior, such as how many people can be in a meeting at any one time and what information technology is or is not available, virtual space means that people determine their needs first and design the space to fit those needs. It is an entirely different way of thinking about space. Most important, virtual or flexible space does not mean open, fixed cubicles. For example, Allan Alley, vice president of Focus Systems Inc., a Wilsonville, Oregon maker of computer-projection systems, states that open cubicles are the "worst of both worlds. . . . No impromptu meetings and a lot of wasted space" (O'Hamilton et al., 1996, p. 113).

A prime example of virtual or flexible space is the "cave and commons" design: The idea is to balance individual work and teamwork, as well as privacy and community. At Minneapolis-based advertising agency Fallon-McElligott, when it is time to brainstorm, art directors, space buyers, account managers, and copywriters wheel special desks equipped with an employee's computer, files, and phone into flexible space. The room may hold 30 employees on Monday, none on Tuesday, and 10 or so on Wednesday, depending on what needs to be done. At any given time, team members may be working independently in their own cubicles or meeting at a center table.

At Procter & Gamble, project groups were the central design theme in their Cincinnati building. Members of teams work in open cubicles grouped together, and can all see each other, regardless of rank. File cases are on wheels, and offices are designed out of "bricks" that can be reconfigured in a jiffy. P&G personnel travel between floors by escalator, instead of elevators, which tend to halt conversation. "Huddle rooms" are strategically placed where teams can come together to brainstorm; and electronic whiteboards, which can convert scribble to e-mail, are present in lunchrooms and lounges. Corridors are deliberately wide so employees can stop for a chat. Furthermore, P&G designed features to help dual-career families: A dry cleaner, shoe repair shop, and take-out cafeteria are all on site.

FLEXIBLE FURNITURE

Furniture for the new space is key for productivity. Consider the "personal harbor," a small, cylindrical booth made by Steelcase Inc., with a door that can be closed; because it is curved, it has the effect of increasing interior space. There is enough room inside for a flat work surface, computer setup, phones, file drawer, and other standard desk items. There's even a whiteboard and built-in CD player. The important design feature is that the harbors are grouped around a large puzzle-like table that can be broken into several pieces. When harbor doors are open, people move in and out of the group space to talk to colleagues and participate in meetings. Whereas most norms state that people should never leave a traditional meeting room, with the personal harbor, people stay in a meeting long enough to contribute and then go back to work.

Some companies are even turning to custom designers and artists to get what they want. For example, when Fallon McElligott wanted to create its flexible space, interior designer Gary E. Wheeler created the award-winning "free address lockers" that resemble armoires on wheels. They hold a computer, files, phone, and a desktop, as well as a special universal plug to simplify "docking" all the electronics (O'Hamilton et al., 1996).

Inhale Therapeutic Systems, a small Palo Alto start-up working on novel drug delivery technology, uses "bullpens"—large cubicles containing four people of various ranks and functions—with no walls or barriers of any kind between people (O'Hamilton et al., 1996). These bullpens enable the employees to communicate more frequently and informally.

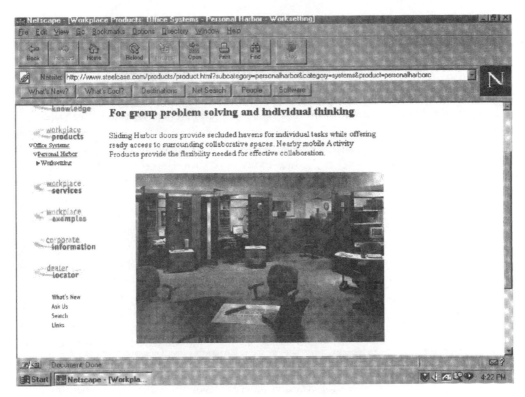

FIGURE 3-14

An Office Space Using Personal Harbors Designed by Steelcase, Inc.

Source: Steelcase Inc.'s Web site at *www.steelcase.com*.

HOTELING

Employees are increasingly mobile, spending more of their work time on the road than in the office. However, the mobile employee still needs a place to meet with the rest of the sales team or client team. **Hoteling** is the provision of a building, office, or meeting rooms that can be reserved in advance, just like a hotel. For example, at Ernst & Young's Washington office, when employees call, they are asked for a personal ID and the dates they need "hotel" space. Within 30 seconds, the system confirms whether a workstation or a meeting room is available. Each hotel has a concierge to meet and help guests. When employees arrive, their name is on a door, and any files or supplies the employees have requested will be there too. Also, their phone numbers are forwarded. IBM has about 20,000 sales and service professionals nationwide using shared offices, which has cut about $1.4 billion from real-estate expenses (O'Hamilton et al., 1996). For hoteling to be effective, it must be hassle-free for the employee (Smith, 1997).

Hoteling can be extraordinarily cost-effective. It has allowed KPMG Peat Marwick LLP to hire new employees without leasing extra space. At Ernst & Young, staffers realize that the lack of individual offices shows up in the firm's profit margin, which, in turn, shows up in their bonuses (Smith, 1997).

BEFORE IMPLEMENTING ALTERNATIVE FORMS OF OFFICE SPACE ...
(Becker, Quinn, Rappaport, & Sims, 1994)

1. The presence or absence of a strong champion is very important to the success/failure of the project.

2. Many issues that management may feel are barriers to implementing innovative ideas are perceived barriers.

3. A richer, more varied set of work settings that truly support the range of work activities must be provided.

4. A business approach to implementing innovations must be used instead of a cost approach.

5. User involvement is very critical to the success of the project.

6. Reinvesting a portion of the innovation cost savings is likely to result in a far higher level of employee satisfaction.

7. Using a pilot project to apply a standardized solution is ineffective.

8. The reassessment and data collection phase must not be eliminated.

9. Employees must be given time to adjust to the new work patterns.

However efficient, alternative forms of office space are not without problems. Implementing these types of alternative office space should be considered carefully. Consider the lessons in the box titled: Before Implementing Alternative Forms of Office Space.

The new design of offices and furniture indicates that most managers and executives regard face-to-face communication to be the ideal—and the more of it the better. However, it is not always possible to bring team members together, especially those who are spread across the globe. The answer is the virtual team.

*V*irtual Teams

A virtual team is a task-focused group that meets without all members necessarily being physically present or even working at the same time. Virtual teams work closely together even though they may be separated by many miles or even continents. Virtual teams may meet through conference calls, video conferences, e-mail, or other communications tools, such as application sharing. Teams may include employees only, or they may include outsiders, such as a customer's employees. Virtual teams work well for global companies, but they can also benefit small companies operating from a single location, especially if decision makers are often at job sites or on the road. They can be short-lived, like the one that helped the VeriFone sales rep in Greece, or permanent, such as operational teams that run their companies virtually.

If a company has a need for virtual teams, the biggest challenge for productivity is *coordination of effort*: How to get people to work together compatibly and productively, even though face-to-face contact is limited and communication is confined to phone, fax, and e-mail. To deal with the coordination problem, the leaders of every virtual team at VeriFone must know and follow written procedures put together by the company's senior managers, whether the team is appointed (as in the case of the San Francisco staffer heading the team aiding the Greek sales rep), or self-selected (as in the case of a director of a long-term team monitoring day-to-day operations).

Furthermore, before employees are permitted to form one of VeriFone's process-improvement teams, they must complete a 40-hour training program.

There are five crucial steps to creating (and maintaining) a successful virtual team (Pape, 1997). The first three steps are those that are required of any team.

1. *Have a clear, shared goal.* Teams must always be guided by a clear purpose, one that is shared by all team members. The purpose of the team will largely define issues such as who will be on the team, the process design, and the criteria that will be used to measure performance.

2. *Select members.* As with most teams, more is not better. The same is true for virtual teams: Most virtual teams should have three to seven members. More members mean greater process losses.

3. *Chart the course.* Team members tend to work to fill their time. Members of virtual teams will often be serving double or triple duty on other, local teams. It is important to set clear milestones for progress and give team members a clear sense of the likely duration of their work activity.

4. *Select technology tools.* Perhaps the most distinguishing aspect of virtual teams is the need to select a medium or media of communication. Any non-face-to-face communication medium will often entail considerable coordination loss if problems in using the technology are not adequately anticipated. Knowing what information technology to use when is key. For example, VeriFone teams use beepers, cellular phones, and voice mail for keeping in contact; and fax, e-mail, conference calls, and video conferencing for disseminating information.

5. *Focus on the human factor.* Do not take it for granted that team members working virtually will develop cohesion on their own. However, it is neither practical nor realistic to create special face-to-face bonding opportunities for virtual teams before they work together. For example, Price-WaterhouseCoopers has 45,000 employees in 120 countries, and people work on projects with each other without having ever met in person. We discuss the human factor in more detail in the next section.

*S*trategies for Enhancing the Virtual Team

There are a variety of methods for creating rapport among team members. The tradeoffs involve money and time. The following methods are used by various companies to address the rapport and trust problem that virtual teams encounter. Few of these methods have been tested in rigorous controlled research. We begin by discussing the most elaborate (and most expensive).

COLLABORATORY

A **collaboratory** is the combination of technology, tools, and infrastructure that allows scientists to work with remote facilities and each other as if they were co-located (Lederberg & Uncaphor, 1989). It is a center without walls, in which scientists and technicians can perform research without regard to geographical location. Parallels in the business world include virtual corporations in the place of physical corporations (Davidow & Malone, 1992) and a global workplace instead of national or local workplaces (O'Hara, Devereaux & Johansen, 1994). Although the collaboratory requires no face-to-face contact, teams often need some degree of actual face-to-face contact to establish rapport. There are several types of interaction that will help develop rapport among team members and force them to work in a single geographic location. The length of the face-to-face interaction varies by method. Among them are initial face-to-face experience, temporary engagement, or the one-day video conference.

INITIAL FACE-TO-FACE EXPERIENCE

Bringing together team members for a short, face-to-face experience is often used by companies who want to lay a groundwork of trust and communication for later teamwork that will be conducted strictly electronically. The idea here is that it is much easier for people to work together if they have actually met in a face-to-face encounter. Face-to-face contact humanizes people and creates expectations for team members to use in their subsequent long-distance work together.

TEMPORARY ENGAGEMENT

The idea here is to allow team members to work together in a sustained face-to-face fashion before separating them. For example, John Spencer, worldwide manager for the design and development of single-use cameras for Eastman Kodak Company in Rochester, New York, pulled together a project development team to design a new product that required the involvement of German design engineers. Spencer brought the German engineers to the United States for the initial 6 months of the project.

ONE-DAY VIDEO CONFERENCE

Chris Newell, executive director of the Lotus Institute, the research and education arm of Lotus Development Corp. in Cambridge, Massachusetts, believes that introductions via video conference are crucial to develop trust and relationships before doing teamwork electronically. Thus, if an initial, face-to-face meeting is out of the question, an alternative may be to at least get everyone on-line so that people can attach a name to a face. Depending upon the size of the team and locations of different members, this alternative may be more feasible than a face-to-face meeting.

TOUCHING BASE

If teams do not have an opportunity to work together at the outset of a project, then providing an opportunity for them to touch base at some later point can be helpful. This method is most useful for teams in which one or two members are remotely located. For example, Barbara Recchia, communications program manager at Hewlett Packard in Palo Alto, California, lives and works in Santa Rosa. In the early months of her remote work arrangement, she felt hopelessly out of touch with her colleagues (Geber, 1995). Eventually, she decided to drop in once a week instead of once a month to maintain her connection to her team. There are often special problems when just one member of the team is remotely located from the rest of the local team. Because much teamwork is done informally at the water cooler or at lunch, the remote person often feels lonely and disconnected from the rest of the team, and the rest of the team may leave that person out of the loop—if not deliberately, then just because it is cumbersome to bring the outsider up to date on all team actions.

SCHMOOZING

Schmoozing is our name for superficial contact between people that has the psychological effect of having established a relationship with someone. There are a variety of non-face-to-face schmoozing strategies, such as exchanging pictures or biographical information or engaging in a simple get-acquainted e-mail exchange. The effectiveness of electronic schmoozing has been put to test and the results are dramatic: schmoozing increases liking and rapport and results in more profitable business deals than when people just get down to business (Moore, Kurtzberg, Thompson, & Morris, 1999). Perhaps the most attractive aspect of schmoozing is that it is relatively low-cost and efficient. Merely exchanging a few short e-mails describing yourself can lead to better business relations. However, you should not expect people to naturally schmooze—at least at the outset of a business relationship. Team members working remotely have a tendency to get down to business. As a start toward schmoozing, begin by telling the other person something about yourself that does not necessarily relate to the business at hand (e.g., "I really enjoy kayaking"); also, provide a context for your own work space (e.g., "It is very late in the day and there are 20 people at my door, so I don't have time to write a long message"). Furthermore, ask questions that show you are interested in the other party as a person; this is an excellent way to search for points of similarity. Finally, provide the link for the next e-mail or exchange (e.g., "I will look forward to hearing your reactions on the preliminary report and I will also send you the tapes you requested").

TRANSNATIONAL TEAMS[1]

Thus far, we have discussed teamwork via information technology as if it were strictly a burden or nuisance to be overcome. However, depending upon the goals of the company, it may be highly desirable to put together virtual teams, even when local teamwork is an alternative.

---

[1]This section draws heavily upon the work of Snow, Snell, Davison, and Hambrick (1996).

Many companies are international or multinational. A better goal might be to become a transnational company or team. A **transnational team** is a work group composed of multinational members whose activities span multiple countries; transnational teams have successfully transcended the cultural, geographic, and managerial barriers to team effectiveness (Snow, Snell, Davison, & Hambrick, 1996). Global teamwork may be the best ticket going to becoming truly transnational. As cases in point, consider the following companies (Snow et al., 1996):

- In 1985, Fuji-Xerox sent 15 of its most experienced Tokyo engineers to a Xerox Corporation facility in Webster, New York. For the next 5 years, the Japanese engineers worked with a group of American engineers to develop the "world copier"—a huge success in the global marketplace.

- In 1991, Eastman Kodak formed a team to launch its latest consumer product, the photo CD. That group of experts, based in London, developed a strategy for the simultaneous introduction of the photo CD in several European countries. The photo CD was Kodak's most successful multi-country product introduction in the 1990s.

- At IBM-Latin America, in 1990, a group of managers and technical specialists formed their own team to market, sell, and distribute personal computers in 11 Latin American countries. It took the team leader about a year to convince his boss that the team should be formally recognized and allowed to operate as an autonomous business unit.

In each of these cases, a transnational team was key to the company's efforts to globalize and extend the firm's products and operations into international markets. Global competitive strategies are complex and expensive, and they are often administered by a transnational team of managers and specialists. For some examples of companies that missed the mark when attempting to cross cultural borders, see the box titled: Marketing "Cam-pains".

Like the other types of teams we have discussed, transnational teams come into existence in one of two primary ways: From the top down or from the bottom up. Most transnational teams are formed from the top down, as in the case of manager-led or self-managing teams. That is, senior managers see a competitive need, decide a transnational team should be formed, and put together a team with a particular mandate. For example, in 1991, Heineken formed the European Production task force, a 13-member team representing five countries. The task force wrestled with the issue of how many breweries the company should operate in Europe, what size and type they should be, and where they should be located. Eighteen months after it was formed, the task force presented its findings and recommendations to Heineken's board of directors, who enthusiastically accepted the recommendations.

In contrast, other transnational teams are emergent; like self-directing and self-governing teams, they evolve naturally from the existing network of individuals who depend on each other to accomplish their work objectives. These teams may cut across functions, business units, and countries and may even incorporate "outsiders" from other organizations, either temporarily or permanently. These teams may develop their own mandate and challenge

MARKETING "CAM-PAINS"

- Coors put its slogan, "Turn it loose," into Spanish, where it was read as "Suffer from diarrhea."
- Clairol introduced the Mist Stick, a curling iron, into Germany, only to find out that *mist* is slang for *manure*. Not too many people had use for the "manure stick."
- Scandinavian vacuum manufacturer Electrolux used the following in an American campaign: "Nothing sucks like an Electrolux."
- In Chinese, the Kentucky Fried Chicken slogan "Finger-lickin' good" came out as "Eat your fingers off."
- The American slogan for Salem cigarettes, "Salem—feeling free," was translated into the Japanese market as "When smoking Salem, you will feel so refreshed that your mind seems to be free and empty."
- When Gerber started selling baby food in Africa, they used the same packaging as in the United States, with the beautiful Caucasian baby on the label. Later, they learned that in Africa, companies routinely put pictures on the label of what's inside, since most people can't read English.
- Colgate introduced a toothpaste in France called Cue, the name of a notorious porno magazine.
- An American T-shirt maker in Miami printed shirts for the Spanish market which promoted the Pope's visit. Instead of "I saw the Pope" (el Papa), the shirts read "I saw the potato" (la papa).
- In Italy, a campaign for Schweppes Tonic Water translated the name into "Schweppes Toilet Water."
- Pepsi's: "Come alive with the Pepsi Generation" translated into "Pepsi brings your ancestors back from the grave" in Chinese.
- We all know about GM's Chevy Nova meaning "won't go" in Spanish markets, but did you know that Ford had a similar problem in Brazil with the Pinto? *Pinto* was Brazilian slang for "tiny male genitals." Ford renamed the automobile Corcel, meaning "horse."
- Hunt-Wesson introduced Big John products in French Canada as "Gros Jos." Later, they found out that in slang it means "big breasts."
- Frank Perdue's chicken slogan, "It takes a strong man to make a tender chicken," was translated into Spanish as "It takes an aroused man to make a chicken affectionate."
- When Parker Pen marketed a ball-point pen in Mexico, its ads were supposed to have read, "It won't leak in your pocket and embarrass you." Instead, the company thought that the word *embarazar* meant "to embarrass," when it actually meant "to impregnate," so the ad read: "It won't leak in your pocket and make you pregnant."
- The Coca-Cola name in China was first read as "Ke-kou-ke-la," meaning "Bite the wax tadpole" or "Female horse stuffed with wax," depending on the dialect. Coke then researched 40,000 characters to find a phonetic: equivalent, "Ko-kou-ko-le," translating into "Happiness in the mouth."
- Some folks from England got a huge laugh from the name of an airline: The Trump Shuttle (Donald Trump's airline). They said that in England, *Trump* translated into "fart."
- And finally, not even Nike is exempt. Nike has a television commercial for hiking shoes that was shot in Kenya using Samburu tribesmen. The camera closes in on one tribesman who speaks in native Maa. As he speaks, the Nike slogan "Just do it" appears on the screen. Lee Crank, an anthropologist at the University of Cincinnati, says the Kenyan is really saying, "I don't want these. Give me big shoes." Says Nike's Elizabeth Dolan, "We thought nobody in America would know what he said."

higher managers to accept and support it. For example, the concept of one transnational team was initiated around a dinner table at an annual quality assurance convention held internally by Glaxo-Wellcome. They chose their own leader—a medical doctor—and she approached senior executives to obtain authorization and funding for the team.

Transnational teams are distinguished from other teams in terms of the complexity of their work and their multicultural membership. Transnational teams work on projects that are highly complex and have considerable impact on company objectives. It is imperative that transnational teams adeptly handle a variety of cross-cultural issues. In particular, transnational teams must take into account the degree of similarity among the cultural norms of the individuals on the team, language fluency, and leadership style (Snow et al.,1996). Here's where a clearly shared goal, well-articulated team member roles, shared values, and agreement upon performance criteria are critical. The more deliberate planning centered upon these factors that occurs on the front end of teamwork, the better.

Once formed, transnational teams can be used to accomplish a number of different objectives. Some firms use the teams primarily to help achieve global efficiency, to develop regional or worldwide cost advantages, and to standardize designs and operations (Ghoshal & Barlett, 1988). Other teams enable their companies to be locally responsive; they are expected to help their firms attend to the demands of different regions' market structures, consumer preferences, and political and legal systems. For example, local responsiveness was the main concern of Eastman Kodak's photo CD team as it sought to tailor the marketing strategy for the new product to each major country in the European market. A third use of transnational teams is for organizational learning, bringing together knowledge from various parts of the company, transferring technology, and spreading innovations throughout the firm. For example, IBM has a global network of experts, led by a core team of six people headquartered outside of London, that consults around the world for clients in the airline industry. That team, the International Airlines Solution Centre, is composed of permanent and temporary members who fuse technical, consulting, and industry expertise to provide information technology to airlines and airport authorities. The team identifies knowledge located in one part of the world and applies it to problems that arise in another.

*C*onclusions

Change is often disturbing for the corporate world, and technological change is often thought to be a "Frankenstein's monster." However, teams have been dealing with place and time issues for several decades. The older solution was to relocate employees; newer solutions are more varied, creative, (often) cheaper, and less permanent. There is a strong intuition in the business world that face-to-face communication is necessary for trust, understanding, and enjoyment. However, face-to-face communication in no way ensures higher team productivity—especially in the case of creative teams. Information technology can increase productivity of teams. The skilled manager knows when to use it, which obstacles are likely to crop up when using it, and how to address those obstacles.

Conflict Happens

Introduction

So what did we expect? We're dealing with human beings here, aren't we? In every other area of our lives we know and expect that there will be conflicts to work through. In our marriages or relationships, with our children, with friends, with co-workers, in politics—we all accept conflict as a normal part of the equation.

Why then do we seem so surprised when conflicts arise in our teams? Perhaps the problem can be found in our definitions. The word "team" conjures a vision of a group working together unselfishly to achieve a common goal. We see what happens after the last out of the World Series—the hugging, the laughing, the flowing champagne—and may tend to forget leading up to this wonderful moment there was a whole lot of sacrifice, pain, *and conflict*.

One of the models in Section Two identified "storming" as a natural part of the team process. In cases where the task is simple, the timeline is short, and the members are like-minded, this phase is likely to be short and relatively painless; primarily the process of agreeing on ground rules and sorting out responsibilities. It's usually not that simple, though. Add any level of complexity, pressure, personality, politics, or economic impact and you've got a recipe for a big helping of conflict.

Realizing that conflict is unavoidable is crucial if we hope to be effective in our teams. In my consultations with teams in varying stages of dysfunction, I'm often struck with how comforted they seem when I explain that conflict is a natural, and often important, part of the teaming process. There's an old saying that "if everyone thinks alike, some of us aren't necessary." That's true of teams. If every member is of the same mind all the time, it's likely that the team isn't looking at every side of the issue.

To get to the best result often means looking at a situation from several different points of view. As we team in a virtual and global environment, our membership will represent a much higher level of diversity. That's a great benefit because we'll see something from numerous points of view. It also guarantees more conflict because the cultural and contextual differences are magnified.

Being an effective team leader or team member requires becoming an effective conflict manager and dispute-resolver. Negotiation and mediation have always been important skills. As our organizations move more to team environments, they are even more critical.

Taking the time to create a comprehensive and well thought-out team charter can help us minimize conflict. Effective chartering allows us to set the ground rules by which we'll operate and come to an agreement about how we'll deal with conflict <u>before</u> it occurs. It's probably the most important step we can take.

We should not be so naïve as to think however, that our charter will eliminate conflict. Things change and when the pressure is on and the blood pressure rises, our warm feelings and good intentions can be forgotten. Knowing how to get through the messy emotions and tangled facts is a critical competency for an effective team leader or member. Getting to and through the performing stage of the team process will depend in large measure on our ability to manage the natural conflicts that arise in any team setting. That's what Section Four is all about.

Dealing with Team Conflict

Conflict in Teams: Leveraging Differences to Create Opportunity

At Emap, the fast-growing media company, an extraordinary general meeting had to be called to expel two nonexecutive directors, Professor Ken Simmonds and Joe Cooke, from the board. Earlier the pair had called on the chairman, Sir John Hoskyns, to resign, and although the dispute was positioned by both sides as being purely about matters of corporate governance, it was difficult for impartial observers to escape the conclusion that the men involved simply did not want to have to sit around the same table any more (Lynn, 1997).

At Cable & Wireless (C&W), there was an even more spectacular clash at the close of 1995 between the company's chairman, Lord Young, and chief executive James Ross. Both men wanted to stay in ultimate command of the firm, and through weeks of public squabbling, the pair waged a bitter battle with one another. In the end, both turned out to be losers: The nonexecutives despaired of finding any workable solution to the painfully protracted conflict, and it was agreed that both men would simply have to go, while the company started merger talks with British Telecom (Lynn, 1997).

Our survey of executives and managers, revealed that team conflict is one of the top three concerns of team management.[1] Conflict that is not properly managed may lead to hostility, performance deficits, and, in extreme

---

[1]Survey of Kellog Executive Program's Team Building for Managers.

cases, dissolution of the team. Most people regard conflict to be detrimental to effective teamwork and believe that differences between team members should be immediately eliminated. However, differences in interests, perception, information, and preference cannot be avoided, especially in teams that work together closely for extended periods of time. Moreover, conflict can be good for the team—when managed properly. The challenge for the manager is to transform conflict into opportunity. Conflict can have positive consequences, such as enhancing creativity or fostering integrative solutions reflecting many points of view. However, effective conflict management is not intuitive, as illustrated in the box titled: Check Your Intuition About Conflict.

This chapter begins by distinguishing between two types of conflict: Emotional conflict and cognitive conflict. We then discuss the team dilemma, which centers on the tension between one's own and the team's interests. Next, we describe voting and majority rule and when they are appropriate to use in teams. Finally, we discuss team negotiation and how to maximize mutual interests.

*T*ypes of Conflict

All conflict is not created equal. Many types of conflict can threaten teamwork. Before a manager launches into conflict management mode, it is important to accurately diagnose the type of conflict that plagues the team. There are two basic types.

Emotional conflict is personal, defensive, and resentful. Also known as **A-type conflict** or **affective conflict** (Guetzkow & Gyr,1954), it is rooted in anger, personal friction, personality clashes, ego, and tension.

Cognitive conflict is largely depersonalized; also known as **C-type conflict**, it consists of argumentation about the merits of ideas, plans, and projects. Cognitive conflict is often effective in stimulating creativity because it forces people to rethink problems and arrive at outcomes that everyone can live with. This is why having divergent views in a team is beneficial for creativity and innovation. For example, when a majority of members in a team is confronted by the differing opinions of minorities, the majority is forced to think about why the minority disagrees. This thought process can instigate novel ideas (Levine & Moreland, 1985; Nemeth, 1995). As a general rule, A-type conflict threatens team productivity, whereas C-type conflict benefits team functioning.

Why is A-type conflict bad for team functioning? Affective conflict interferes with the effort people put into a task because members are preoccupied with reducing threats, increasing power, and attempting to build cohesion rather than working on the task. In contrast, C-type conflict can improve decision-making outcomes and team productivity by increasing decision quality through incorporating devil's advocacy roles, constructive criticism, and stimulation of discussion.

Clear evidence for the advantages to C-type conflict over A-type conflict is found in observations of actual organizational work teams. According

CHECK YOUR INTUITION ABOUT CONFLICT

Our intuitions about conflict are not always accurate. Faulty information about the causes of conflict can have unintended consequences which can exacerbate, rather than reduce, conflict. Below are 10 observations pertaining to conflict in teams and organizations.

As you read each statement, note whether you think the observation is generally true or false (there will always be some qualifiers) and justify your answer. Do this first to avoid hindsight bias: The tendency to think the answer is obvious—once you know it.

_____ 1. You can weaken an opposing group's resolve (i.e., their motivation to continue conflict escalation) by using coercive, rather than conciliatory, strategies.

_____ 2. When people engage in competitive, as opposed to cooperative, strategies to resolve conflict, this stems from a basic need to take advantage of the situation—in short, one-upmanship.

_____ 3. Most people in the competitive business world will take advantage of others whenever and however they can.

_____ 4. The best method of reaching settlement and avoiding costly delays (such as strikes) is to get the other party to empathize with your position.

_____ 5. People who are friends are most likely to come up with creative solutions (i.e., win-win solutions) to conflict situations, as compared with non-acquaintances.

_____ 6. In conflict situations, giving both sides more and accurate information about the situation is an effective method of reducing conflict.

_____ 7. The more successful people (or teams) are in achieving their desired outcomes in conflict situations, the happier they are.

_____ 8. Conflict among team members hinders their productivity.

_____ 9. For the most part, the key to reaching win-win outcomes is to build trust between parties in conflict.

_____ 10. Voting, and in particular, majority rule, is the best way to resolve conflicts among team members.

After you have read this chapter, review the questions again and see whether your answers—or explanations—change.

to Jehn (1997), who investigated everyday conflicts in six organizational work teams, A-type conflict is detrimental to performance and satisfaction (two major indices of team productivity); furthermore, emotionality reduces team effectiveness. Groups that accept task (C-type) conflict but not A-type conflict are the most effective.

In Jehn's (1997) investigation, cognitive conflict was associated with higher decisionmaking quality, greater understanding, higher commitment, and more acceptance. In contrast, emotional conflict significantly reduced decision quality, understanding, commitment, and acceptance. (For another illustration of the deleterious effects of A-type conflict, see the box titled: The Effects of A-Type Conflict.)

THE EFFECTS OF A-TYPE CONFLICT

Amason (1996) interviewed 48 top-management teams in small and mid-sized food processing firms across the United States and 5 top-management teams in furniture manufacturing firms in the southeastern United States. Both CEOs and managers were asked about
strategic decisions and team behavior. Questions to assess A-type conflict included: How
much anger was there among the group over this decision? How much personal friction
was there in the group during this discussion? How much were personality clashes between
group members evident during the decision? How much tension was there in the group during this decision?

Questions to assess C-type conflict included: How many disagreements over different
ideas about this decision were there? How many differences about the content of this decision did the group have to work through? How many differences of opinion were there
within the group over this decision?

The results were striking: The presence of cognitive conflict was associated with higher
decision-making quality, greater understanding, higher commitment, and more acceptance.
In contrast, the presence of affective conflict significantly reduced decision quality, understanding, commitment, and affective acceptance.

Cognitive conflict is productive because when people are in conflict about
ideas, they are forced to consider the ideas of others. For example, consider
a debate between two managers concerning how to market a company's product. Although they have their own individual ideas, when they try to persuade the other by presenting a rationale for their approach, each is forced,
on some level, to integrate the other's point of view. It is possible, of course,
to completely reject the other's arguments, but this is inappropriate in a
healthy working relationship. It would also represent A-type rather than C-
type conflict.

TRANSFORMING A-TYPE INTO C-TYPE CONFLICT

The key, of course, for the manager is to learn how to turn A-type conflict into
C-type conflict; or, ideally, design the team so that A-type conflict does not
erupt and, instead, only healthy C-type conflict exists. It is interesting to note
that teams of friends are better at applying effective conflict management
strategies to suit the task at hand than are teams of strangers, whose conflict
management approaches are less sophisticated (Shah & Jehn, 1993). Some
specific strategies follow.

Agree on a Common Goal or Shared Vision

The importance of a common goal is summed up in a quote by Steve Jobs,
who is associated with three highprofile Silicon Valley companies—Apple,
NeXT, and Pixar: "It's okay to spend a lot of time arguing about which route
to take to San Francisco when everyone wants to end up there, but a lot of
time gets wasted in such arguments if one person wants to go to San Francisco and another secretly wants to go to San Diego" (Eisenhardt, Kahwajy,
& Bourgeois, 1997, p. 80). Shared goals do not imply homogeneous thinking,
but they do require everyone to share a vision. Steve Jobs is not alone in his

---

CREATING A FORUM FOR CONFLICT

Bovis Construction Corporation, which has worked on the renovation of Los Angeles City Hall and the construction of a football stadium in Nashville, deals with conflict in an open fashion. Prior to each project, Bovis construction teams hold a planning session in which team members openly address potential conflicts. These planning sessions are conducted by company facilitators who encourage the project owner, architects, contractors, and other players to map out processes they plan to follow to get the job done. During the session, participants draft and sign a "win-win agreement," which includes a matrix that lays out what team members expect from one another. The first box in a matrix may detail the owner's responsibilities on the project, whereas the next box may look at the owner's expectations of the construction manager. Teams then use this matrix to review their progress on the project. Bovis managers agree that the process has not only decreased the adversity that is so prevalent on construction sites, but the firm has also saved millions of dollars and has completed projects on time (Oldham, 1998).

---

thinking. Colin Sewell-Rutter, a director of The Results Partnership, a consultancy that specializes in improving board-level communications, concludes that "The single most important source of problems within the boardroom is the lack of a shared vision, and shared corporate goals. . . . All the major difficulties ultimately stem from that" (Lynn, 1997, p. 31).

The 1993 departure of Ernest Mario as chief executive of pharmaceutical firm Glaxo (as it then was) illustrates how conflicts can also mask the fact that teams never fundamentally agreed on what the company is about. Mario was thought to have been preparing a takeover of American rival Warner-Lambert, even though the then chairman, Sir Paul Girolami, believed that the company should stick with its strategy of investing for organic growth. The result was a bitter conflict that culminated in Mario's departure with a $3 million payoff (it was only after Girolami retired that Glaxo made its first takeover in decades when it bid for Wellcome).

Create a Place for Conflict and Get It Out in the Open

Most people, even seasoned managers and executives, feel uncomfortable about conflict. It is much easier to capitalize on constructive conflict by creating a time and place for it to occur, rather than expecting it to naturally erupt. Furthermore, discussing the potential for conflict before it erupts is a lot more effective than trying to deal with it after the fact. As an example of how companies create a forum for conflict, see the box titled: Creating a Forum for Conflict.

*T*eam Dilemma: Group Versus Individual Interests

In most teams, members have both cooperative and competitive motives (Deutsch, 1973). Team members share a common objective when they work together—this is the cooperative aspect. Yet in many teams, individual members have an incentive to further their own interests. Team efforts are often subverted when individual agendas lead to competition between members, and members become preoccupied with what others are getting, relative to what they themselves are getting. Sometimes the way teams are set up can lead to these kinds of conflict. For example, when individuals are compensated according to team rather than individual performance, conflict may arise to the detriment of the team if members' skills, abilities, or effort vary to a significant degree.

In many team situations, members face a choice between furthering team-level interests or their own personal interests. For example, consider project teams composed of various members within a company. Each employee may be, at any time, a member of four or more project teams. Consequently, the team members have other projects vying for their attention and have an incentive to work on pet projects, letting the rest of the team carry them on the other project. However, if everyone does this, each project suffers. The choice between individual and group interests is a **team dilemma**. The hallmark features of a team dilemma are when members are *interdependent* with regard to resources, and each person has an *incentive to free ride* on the group's efforts. The resources may be tangible outcomes, such as salaries, office space, or equipment; or intangible outcomes, such as information, services, or social support (Foa & Foa, 1975).

Team members in this case must choose between the team and self-interest. Consider the following team dilemmas:

- A group of M.B.A. students is working on a class project that counts for 50 percent of their grade. Some take a higher course load than others; some are taking the course pass-fail; some are second-year students who already have jobs. How should the work be divided?

- Firms with significant R&D activities frequently use cross-functional teams. However, when the R&D is spread across different parts of the firm, members may want to retain control of the project in their own division, rather than collaborating with others across divisions, which might add substantial value.

- In large law firms, partners act as their own profit centers and, thus, have little incentive to provide knowledge to attorneys outside their group. Yet doing so improves the long-term viability of the firm in a competitive marketplace.

Team dilemmas pit individual incentives against group incentives in such a way that a poorer outcome for the firm is likely if each member acts in a self-interested way. The dilemma lies in the fact that members cannot simultaneously choose to cooperate and avoid exploitation by other members.

STRATEGIES TO ENHANCE COOPERATION AND MINIMIZE COMPETITION

There are some specific strategies to reduce free riding. Here, we add to the list.

Build Team Identity

The stronger a team's identity, the less sharply members distinguish between their selfinterest and that of the group (Dawes, van de Kragt, & Orbell, 1990).

There are several ways to increase team identity, such as linking individual outcomes (i.e., compensation) to team outcomes (i.e., performance). Recognition of individual efforts can also be effective. Sometimes, emphasizing team identity as being an integral part of a larger team effort, such as that of a plant, division, or firm, is effective, particularly when a conscious challenge is presented in which the team can either succeed or fail—for example, beating the competition to market with a new product. If the team has an identity or reputation of its own, that can also make members want to uphold their end of the work.

Certain things detract from team identity, the most important of which is whether members expect to work together in the future. If the cooperative effort is shortlived, individuals have less incentive to invest in the team. Hence, another way of enhancing team identity is to extend the length of time people expect to work as a team. Moreover, members who believe that other members will leave cooperate less than those who expect the team to remain intact (Mannix & Loewenstein, 1993). Therefore, preserving continuity in membership can also be important.

Make Pledges

To the extent that team members make pledges, cooperation is greatly enhanced (Chen, 1996). Pledges or social contracts come in all shapes and forms, the most common being the business handshake, or the simple statement "You have my word." Social contracts are sometimes explicit ("You can count on me") and sometimes implicit (such as a wink, a nod, or a handshake). Social contracts capitalize on a basic psychological need for commitment and consistency. The power of pledges cannot be underestimated. In many instances, team members who make specific pledges or commitments to their team will act in ways that benefit the group, even at the expense of self-interest.

Change the Incentive Structure

When it is more cost-effective for group members to cooperate rather than adopt self-interested behavior, cooperation increases. This is precisely why many organizations are moving toward team-based pay. However, team-based pay must be structured in such a way that everyone feels they are being treated fairly (so, for instance, there is no antagonism between members with different skill levels).

Perils and Pitfalls of Democracy

In some teams, the choice facing members does not center upon a choice between the team and self-interest. Rather, members must agree on some course of action. This is particularly true when the decisions facing the team are complex. Consider, for example, team members who disagree about their weekly meeting time. This cannot be resolved by individual members simply deciding the time that is best for them. Effective conflict resolution requires coordination and consensus among members. Voting is one method for reducing conflict, in which members agree to adopt the choice preferred by the majority. Voting is commonly used in organizational hiring, promotion, and firing decisions. Team members who vote among alternatives acknowledge that conflict exists, but agree to accept the outcome of the vote. The key issue becomes how to develop and utilize a suitable voting scheme.

VOTING RULES

There are several kinds of voting rules, and different rules are used in different situations. The objective of voting rules can be to find the alternative that the greatest number of team members prefer, the alternative the fewest members object to, or the choice that maximizes team welfare. Anything short of unanimity indicates disagreement or conflict within the team. In most cases, conflict will be reduced or eliminated following the conclusion of voting, although there are exceptions. For example, individuals who "lose" the vote may assert that the voting procedure was fraudulent or not carried out as agreed upon (Tyler & Smith, 1998).

Voting does not guarantee conflict resolution. First, members may not agree on a method for voting. For example, how is a winning choice to be determined? Some members may insist on unanimity, others on simple majority rule, and still others on a weighted majority rule. Second, even if a voting method is agreed on, it may not yield a decision (in the case of a tie, for instance) or may not yield a single decision. Finally, because voting does not eliminate conflicts of interest, but rather provides a way for members to live with conflict, such decisions may not be stable. In this sense, voting masks disagreement within teams, potentially threatening longterm group and organizational effectiveness.

Majority Rule

The most common voting procedure is majority rule. However, it presents several problems in the attainment of consensus. Despite its democratic appeal, majority rule does not reflect the strength of individual preferences. The vote of a person who feels strongly about an issue counts only as much as the vote of a person who is virtually indifferent. Consequently, majority rule does not promote creative tradeoffs among issues. For example, groups that use unanimous rule reach more win-win outcomes (i.e., profitable outcomes for everyone involved) compared to groups that use majority rule (Mannix, Thompson, & Bazerman, 1989; Thompson, Mannix, & Bazerman, 1988). When groups use voting in combination with strict agendas (in which the order of issues is discussed sequentially, rather than simultaneously), outcomes for the team as a whole plummet. Why? One of the successful keys to conflict management is the ability to make tradeoffs between issues under discussion (i.e., "I will do this for you if you do such-and-such for me"; Mannix et al., 1989; Thompson et al., 1988). In short, when teams discuss only one issue at a time and vote on outcomes under consideration, this results in less profitable outcomes than when teams discuss issues simultaneously and seek consensus.

Unanimous Decision-Making

Although unanimous decision-making is time-consuming, it encourages team members to consider creative alternatives to expand the size of the pie and satisfy the interests of all members. On the other hand, unanimous rule

---

WHEN VOTING GOES AWRY

Suppose a three-person product development team (Raines, Warner, and Lassiter) is choosing among designs *A, B,* or *C.* Each manager's preference ordering is depicted below. As a way of resolving the conflict, Warner suggests voting between designs *A* and *B.* In that vote, *A* wins over *B.* Warner then proposes a vote between *A* and *C.* In that vote, *C* wins. Warner then declares design *C* the consensus choice—which Lassiter agrees to. However, Raines proposes a new vote, but this time starting with a contest between *B* and *C. B* wins this vote, eliminating *C.* Between *A* and *B, A* beats *B,* so Raines happily declares *A* the winner. Lassiter complains the whole voting process was fraudulent; but cannot explain why.

Manager	*Design A*	*Design B*	*Design C*
Raines	1	2	3
Warner	2	3	1
Lassiter	3	1	2

Note: Numbers represent rank-ordered choices.

---

can
present formidable obstacles, such as when members refuse to compromise. By holding out, these members can force decisions their way when considerations like timeliness are important. When a decision reached in these circumstances goes against what most members believe is right, it can lead to poor outcomes.

DRAWBACKS TO VOTING

Arrow Paradox

Consider the situation described in the box titled: When Voting Goes Awry. The product development team members are victims of the **Arrow paradox**, in which the winners of majority rule elections change as a function of the order in which alternatives are proposed. In fact, any system of weighted voting (such as when members give three points to their first choice, two to their second, and one to their third) produces the same problem.

Impossibility Theorem

The unstable voting outcomes of the product development team illustrate the **impossibility theorem** (Arrow, 1963), which states that the derivation of team preference from individual preference is indeterminate. Simply put, there is no method of combining group members' preferences that guarantees that group preference has been maximized when groups have three or more members and there are three or more options.

The context of voting often involves people explaining the reasons for their preferences. Sometimes they persuade others with their arguments; other times, the holes in their arguments become illuminated. Therefore, aside from the mathematical complexities involved in voting rules, voting serves an important function. The process itself can lead to buy-in, if not downright consensus, by the time the vote is through.

Strategic Manipulation

Strategic manipulation further compounds the problem of indeterminacy of team choice (Chechile, 1984; Ordeshook, 1986; Plott, 1976; Plott & Levine, 1978). Consider a situation in which members do not vote for their first choice because by voting for another choice, some other, undesirable option is sure to lose. This is an example of strategic manipulation—people do not vote in accord with their true preferences. Furthermore, members may manipulate the order in which alternatives are voted on, because when the alternatives are voted on sequentially in pairs, those voted on later are more likely to win (May, 1982).

$\mathcal{G}$roup Negotiation

Some situations call for team members to discuss issues and build consensus—for example, when a team of professionals must divide responsibilities among themselves, or members of a department must allocate funds. In both cases, members must arrive at a mutually satisfactory outcome although each may have different interests. This involves negotiation.

Negotiation occurs when interdependent parties make mutual decisions regarding the allocation of scarce resources (Bazerman, Mannix, & Thompson, 1988). Negotiation is necessary when no one can dictate a solution. Furthermore, team members must agree for any decision to be binding. Failure to reach consensus can be costly for the team if, for example, it cannot move forward because it fails to reach agreement, if opportunities are missed due to protracted negotiations, if costs of negotiation increase over time (such as if lawyers or arbitrators must be paid), or if the rights to decision-making are lost and must instead be sent to a higher level. An example of opportunity lost due to impasse occurred at a prominent state university. A department had been granted special funds to create a badly-needed additional wing of a new building. Unfortunately, department members could not agree on how to allocate the new space among themselves, preventing the drafting of final blueprints. Because no plans were forthcoming, the university withdrew the funding. This is an example of a **lose-lose outcome** (Thompson & Hrebec, 1996). When group members fail to reach consensus, it can be costly for everyone. In retrospect, the members of the department would have all been happier had the new wing been built, but at the time, they were absorbed in paralyzing conflict with one another.

What are some strategies that teams can use to avoid lose-lose outcomes and move toward mutual agreement? Most conflict situations contain the potential for joint gain, or integrative outcomes, although these may be obvious only after the fact. The following strategies are aimed at uncovering the win-win potential existing in most conflicts.

THE BATNA PRINCIPLE

Team consensus is only feasible if it represents an improvement over each member's **best alternative to a negotiated agreement**, or **BATNA** (Fisher & Ury, 1981). If members have better options outside the team (such as with another team or different company), then group dissolution is inevitable. Thus, for consensus to be viable, the outcome must be at least as attractive as each person's best available outside option. Knowing the BATNAs of the parties involved greatly enhances the ability to achieve consensus.

AVOID THE FIXED-PIE FALLACY

The fixed-pie fallacy is the tendency of people in conflict to assume that their interests are completely opposed to those of others. The fixed-pie mentality can be extremely detrimental in negotiations (Thompson & Hastie, 1990). Although most negotiations contain potential for mutually beneficial agreements, the belief that the pie is fixed and successful negotiation means grabbing the biggest slice is so pervasive that most people fail to recognize opportunities for win-win agreements.

For example, Thompson and Hrebec (1996) found that about 50 percent of people fail to realize when they have interests that are completely compatible with others, and about 20 percent fail to reach optimal agreements even when their interests are completely compatible. A key reason for such breakdowns is that people in negotiations fail to exchange information about their interests, making it unlikely that faulty judgments will be challenged and corrected (Thompson, 1991). Furthermore, when people are provided with information about others' interests, they often overlook areas of common interest (Thompson & DeHarpport, 1994; Thompson & Hastie, 1990).

BUILD TRUST AND SHARE INFORMATION

Rapport between members of the team makes mutually beneficial agreement more likely (Moore, Kurtzberg, Thompson, & Morris, 1999). Rapport is usually established when people find points of similarity. Surprisingly, it does not take much to find something in common with another person. For example, in one investigation (Nadler, Thompson, & Morris, 1999), students from two highly competitive rival M.B.A. programs negotiated with one another via electronic mail. The bargaining zone was small and reputations were at stake. All buyer-seller pairs had exactly 8 days to reach some kind of settlement. Some of the negotiators were randomly selected to have a "get acquainted" phone call with their opponent immediately before getting down to the business of negotiation. Others just immediately commenced negotiations. The results were dramatic: The impasse rate was cut nearly in half when negotiators spent a few minutes on the phone with the other person— a strong testament to the power of rapport in building trust in negotiations. Furthermore, those who had the phone call were convinced that their opponent had been especially selected for them on the basis of similarity, when in actual effect, the opponent was chosen at random.

These results may suggest that the better two persons know one another, the stronger their rapport should be and, consequently, the better they should be at finding common ground. However, this is not always the case. In fact, when friends negotiate, they often do worse than complete strangers (Fry, Firestone, & Williams, 1983; Thompson & DeHarpport, 1998). Friends are often uncomfortable negotiating with each other, and so may make premature concessions; as a result, they may overlook opportunities for expanding the pie in their hurry to reach a deal. Friends may also presume they know each other's interests, when this may not be the case. However, it can be awkward trying to explain your side to someone who knows you. Strangers, by contrast, do not need a pretense to clarify their point of view. The key takeaway message goes back to our earlier point: It is important to create a forum for C-type conflict.

ASK QUESTIONS

Integrative negotiation often requires that people have information about each other's preferences (Pruitt & Lewis, 1975; Thompson, 1991). Most people in negotiations neither provide nor seek the information necessary to reach such agreements. The most important question a team member can ask of another is: "What are your priorities in this situation?" (Thompson, 1991).

PROVIDE INFORMATION

The distinction between this strategy and building trust and providing information has to do with bilateral versus unilateral strategies. In the earlier strategy, it was assumed that teammates were mutually engaged in a process of information exchange. However, if that strategy fails, then we encourage some degree of unilateral (i.e., one-sided) information sharing. It would seem that individuals should always reveal their interests to fellow team members. However, they may hesitate to do so if they feel this will place them in a strategically disadvantageous position. Consider a team negotiating the allocation of scarce resources (research money, secretarial assistance, and travel support) among its members. One member may feel that, of these scarce resources, research support is most important, although secretarial and travel support are also valuable. This person may reason that a mutually beneficial agreement is possible by "trading" secretarial support for research support. However, he may hesitate to reveal his priorities, fearing that other members will demand large concessions on the secretarial and travel support issues in exchange for conceding research support. There are several advantages of revealing information: It builds trust, convinces others of your sincerity in achieving the priorities you do reveal, encourages others to incorporate your priorities in their proposals, and leads to faster agreements.

MAKE MULTIPLE OFFERS SIMULTANEOUSLY

In some cases, team members are frustrated when their attempts to provide and seek information are not effective. This happens most commonly in the face of high distrust and less than amicable relations. The strategy of multiple offers can be effective even with the most uncooperative of negotiators. The strategy involves presenting the other party with at least two (and preferably more) proposals of equal value to yourself. The other party is asked to indicate which of the proposals they prefer. This should reveal information about how the other side values trade-offs between different components of the negotiations. There are psychological benefits as well: When people believe they have more choices, they are more inclined to cooperate.

AVOID SEQUENTIAL DISCUSSION OF ISSUES

There is a pervasive tendency in teams to discuss issues sequentially. This usually stems from the belief that making progress on some issues will grease the wheels of cooperation for more difficult ones. However, sequential discussion inhibits joint discussion of sets of issues, reducing the likelihood that team members will identify potentially beneficial trade-offs between issues (Mannix et al., 1989; Thompson et al., 1988; Weingart, Bennett, & Brett, 1993). Just as we saw in the Arrow paradox, it may not be possible to find the best outcome if tradeoffs are only considered pairwise.

Team members who discuss issues simultaneously exchange more information and have greater insight into other members' interests (Weingart et al., 1993). Teams following sequential agendas under majority rule are less likely to reach integrative agreements. This may stem from the fact that coalitions often form, preventing information exchange and discussion of members' underlying interests. It may also be that the full set of trade-offs cannot be evaluated one pair at a time. For instance, you may prefer A over B and C over D, and so think that in a negotiation over four such possibilities, your position would be AC. However, you may also prefer AD over BC, and this could be a potential compromise that you would accept. If you proceed with pairwise trade-offs, this opportunity may never arise.

CONSTRUCT CONTINGENCY CONTRACTS AND LEVERAGE DIFFERENCES

Team members differ in their forecasts about what they think will happen in the future. These different expectations may make negotiation difficult. For example, one member wants to protect against disaster stemming from a potentially bad investment; another may worry about how to spend the vast riches that are sure to follow. Each may have difficulty taking the other's position seriously, because each has very different expectations about what the consequences (and the value) of a decision may be. However, such differences in beliefs can actually improve the possibility of integrative agreements.

This is possible through the formation of **contingency contracts**. Consider the case of a cross-functional team in which a sales manager is more optimistic than the manufacturing manager about product sales. A contingent contract can be constructed, establishing that manufacturing will produce more products, but if sales fail to meet an agreed upon level, the sales department will cover all manufacturing costs.

In other situations, team members may agree on the probability of future events, but feel differently about taking risks. For example, two colleagues may undertake a collaborative project, such as writing a novel, for which they both agree that the probability of success is only moderate. The colleague with an established career can afford to be risk seeking; the struggling young novelist may be risk averse. The two may capitalize on their different risk-taking profiles with a contingent contract: The more risk-averse colleague receives the entire advance on the book; the risk-seeking colleague receives the majority of royalties after publication of the novel.

People may value the same event quite differently depending on when it occurs. If one party is more impatient than the other, mechanisms for sharing the consequences over time may be devised. Two partners in a joint venture might allocate the initial profits to the partner who has high costs for time, whereas the partner who can wait will achieve greater profits over a longer, delayed period.

Capitalizing on differences often entails contingency contracts, in which team members make bets based upon different possible outcomes. For contingency contracts to be effective, they should be easy to evaluate and leave no room for ambiguity of interpretation. Conditions and measurement techniques should be spelled out in advance.

BE WARY OF INTUITION

Many people make the mistake of relying on intuition to guide their negotiations. This is a mistake because they frequently make faulty assumptions about what the other person wants—an example of the fixed-pie perception. Furthermore, people are not very good at reading others' emotions in mixed-motive situations. In fact, intuition is almost completely unrelated to how well people actually do in negotiations. For example, an investigation examined M.B.A. students at Stanford University who engaged in simulated negotiations (Thompson, Valley, & Kramer, 1995). Prior to receiving feedback on how well they actually did, they were asked to indicate how "successful" they felt. Most students reported feeling extremely successful and confident about the quality of their negotiated settlements. However, these same students were often dismayed to learn that they failed to capitalize on a number of integrative opportunities.

In the absence of any objective indices of their performance, people rely on the emotional expressions and reactions of others to assess their own success at the bargaining table. People appear to follow a simple rule of thumb: "If the other party is happy, then I probably did not do so well; if the other party is disappointed, then I probably did pretty well." This rule of thumb is based upon a false heuristic—namely, the fixed-pie fallacy. If the situation is strictly fixed-pie in nature—meaning that whatever one person gains, the other loses—then whenever one person is happy about something, the other person should be disappointed.

SEARCH FOR POST-SETTLEMENT SETTLEMENTS

Team members may decide to renegotiate after reaching a mutually agreeable settlement. It may seem counter-intuitive or counterproductive to resume negotiations once an acceptable agreement has been reached, but the strategy of post-settlement settlements can be remarkably effective in improving the quality of negotiated agreements (Raiffa, 1982). In the post-settlement settlement, team members agree to explore other options with the goal of finding another that both prefer more than the current one. The current settlement becomes the new BATNA. The post-settlement settlement strategy is effective because it allows team members to reveal their preferences without fear of exploitation; they can safely revert to their previous agreement if the post-settlement settlement discussion does not prove fruitful. If better terms are found, parties can be more confident they have reached a truly integrative agreement. If no better agreement is found, the parties may be more confident that the current agreement is really a win-win outcome.

USE TEAM-ON-TEAM NEGOTIATION

Consider the following situations:

- A group of employees approaching management about wages and working conditions
- A small software company approaching a large software company concerning a joint venture
- A functional team approaching upper management about increasing resources

In each of these examples, a team needs to negotiate with another group. Is a team best advised to send one person to negotiate on their behalf or a team?

To answer the question of whether teams are more effective than solos at the bargaining table, Thompson, Peterson, and Brodt (1996) compared three types of negotiation configurations: Team versus team, team versus solo, and solo versus solo. The presence of at least one team at the bargaining table dramatically increased the quality of agreements reached. The question is, why? It turns out that people exchange much more critical information when at least one team is at the bargaining table than when two individuals negotiate (O'Connor, 1994; Rand & Carnevale, 1994; Thompson et al., 1996). Apparently, team members who negotiate as a team create a kind of transactive memory system or shared mental model that forces them to be more explicit about what they know. The team effect (i.e., the ability of teams to expand the pie of value for everyone involved) is quite robust. It is not even necessary that members of teams privately caucus with one another to be effective (Thompson et al., 1996).

AVOID MAJORITY RULE

Because team negotiation is so complex, members often use simplifying procedures to reach decisions (Bazerman et al., 1988). For example, teams may use majority rule as a decision heuristic because of its ease and familiarity (Hastie, Penrod, & Pennington, 1983; Ordeshook, 1986). However, as noted, majority rule ignores members' strength of preference for alternatives. Teams that use majority rule are less likely to reach mutually beneficial, integrative outcomes than are teams requiring unanimity (Thompson et al., 1988). Majority rule inhibits the discovery of integrative agreements because it discourages information exchange about preferences (Castore & Murnighan, 1978).

BEWARE OF COALITIONS

A **coalition** is a group of two or more members who join together to affect the outcome of a decision involving at least three parties (Komorita & Parks, 1994). Coalitions involve both cooperation and competition: Members of coalitions cooperate with one another in competition against other coalitions but compete within the coalition regarding the allocation of rewards the coalition obtains. Power is intimately involved in both the formation of coalitions and the allocation of resources among coalition members. In some cases, members of an organizational coalition might be relatively equal in power (e.g., all may be of the same rank); however, in other cases, there might be extreme differences in power (e.g., a team of senior executives and junior hires). Although members of a coalition cooperate in joining resources (e.g., a team might rally together in an organization to gain a greater budget), eventually, they need to allocate the resources they attain among themselves (e.g., individual team members may think they deserve a higher percentage of the budget).

Power imbalance among coalition members can lead to a number of detrimental consequences, including more defecting coalitions (Mannix; 1993), fewer integrative agreements (Mannix, 1993; McAlister, Bazerman, & Fader, 1986), greater likelihood of bargaining impasse (Mannix, 1993), and more competitive behavior (McClintock, Messick, Kuhlman & Campos, 1973).

APPEAL TO NORMS OF JUSTICE

Team members in conflict who use objective appearing arguments are more effective than those who use subjective arguments. However, there are many different objective arguments. Consider the following:

- **Equity** (or contribution-based distribution) prescribes that benefits should be proportional to members' contributions (Adams, 1965).
- **Equality** (or blind justice) specifies that all team members should suffer or benefit equally (Messick, 1993).
- **Need** (or welfare-based justice) specifies that benefits should be proportional to members' needs (Deutsch, 1975).

Characteristics of Fairness-Based Arguments

The effectiveness of any given principle will be enhanced to the extent that it is simple, clear, justifiable, popular, and general. To be more specific, a fairness-based argument that has the following characteristics is more likely to win the support of team members and other relevant organizational actors (Messick, 1993):

- **Simplicity:** Team members should be able to articulate the procedure easily. This reduces the chances of misunderstanding and makes it easier to evaluate how accurately the procedure is being implemented.
- **Clarity:** The allocation procedure should be clear; if not, conflict may erupt concerning its interpretation.

- **Justifiability:** The procedure should be consistently applied across different individuals, time, and situations.

- **Consensus:** Team members should agree on the method of allocation. Team members often internalize effective social justice procedures, and such norms act as strong guidelines for decision-making in teams. Because these norms often outlive current team members, new members are frequently indoctrinated with procedures the team found useful in the past (cf. Bettenhausen & Murnighan, 1985; Levine & Moreland, 1991, 1994).

- **Generality:** The procedure should be applicable to a wide variety of situations.

The Many Faces of Fairness

No matter how objective a fairness rule may appear, fairness is not an absolute construct. And, people's uses of fairness are for the most part self-enhancing. We do not wish to evaluate here what is really fair, but rather to stress the importance of arriving at an outcome that is perceived as fair by everyone concerned.

Reputations for fairness can be extremely important in business and employment relationships and often set the background against which a negotiation takes place. Generally speaking, people with a reputation for fairness will be trusted more than those who are viewed differently. We are not saying that being "fair" or "not fair" is the right or moral thing to do in every circumstance, simply that a reputation for fairness can be beneficial in many negotiating contexts. Moreover, an expectation of fairness as a splitting rule is pervasive—despite the emphasis in virtually every business publication, textbook, and so on, for competitive behavior.

*W*hat to Do When Conflict Escalates?

Sometimes a firm will set up teams within the organization to compete with one another. The idea is to create a healthy competition to spur motivation. However, this can lead to escalating conflict and destructive outcomes that need special interventions. As an example, see the box titled: Strike Behavior.

Conflict often escalates because people believe that coercion is effective in reducing the resolve of others. Paradoxically, most people believe that when others use coercion on them, that it increases their resolve (Rothbart & Hallmark, 1988). The unfortunate consequence is that this perception encourages mutually aggressive behavior.

The likelihood of protracted conflict is intimately linked to the beliefs each party holds about what they regard to be a fair settlement (Thompson & Loewenstein, 1992). People in conflict have different ideas about what is fair, and the most difficult conflicts are ones in which the parties' ideas of fairness are highly discrepant. In fact, the length of costly strikes can be directly predicted by the discrepancy between what the parties involved regard to be a fair outcome: The greater the discrepancy, the longer the strike—and both parties ultimately lose. Thus, to reduce conflict, it is critical to understand how to get parties to move away from egocentric perceptions of fair outcomes to

STRIKE BEHAVIOR

To paraphrase a General Motors Corp. official, strikes hurt both the company and the workers and so are designed to put each of them in the mood to get together and compromise. However, bad blood can often escalate to a point where parties look beyond their own welfare to inflict punishment on the other party. Strikes are influenced by fairness perceptions; for instance, the likelihood and length of strikes is influenced by the difference in perceived fair wages between management and the union. That is, if management and the union have widely differing perceptions of what constitutes a fair settlement, a strike is more likely. Furthermore, teams on opposite sides of a conflict. Indeed such as management and union, hold biased perceptions about the strategies that will effectively settle conflict (Babcock & Olson, 1992; Thompson & Loewenstein, 1992).

more reasonable ones. The key problem is that most people regard themselves to be uniquely immune to bias and benevolent in their own motivations (Farwell & Weiner, 1996); they regard bias to be something that afflicts the other party in conflict. Most people involved in really difficult conflicts hold the following perceptions: (1) they are fairer than others; (2) the other party's view is egocentrically motivated (and, hence, unfair); and (3) there is only one correct (and fair) way to view the situation. This trilogy of beliefs is a recipe for disaster, unless something can be done to move parties away from one (and hopefully more) of these views.

Most people are not aware that their own perceptions of fairness are egocentrically biased. For example, van Avermaet (1974) asked team members to complete several questionnaires. These took either 45 or 90 minutes. The questionnaires were constructed so that, for each duration, some participants completed six questionnaires, while others completed only three. When asked to allocate monetary rewards, participants emphasized the dimension that favored them in the allocation procedure (those who worked longer emphasized time; questionnaire completion was emphasized by those who worked on more questionnaires).

It is not surprising, then, that members who contribute less prefer to divide resources equally, whereas those who contribute more prefer the equity rule (Allison & Messick, 1990). In groups containing members having different power or status levels, those with low power want equality, whereas those with high power desire equity (Komorita & Chertkoff, 1973; Shaw, 1981).

As a way of dealing with how to minimize egocentric perceptions of conflict it is probably most useful to first indicate which strategies seem like they would work, but usually don't. We are not saying that these strategies are doomed to failure, but rather that they have been tried and have not been shown to work, at least in simulated (yet realistic) conflict situations. It would seem that providing both parties with veridical information pertaining to the conflict situation (statistics on the labor supply, competitive analysis, etc.) would be helpful, at the very least serving as a reality check; however, this has not shown to be helpful. That is, when management and labor are provided with additional, unbiased information concerning disputes, this has the effect of further entrenching both parties more firmly in their own positions (Thompson & Loewenstein, 1992). To understand this backfire effect, it is important to recall our discussion of the confirmation bias. Parties interpret information in a way that is most favorable to their own position. Thus, they put their own spin on the facts in a way that gives them more confidence in their position.

It may seem that warning disputants about the existence of bias may be effective in reducing conflict and, at the very least, getting parties to perform a reality check of their own positions and beliefs supporting those positions. However, this does little to assuage biased perceptions (Babcock, Loewenstein, Issacharoff, & Camerer, 1995). Apparently, people regard bias as something that afflicts the "other guy"—not themselves. For similar reasons, taking the other person's point of view is generally not effective in reducing bias and conflict.

So much for what does not work; what does work to reduce egocentric perceptions of fairness? The key is to get parties to change their own perceptions about what is fair. Inducing parties to actively think about the weaknesses in their own position can be effective in reducing the length of costly strikes (Babcock et al., 1995). Furthermore, inviting a respected, neutral outsider to mediate can be effective.

*C*onclusions

Conflict in teams is unavoidable. However, it does not have to result in decreased productivity. Managed effectively, conflict can be key to leveraging differences of interest to arrive at creative solutions. However, many people intuitively respond to conflict in a defensive fashion, and this emotional type of conflict can threaten productivity. To the greatest extent possible, team members should depersonalize conflict. We have presented a variety of ways to achieve this. We have also cautioned against using majority rule, splitting the difference, and strict agendas, which might stifle the opportunity for team win-win gains.

Resolving Conflict

A CASE STUDY ON CONFLICT MANAGEMENT

Editor's Note:
A different slant on managing conflict. Be sure to check out "Creative Ways to Manage Conflict" near the end of the section.

He Said, She Said . . .

Shirley and Abdul both work for a software development company. The manager of the new product division was originally the leader of a project team for which she interviewed and hired Abdul. Shirley, another project team member, also interviewed Abdul but strongly opposed hiring him for the project because she thought he was not competent to do the job.

Seven months after Abdul was hired, the manager left the project to start her own company and recommended that Abdul and Shirley serve as joint project leaders. Shirley agreed reluctantly—with the stipulation that it be made clear she was not working for Abdul. The General Manager consented; Shirley and Abdul were to share the project leadership.

Within a month Shirley was angry because Abdul was representing himself to others as the leader of the entire project and giving the impression that Shirley was working for him. Now Shirley and Abdul are meeting with you to see if you can help them resolve the conflict between them.

Shirley says: "Right after the joint leadership arrangement was reached with the General Manager, Abdul called a meeting of the project team without even consulting me about the time or content. He just told me when it was being held and said I should be there. At the meeting, Abdul reviewed everyone's duties line by line, including mine, treating me as just another team member working for him. He sends out letters and signs himself as project director, which obviously implies to others that I am working for him."

Abdul says: "Shirley is all hung up with feelings of power and titles. Just because I sign myself as project director doesn't mean that she is working for me. I don't see anything to get excited about. What difference does it make? She is too sensitive about everything. I call a meeting and right away she thinks I'm trying to run everything. Shirley has other things to do—other projects to run—so she doesn't pay too much attention to this one. She mostly lets things slide. But when I take the initiative to set up a meeting, she starts jumping up and down about how I am trying to make her work for me."

DISCUSSION QUESTIONS

A variety of strategies can be used to help resolve the conflict between Abdul and Shirley. As you explore and develop concepts on conflict management presented in this chapter, keep this situation in mind. At the conclusion of this chapter you should be able to recognize the warning signs and know how to prevent this type of conflict from becoming a reality. But before reading the chapter, put yourself in the position of mediator between Abdul and Shirley and consider the following questions:

Interpersonal Skills for Leadership, Second Edition, by Susan Fritz, F. William Brown, Joyce Poulacs Lunde, and Elizabeth A. Banset. Copyright © 1997 by Simon and Schuster Custom Publishing (now Pearson Custom Publishing).

1. Abdul and Shirley seem to have several conflicts occurring simultaneously. Identify as many of these individual conflicts as possible.

2. Are there any general statements you can make about the overall nature of the conflict between Abdul and Shirley?

3. What are the possible ways to deal with the conflict between Abdul and Shirley (not just the ones that you would recommend, but all of the options)?

4. Given the choices identified in item three, what is the best way for Abdul and Shirley to deal with the conflict between them?

5. Given all the benefits of retrospection, what could or should have been done to avoid this conflict in the first place?

Introduction to Theories of Conflict Resolution

What is conflict? Is it the same as a disagreement or an argument? Typically, conflict is characterized by three elements: 1) interdependence, 2) interaction, and 3) incompatible goals. We can define conflict as the interaction of interdependent people who perceive a disagreement about goals, aims, and values, and who see the other party as potentially interfering with the realization of these goals. Conflict is a social phenomenon that is woven into the fabric of human relationships; therefore, it can only be expressed and manifested through communication. We can only come into conflict with people with whom we are interdependent; that is, only when we become dependent on one another to meet our needs or goals does conflict emerge.

Conflicts are differentiated in a number of ways. One method of distinguishing among conflict situations is based on the context in which the conflict occurs. Barge (1994) indicates that traditionally conflict is viewed as occurring in the following three contexts:

Interpersonal conflict exists between two individuals within a group.

Intergroup conflict occurs between two groups within the larger social system.

Interorganizational conflict occurs between two organizations.

UNDERSTANDING CONFLICT

Most authorities claim some conflict is inevitable in human relationships when people and groups are interdependent. Clashes occur more often over perceived differences than over real ones. People anticipate blocks to achieving their goals that may or may not be there. Thus conflict can be defined as two or more people independently perceiving that what each one wants is incompatible with what the other one wants.

There is a normal process of development in any conflict and this process tends to be cyclical, repeating itself over and over. At each stage of the cycle, the potential for conflict grows stronger. The table on the next page describes each stage of the conflict development process in terms of the thoughts or actions an individual experiences as the conflict develops.

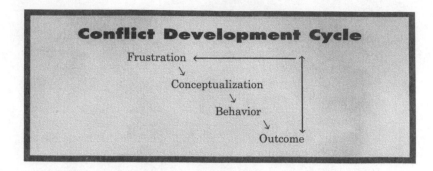

Conflict often results when we fail to check our perceptions and assumptions about the other party's attitudes and motives. Our subsequent behavior and the outcome of the conflict are directly determined by the conceptualization phase.

We act on our beliefs about the other party. For example, we may decide that the person rejected our idea because he or she is threatened by or does not like us when, in fact, we did not communicate clearly or give enough information. We will respond quite differently depending on which case we believe to be true.

Rees (1991) suggests that conflict, like power, is neither good nor bad. It is what we do with it that makes the difference. Although conflict is generally viewed in a negative way and as something to avoid, when appropriately managed it can generate beneficial results. Conflict management theorists distinguish between constructive and destructive conflict. Constructive conflict is functional because it helps members accomplish goals and generate new insights into old problems. Destructive conflict is dysfunctional because it negatively affects group members by disrupting their activity. Bennis (1989) lists several characteristics that distinguish constructive and destructive conflict.

Constructive Conflict

- Allows constructive change and growth to occur within a system or group.
- Provides the opportunity for resolving problems associated with diversity of opinion.
- Provides a forum for unifying the group.
- Enhances group productivity.

Stage	Individual Thought or Action
Frustration	I am blocked from satisfying a goal or concern.
Conceptualization	I begin to determine in my mind what the problem is. I begin to attribute motives and blame based on my perceptions.
Behavior	I act on the perceptions above. (There is a cycle of reinforcement between conceptualization and behavior. How I act is determined by what I believe about the other party. How I act determines how the other perceives my motives and how he or she consequently acts.)
Outcome	The conflict is resolved in one of three ways: win/lose, lose/lose, or win/win, depending on the behavior of both parties.

■ Enhances group commitment.

Destructive Conflict

■ Develops when lack of common agreement leads to negativism.

■ Leads to hardening of respective positions and diminished likelihood of a resolution.

■ Causes the group to divide into camps, each supporting a different position.

■ Results in a decrease in group productivity, satisfaction, and commitment.

MISCONCEPTIONS ABOUT CONFLICT

Smith and Andrews (1989) suggest that people still hold negative opinions about the advisability of conflict resolution because of the following misconceptions:

1. *Harmony is normal and conflict is abnormal.* This belief is erroneous. Conflict is normal; in fact, it is inevitable. Whenever two people must interact in order to achieve goals, their subjective views and opinions about how to best achieve those goals will lead to conflict of some degree. Harmony occurs only when conflict is acknowledged and resolved.

2. *Conflicts and disagreements are the same.* Disagreement is usually temporary and limited, stemming from misunderstanding or differing views about a specific issue rather than a situation's underlying values and goals. Conflicts are more serious and usually are rooted in incompatible goals.

3. *Conflict is the result of personality problems.* Personalities themselves are not cause for conflict. While people of different personality types may approach situations differently, true conflict develops from and is reflected in behavior, not personality.

4. *Conflict and anger are the same thing.* While conflict and anger are closely merged in most people's minds, they don't necessarily go hand in hand. Conflict involves both issues and emotions—the issue and the participants determine what emotions will be generated. Serious conflicts can develop that do not necessarily result in anger. Other emotions are just as likely to surface: fear, excitement, sadness, frustration, and others.

Getting beyond the misconceptions described above is crucial to effective conflict resolution.

LEVELS OF CONFLICT

One thing that determines the depth and complexity of conflict is the type of basic issue at stake. Most experts identify four levels of issues that may be the bases for conflict. Conflicts that escalate to higher levels become more complex and thus more difficult to resolve. See the table on the next page for a description of the four levels of conflict.

WARNING SIGNS

Being aware of conflict warning signs can minimize conflict situations. The following social relationship characteristics should alert us to the potential for conflict.

1. *Ambiguous Jurisdictions.* If divisions of responsibility and authority are unclear, the possibility of conflict increases.

2. *Conflict of Interest.* Competition for perceived scarce resources (or rewards) escalates conflict possibilities.

3. *Communication Barriers.* Lack of communication, misunderstanding in terminology, unwillingness to listen to another person, etc., increase conflict possibilities.

4. *Overdependency of One Party.* If one person depends too heavily on another for information or assistance, conflict is more apt to occur.

5. *Differentiation in Organization.* The greater the degree of differentiation in a group (e.g., levels of authority, types, and numbers of specific tasks), the greater the potential for conflict.

6. *Association of the Parties.* The more individuals interact, both informally and in decision-making situations, the greater the opportunity for conflict. However, major incidents of conflict decrease as interaction increases.

7. *Need for Consensus.* When all parties must agree on the outcome, disagreements tend to escalate.

8. *Behavior Regulations.* Conflicts are greater when controls like rules, regulations, and formal policies are imposed.

Level Number	Type of Issue	Description
I	Facts or Data	The parties simply have different information. Conflict at this level is often a basic communication problem; when all pertinent information is shared with those concerned, differences usually disappear.
II	Process or Methods	The parties disagree over the best way to achieve a goal or solve a problem. Conflicts at this level are somewhat more difficult to resolve, but by using sound problem solving techniques they can usually be settled.
III	Goals or Purpose	The parties cannot agree on what the group's basic purpose or mission is. Negotiating goals takes patience and skill, but it is vital if collaboration is ever to be achieved.
IV	Values	The parties disagree about the basic meanings of the situation and things they hold dear. The bases for the conflict are highly subjective and at this level, conflicts are extremely difficult to resolve. In such cases, an expert third party may be needed to help resolve the conflict.

9. *Unresolved Prior Conflicts.* As the number of past unresolved conflicts increases, so does the possibility for more conflicts in the future. (This underlines the importance of managing conflicts at their earliest stages, since they do not go away!)

PHASES OF CONFLICT MANAGEMENT

When parties in conflict agree that conflict resolution is needed, they are more likely to succeed if they move through prescribed phases to reach resolution (Johnson & Johnson, 1994).

1. *Collect data.* Know exactly what the conflict is about and objectively analyze the behavior of parties involved.
2. *Probe.* Ask open-ended, involved questions; actively listen; facilitate communication.
3. *Save face.* Work toward a win/win resolution; avoid embarrassing either party; maintain an objective (not emotional) level.
4. *Discover common interests.* This will help individuals redefine dimensions of the conflict and perhaps bring about a compromise.
5. *Reinforce.* Give additional support to common ideas of both parties and know when to use the data collected.
6. *Negotiate.* Suggest partial solutions or compromises identified by both parties. Continue to emphasize common goals of both parties involved.
7. *Solidify adjustments.* Review, summarize, and confirm areas of agreement. Resolution involves compromise.

STRATEGIES FOR COPING WITH CONFLICT

There are a variety of strategies available for dealing with conflict. Some of us are more comfortable with some of these strategies than with others, but we all can be better conflict managers if we develop skills to implement several strategies and adapt resolution strategies to suit the particular conflict situation. Johnson and Johnson (1994) describe five possible approaches to conflict management: avoidance, accommodation, compromise, competition, and collaboration.

Avoidance

Avoidance occurs when an individual fails to address the conflict, but rather sidesteps, postpones, or simply withdraws. Some people attempt to avoid conflict by postponing it, hiding their feelings, changing the subject, leaving the room, or quitting the project.

Use avoidance when:

1. The stakes aren't that high and you don't have anything to lose.
2. You don't have time to deal with it.
3. The context isn't suitable to address the conflict—it isn't the right time or place.
4. More important issues are pressing.

5. You see no chance of getting your concerns met.

6. You would have to deal with an angry, hotheaded person.

7. You are totally unprepared, taken by surprise, and you need time to think and collect information.

8. You are too emotionally involved and the others around you can solve the conflict more successfully.

Avoidance may not be appropriate when the issue is very important and postponing resolution will only make matters worse. Avoiding conflict is generally not satisfying to the individuals involved in a conflict, nor does it help the group resolve a problem.

Accommodation

Accommodation is the opposite of competition and contains an element of self-sacrifice. An accommodating person neglects his or her own concerns to satisfy the concerns of the other person.

Use accommodation when:

1. The issue is more important to the other person than it is to you.

2. You discover that you are wrong.

3. Continued competition would be detrimental and you know you can't win.

4. Preserving harmony without disruption is the most important consideration.

Accommodation should **not** be used if an important issue is at stake that needs to be addressed immediately.

Compromise

The objective of compromise is to find an expedient, mutually acceptable solution that partially satisfies both parties. It falls in the middle between competition and accommodation. Compromise gives up more than competition does, but less than accommodation. Compromise is appropriate when all parties are satisfied with getting part of what they want and are willing to be flexible. Compromise is mutual. All parties should receive something, and all parties should give something up.

Use compromise when:

1. The goals are moderately important but not worth the use of more assertive strategies.

2. People of equal status are equally committed.

3. You want to reach temporary settlement on complex issues.

4. You want to reach expedient solutions on important issues.

5. You need a backup mode when competition or collaboration don't work.

Compromise doesn't work when initial demands are too great from the beginning and there is no commitment to honor the compromise.

Competition

An individual who employs the competition strategy pursues his or her own concerns at the other person's expense. This is a power-oriented strategy used in situations in which eventually someone wins and someone loses. Competition enables one party to win. Before using competition as a conflict resolution strategy, you must decide whether or not winning this conflict is beneficial to individuals or the group.

Use competition when:

1. You know you are right.
2. You need a quick decision.
3. You meet a steamroller type of person and you need to stand up for your own rights.

Competition will not enhance a group's ability to work together. It reduces cooperation.

Collaboration

Collaboration is the opposite of avoidance. It is characterized by an attempt to work with the other person to find some solution that fully satisfies the concerns of both. This strategy requires you to identify the underlying concerns of the two individuals in conflict and find an alternative that meets both sets of concerns. This strategy encourages teamwork and cooperation within a group. Collaboration does not create winners and losers and does not presuppose power over others. The best decisions are made by collaboration.

Use collaboration when:

1. Others' lives are involved.
2. You don't want to have full responsibility.
3. There is a high level of trust.
4. You want to gain commitment from others.
5. You need to work through hard feelings, animosity, etc.

Collaboration may not be the best strategy to use if time is limited and people must act before they can work through their conflict, or there is not enough trust, respect, or communication among the group for collaboration to occur.

CREATIVE WAYS TO MANAGE CONFLICT

Conflict of some degree is inevitable when individuals or groups work together. Before conflict evolves, decide to take positive steps to manage it. When it does occur, discuss it openly with the group. Here are some useful guidelines to follow when managing conflict:

1. Deal with one issue at a time. More than one issue may be involved in the conflict, but someone in the group needs to provide leadership to identify the issues involved. Then address one issue at a time to make the problem manageable.

2. If there is a past problem blocking current communication, list it as one of the issues in this conflict. It may have to be dealt with before the current conflict can be resolved.

3. Choose the right time for conflict resolution. Individuals have to be willing to address the conflict. We are likely to resist if we feel we are being forced into negotiations.

4. Avoid reacting to unintentional remarks. Words like always and never may be said in the heat of battle and do not necessarily convey what the speaker means. Anger will increase the conflict rather than bring it closer to resolution.

5. Avoid resolutions that come too soon or too easily. People need time to think about all possible solutions and the impact of each. Quick answers may disguise the real problem. All parties need to feel some satisfaction with the resolution if they are to accept it. Conflict resolutions should not be rushed.

6. Avoid name-calling and threatening behavior. Don't corner the opponent. All parties need to preserve their dignity and self-respect. Threats usually increase the conflict and payback can occur some time in the future when we least expect it.

7. Agree to disagree. In spite of your differences, if you maintain respect for one another and value your relationship, you will keep disagreements from interfering with the group.

8. Don't insist on being right. There are usually several right solutions to every problem.

HUMOR AND CONFLICT

Laughter can effectively relieve tension in conflict situations. A well-timed joke can refocus conflict negotiations in a positive direction. Laughter gives people time to rethink their positions and see alternatives that may not have been obvious before (Westcott, 1988).

A leader can read a humorous story at the beginning of a meeting to set the tone or be prepared with a humorous example to use in case conflict occurs. Laughing together helps individuals accept differences and still enjoy one another as group members.

Humor is most effective when it relates to the situation at hand. The best source of humor is personal experience and it's usually safe to use oneself as the target of the humor. However, humor should never belittle or insult anyone. Use humor to support talent within the group rather than as a way to cover lack of skill.

SUMMARY

Leaders should learn how to manage and use conflict creatively for the betterment of communities, organizations, and personal relationships. We don't need to be devastated by conflict when we can learn to manage it and use the energy it produces. Leaders confront a variety of relational problems as groups and teams develop over time. Some problems may include defining roles, motivating followers, and managing conflict. Such problems can be overcome by leadership that recognizes them and takes appropriate action to resolve them. All leaders can facilitate resolving relational issues through conflict management, bargaining, and feedback.

*T*eam Learning: Marrying Task and Process

Introduction

$\mathcal{S}$ometimes when our teams are finished, they're finished. The task is done or problem is solved, the team adjourns, people go back to their other responsibilities, and life goes on. Except, of course, that there are going to be other teams and other tasks and it's likely that we're going to be asked to serve on those teams and accomplish new tasks. So what did we learn about being an effective team member or team leader? What did we learn about how our organization can improve the team process? If we're not asking ourselves those questions, we're limiting our ability to make our next team assignments as effective as they might be.

Other teams continue on. Self-managed work teams and management teams usually don't end. There is no "adjourning" stage; they just keep going and going and going. Or do they?

What happens when someone is promoted or transferred or leaves the organization? We get a new member or make do with the members who are left. The person who left took with him skills that the group depended on. Or she filled task or maintenance roles that helped the team function effectively and now she's gone. Someone else will have to fill those roles and do those tasks. The personality and culture of the group is unavoidably changed when someone leaves or someone else joins. Like it or not, we have a new team and we can't go on acting as if nothing has changed. The whole process of forming, storming, norming, and performing has to start all over again.

Even if the composition of the team remains constant, things are still changing. The economic or competitive environment changes, the organizational structure outside the team changes, or the task changes. When something significant in our team's operational context changes, the team has to respond. Additionally, a team whose membership stays the same is subject to stagnation. Barring too much external change, teams must learn how to "renew" themselves or risk becoming less and less effective as time passes.

As individuals, learning how to become more effective as team members and leaders requires a process of observation, reflection, and evaluation. It necessitates that we take time periodically to think about what has happened. What has gone well and why has it? What has not gone well and why? Were there conflicts? How were they handled? Could we have done better? Most importantly, we must develop the skill of asking ourselves what steps we can take to be more effective either in our current team or as a member of future teams.

The process is no different for ongoing teams. If teams are to grow and improve, they need to take regular and periodic "process breaks" during which they reflect on what has happened or is happening. By collectively asking what is going well and what isn't, what we can do better, and what we can learn about being more effective in our teams, we ensure that our learning will be passed along to our organizations, as we serve on other teams elsewhere.

How often do we take this time to reflect and question each other and ourselves? Most of us will agree that we don't do it often enough. That's why the material in Section Five has been included. There are three components of this section. The first deals with the team building process: activities and processes we can undertake to strengthen our teams. The second discusses how we can "renew" our ongoing teams. How can we avoid falling into patterns of complacency and convention? How can we continuously learn and improve the team process?

Finally, even when we work together in teams, someone is usually charged with leading the effort. Even if we contend that every member is equally important to the achievement of our task and that our roles complementary roles, we've all been in situations where there are "too many chiefs." Knowing how to be a good follower is as important to ensuring the success of a team as knowing how to lead the team. That's why the concluding portion of this section deals with "followership."

Team Building

For each of the following questions, select the answer that best describes your behavior as a team member.

	Usually	Sometimes	Seldom
1. I seek agreement on a common purpose.	☐	☐	☐
2. I let other members worry about their specific goals.	☐	☐	☐
3. I clarify what each member is accountable for individually and collectively.	☐	☐	☐
4. I focus on home runs versus small wins.	☐	☐	☐
5. I keep my problems and limitations to myself.	☐	☐	☐
6. I respectfully listen to others' ideas.	☐	☐	☐
7. I'm dependable and honest.	☐	☐	☐
8. I don't bug others for feedback on how well I am doing.	☐	☐	☐
9. I offer advice on how group processes can be improved.	☐	☐	☐
10. I give others feedback on their contributions.	☐	☐	☐

Scoring Key

For questions 1, 3, 6, 7, 9, and 10, give yourself 3 points for "Usually," 2 points for "Sometimes," and 1 point for "Seldom."

251

For questions 2, 4, 5, and 8, give yourself 3 points for "Seldom," 2 points for "Sometimes," and 1 point for "Usually."

Sum up your total points. A score of 27 or higher means you're a good team player. A score of 22 to 26 suggests you have some deficiencies as a team member. A score below 22 indicates that you have considerable room for improvement.

Skill Concepts

Groups and teams are not necessarily the same thing. A *group* is two or more individuals who interact primarily to share information and to make decisions to help each other perform within a given area of responsibility. Members of a group have no need to engage in collective work that requires joint efforts so their performance is merely the summation of each group member's individual contribution. There is no positive synergy that would create an overall level of performance that is greater than the sum of the inputs.

But it could be worse. If a group is plagued by factors such as poor communication, antagonistic conflicts, and avoidance of responsibilities, the product of these problems produces negative synergy and a *pseudoteam* where the sum of the whole is less than the potential of the individual parts. Even though members may call themselves a team, they're not. Because it doesn't focus on collective performance and because members have no interest in shaping a common purpose, a pseudoteam actually underperforms a working group.

What differentiates a *team* from a group is that members are committed to a common purpose, have a set of specific performance goals, and hold themselves mutually accountable for the team's results. Teams can produce outputs that are something greater than the sum of their parts. The primary force that moves a work group toward a real high-performing team is its emphasis on performance.

"Going in the right direction but not there yet" is the best way to describe a *potential* team. It recognizes the need for, and is really trying hard to achieve, higher performance, but some roadblocks are in the way. Its purpose and goals may need greater clarity or the team may need better coordination. The result is that it has not yet established a sense of collective accountability. Its goal is to become a *real* team with a set of common characteristics that lead to consistently high performance. We can identify six characteristics of real teams.

Building Real Teams

Studies of effective teams have found that they contain a small number of people with complementary skills who are equally committed to a common purpose, goals, and working approach for which they hold themselves mutually accountable (Katzenback & Douglas, 1993, pp. 43–64) .

Training in Inter-Personal Skills: TIPS for Managing People at Work, Second Edition, by Stephen P. Robbins and Phillip L. Hunsaker. Copyright © 1996, 1989 by Prentice Hall, Inc.

SMALL SIZE

The best teams tend to be small. When they have more than about ten members, it becomes difficult for them to get much done. They have trouble interacting constructively and agreeing on much. Large numbers of people usually cannot develop the common purpose, goals, approach, and mutual accountability of a real team. They tend merely to go through the motions. So in designing effective teams, keep them to ten or less. If the natural working unit is larger, and you want a team effort, break the group into subteams. Federal Express, for instance, has divided the 1000 clerical workers at its headquarters into teams of five to ten members each.

COMPLEMENTARY SKILLS

To perform effectively, a team requires three types of skills. First, it needs people with *technical expertise*. Second, it needs people with the *problem-solving* and *decision-making* skills to identify problems, generate alternatives, evaluate those alternatives, and make competent choices. Finally, teams need people with good *interpersonal skills*.

No team can achieve its performance potential without developing all three types of skills. The right mix is crucial. Too much of one at the expense of others will result in lower team performance.

Incidentally, teams don't need to have all the complementary skills at the beginning. Where team members value personal growth and development, one or more members often take responsibility to learn the skills in which the group is deficient, as long as the skill potential exists. Additionally, personal compatibility among members is not critical to the team's success if the technical, decisionmaking, and interpersonal skills are in place.

COMMON PURPOSE

Does the team have a meaningful purpose that all members aspire to? This purpose is a vision. It's broader than any specific goals. High-performing teams have a common and meaningful purpose that provides direction, momentum, and commitment for members.

The development team at Apple Computer that designed the Macintosh, for example, was almost religiously committed to creating a user-friendly machine that would revolutionize the way people used computers. Production teams at Saturn Corp. are united by the common purpose of building an American automobile that can successfully compete in terms of quality and price with the best of Japanese cars.

Members of successful teams put a tremendous amount of time and effort into discussing, shaping, and agreeing upon a purpose that belongs to them collectively and individually. This common purpose, when accepted by the team, becomes the equivalent of what celestial navigation is to a ship captain—it provides direction and guidance under any and all conditions.

SPECIFIC GOALS

Successful teams translate their common purpose into specific, measurable, and realistic performance goals. Just as goals lead individuals to higher performance, they also energize teams. Specific goals facilitate clear communication and help teams maintain their focus on getting results. Examples of specific team goals might be responding to all customers within twenty-four hours, cutting production-cycle time by 30 percent over the next six months, or maintaining equipment at a level of zero downtime every month.

COMMON APPROACH

Goals are the ends a team strives to attain. Defining and agreeing upon a common approach ensures that the team is unified on the means for achieving those ends.

Team members must contribute equally in sharing the work load and agree on who is to do what. Additionally, the team needs to determine how schedules will be set, what skills need to be developed, how conflicts will be resolved, and how decisions will be made and modified. The recent implementation of work teams at Olin Chemicals' Macintosh, Alabama plant included having teams complete questionnaires on how they would organize themselves and share specific responsibilities. Integrating individual skills to further the team's performance is the essence of shaping a common approach.

MUTUAL ACCOUNTABILITY

The final characteristic of high-performing teams is accountability at both the individual and group level.

Successful teams make members individually and jointly accountable for the team's purpose, goals, and approach. Members understand what they are individually responsible for and what they are jointly responsible for.

Studies have shown that when teams focus only on group-level performance targets and ignore individual contributions and responsibilities, team members often engage in *social loafing* (Sheppard, 1993, pp. 67–81). They reduce their efforts because their individual contributions can't be identified. They, in effect, become "free riders" and coast on the group's effort. The result is that the team's overall performance suffers. This reaffirms the importance of measuring both individual contributions to the team as well as the team's overall performance. And successful teams have members who collectively feel responsible for their team's performance.

 bstacles to Effective Teams

Teams have long been popular in Japan. When they were introduced into the United States in the late 1980s, critics warned that they were destined to fail: "Japan is a collectivist society. American culture is based on the values of individualism. American workers won't sublimate their needs for individual responsibility and recognition to be anonymous parts of a team." While the introduction of work teams in some organizations has met with resistance and disappointment, the overall picture has been encouraging. When teams are properly used in organizations and when the organization's internal climate is one that is consistent with a team approach, the results have been largely positive.

There are, of course, a number of obstacles to creating effective teams. Fortunately, there are also many effective techniques for overcoming those obstacles. The following critical obstacles can prevent teams from becoming high performers.

A WEAK SENSE OF DIRECTION

Teams perform poorly when members are not sure of their purpose, goals, and approach. Add weak leadership and you have the recipe for failure. Nothing will undermine enthusiasm for the team concept as quickly as the frustration of being an involuntary member of a team that has no focus.

INFIGHTING

When team members are spending time bickering and undermining their colleagues, energy is being misdirected. Effective teams are not necessarily composed of people who all like each other; however, members must respect each other and be willing to put aside petty differences in order to facilitate goal achievement.

SHIRKING OF RESPONSIBILITIES

A team is in trouble if members exhibit lack of commitment to the team, maneuver to have others do part of their job, or blame colleagues or management for personal or team failures. The result is a pseudoteam—a team in name only and one that consistently underperforms even what the members could accomplish independently.

LACK OF TRUST

When there is *trust*, team members believe in the integrity, character, and ability of each other. When trust is lacking, members are unable to depend on each other. Teams that lack trust tend to be short-lived.

CRITICAL SKILLS GAPS

When skill gaps occur, and the team doesn't fill these gaps, the team flounders. Members have trouble communicating with each other, destructive conflicts aren't resolved, decisions are never made, or technical problems overwhelm the team.

LACK OF EXTERNAL SUPPORT

Teams exist within the larger organization. They rely on that larger organization for a variety of resources—money, people, equipment—and if those resources aren't there, it's difficult for teams to reach their potential. For example, teams must live with the organization's employee selection process, formal rules and regulations, budgeting procedures, and compensation system. If these are inconsistent with the team's needs and goals, the team suffers.

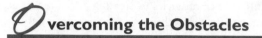vercoming the Obstacles

There are a number of things that can be done to overcome obstacles and help teams reach their full potential.

CREATE CLEAR GOALS

Members of high-performance teams have a clear understanding of their goals and believe that their goals embody a worthwhile or important result. Moreover, the importance of these goals encourages individuals to sublimate personal concerns to these team goals. In effective teams, members are committed to the team's goals, know what they are expected to accomplish, and understand how they will work together to achieve these goals.

ENCOURAGE TEAMS TO GO FOR SMALL WINS

The building of real teams takes time. Team members have to learn to think and work as a team. New teams can't be expected to hit home runs, right at the beginning, every time they come to bat. Team members should begin by trying to hit singles.

This can be facilitated by identifying and setting attainable goals. The eventual goal of cutting overall costs by 30 percent, for instance, can be dissected into five or ten smaller and more easily attainable goals. As the smaller goals are attained, the team's success is reinforced. Cohesiveness is increased and morale improves. Confidence builds. Success breeds success, but it's a lot easier for young teams to reach their goals if they start with small wins.

BUILD MUTUAL TRUST

Trust is fragile. It takes a long time to build and can be easily destroyed. Several things can be done to create a climate of mutual trust (Bartolome, 1989, pp. 135–142).

Keep team members informed by explaining upper-management decisions and policies and by providing accurate feedback. Create a climate of openness where employees are free to discuss problems without fear of retaliation. Be candid about your own problems and limitations. Make sure you're available and approachable when others need support. Be respectful and listen to team members' ideas. Develop a reputation for being fair, objective, and impartial in your treatment of team members. Show consistency in your actions and avoid erratic and unpredictable behavior. Finally, be dependable and honest. Make sure you follow through on all explicit and implied promises.

APPRAISE BOTH GROUP AND INDIVIDUAL PERFORMANCE

Team members should all share in the glory when their team succeeds, and they should share in the blame when it fails. So a large measure of each member's performance appraisal should be based on the overall team's performance. But members need to know that they can't ride on the backs of others. Therefore, each member's individual contribution should also be identified and made a part of his or her overall performance appraisal.

PROVIDE THE NECESSARY EXTERNAL SUPPORT

Managers are the link between the teams and upper management. It's their responsibility to make sure that teams have the necessary organizational resources to accomplish their goals. They should be prepared to make the case to key decision makers in the organization for tools, equipment, training, personnel, physical space, or other resources that the teams may require.

OFFER TEAM-BUILDING TRAINING

Teams, especially in their early stages of formation, will need training to build their skills. Typically, these would include problemsolving, communication, negotiation, conflict-resolution, and group-processing skills. If you can't personally provide this kind of skill training for your team members, look to specialists in your organization who can or secure the funds to bring in outside facilitators who specialize in this kind of training.

CHANGE THE TEAM'S MEMBERSHIP

When teams get bogged down in their own inertia or internal fighting, allow them to rotate members. To manage this change, consider how certain personalities will mesh and reform teams in ways that will better complement skills. If lack of leadership is the problem, use your knowledge of the people involved to create teams where there will be a high probability that a leader will emerge.

ehavioral Checklist

Look for the following behaviors when evaluating your effectiveness in team building.

Effective Team Building Requires

- Establishing a common purpose
- Assessing team strengths and weaknesses
- Developing specific individual goals
- Getting agreement on a common approach for achieving goals
- Encouraging acceptance of accountability for both individual and team performance

- Building mutual trust among members
- Maintaining an appropriate mix of team member skills and personalities
- Providing needed training and resources
- Creating opportunities for small achievements

Team Renewal

Purpose

The purpose of this chapter is to give the team the tools for renewal that it needs so that it can continue to grow and be important to the organization's strategic direction.

There is a tie-in with the purpose and process model that emphasizes the ongoing evaluative measures used to sustain the work of the team. These measures are both individual and team oriented, and they allow the team to make transitions.

Under "process," we discussed two important activities for teams: developing both ground rules and effective decision-making. However, neither of these activities is a onetime event. Both are ongoing practices or skills that need to be continually monitored, adjusted, and upgraded.

Another process skill that is important to a team is assessment. Teams must build assessment into their regular activities and view it as a development activity rather than one that finds fault. Both "progress toward goals" and "team process" need to be included in the assessment process. As with any assessment, criteria should be consistent with the objectives. Samples of tools are given to suggest formats and common criteria, but teams should adapt them using their own specific criteria. Team objectives change, which is why members must periodically evaluate their structure, process, and flexibility in dealing with internal and external political influences.

There are five guidelines for measuring the work of teams. It is important to look at all five to get an accurate picture of work performance. Measuring only one guideline would result in an unbalanced assessment.

Quantity of team work	Is the team making progress toward its goals?
	Are team meetings efficient?
Quality of team work	Is the work of the team based on relevant data and information?
	Are all perspectives considered in developing solutions and making decisions?
	Are team ideas truly innovative?
	Does the team have an external focus?
Team knowledge	Is the team learning the skills needed to accomplish its task?
	Has each person developed as a result of being a member of the team?
	Does the team have a learning program?
	Has the team developed a learning culture?
Initiative	Does the team use an effective method for decision-making?
	Do team members do equivalent amounts of "real" work?
Collaboration	Does the team follow its own ground rules?
	Has the team developed a performance culture?

The initial work of the team includes goal setting as a part of establishing the team's charter.

Teams invariably work under time pressure, and meeting milestones and goals are key measures of the effectiveness of the team. To meet is not enough; the team must show that it is accomplishing what it was chartered to do. This seems obvious, but many teams fall into the trap of thinking they are making progress simply because they keep meeting. By using **quantity of work** measures, the team can hold itself accountable for getting work done.

In addition to moving ahead on its tasks, the team must challenge the quality of its work. This is difficult, because it is hard to be objective about one's own work. Measuring the **quality of work** of the team probably requires the team to do an external reality check with the constituents who must use the outcome of the team's activity.

Learning is a hallmark of an effective team. It is important to understand that the team must gain new skills, both task-oriented skills such as data collection and interpretation, and process-oriented skills such as thinking and evaluating. The team must continually assess where it is gaining **knowledge** on both group and individual levels. Learning assumes a desire for continuous improvement.

Initiative measures assess whether or not the team is taking on challenging tasks and issues. The presence of a risk-taking attitude toward practices is an indication of initiative. Teams can assess themselves and be assessed by external constituents by asking the following questions: Does the decisionmaking process of the team consider new ideas and challenge the current assumptions, or is it a safe discussion likely to reach solutions similar to current practice? Are members of the team engaged in their work? Do they have a commitment to performance? Are they creative and unassuming in their problemsolving discussions?

Teams can quickly fall apart if the process they use does not value both the people and their time commitments. Teams usually recognize this potential pitfall as they set up their ground rules, but they can easily slip back into poor process habits. **Collaboration** assessment lets the team check how well it is working.

These guidelines are meant to be starting points. As discussed early in the book, each team is unique. It will have specific tasks, ground rules, culture, and external expectations that have to be monitored. The essential aspect of assessment is that it must be done on a regular basis. The more measurement is made to be a part of how the team does business, the less the team will generate defensiveness and the easier it will be for the team to correct its course. If the team waits until an external force identifies a need for corrective action, the necessary changes will be difficult indeed.

Measuring performance is only the first part of an assessment process. Performance information must be fed back to team members so that work can be adjusted. How information is fed back to the team is critical to the team's ability to accept and use the information.

The team needs to set up a measurement process as a part of its team charter. It needs to determine what the indicators of success and progress will be; how those indicators will be measured; and when measurement will occur. In addition, the team needs to decide what to do with the information gathered and how to feed that information back to the team. Quarterly reviews and in-depth annual reviews are recommended, as well as specific problem-driven reviews. Team members must commit to this kind of regular assessment if it is to be beneficial.

Without feedback, the information is useless. Sometimes the measures are apparent, as when deadlines are missed. In the case of a missed deadline, teams may address what to do about the missed deadline. However, teams must ask themselves what kind of information is needed in order to know why the deadline was missed; only then is there any assurance that another deadline will not be missed. This process revisits the need for a learning culture. How can a team uncover this information and understand it without creating defensiveness among its members? How can the team identify earlier warning signals so that it does not have to wait until a deadline is missed to make changes in its behavior? These questions speak to the true power of measurement, and they should be the focus of performance feedback.

Process measures for the team are usually more complex than task measures. Teams are often reluctant to do any process measures at all. Both are necessary to quality team performance. Once measures have been taken, the team faces a dilemma: How do we use the information we've created?

Feedback Rules

There are some feedback rules that will help a team accept and use information.

FOCUS ON THE FUTURE

No one can change what he or she did or didn't do in the past. By talking about what went wrong, people become defensive and feel that they have to justify their past actions. That kind of discussion is nonproductive in terms of keeping the problem from occurring again. It doesn't change the current course of action. Instead, it fosters resistance to change. Remember, no one has made a mistake tomorrow. By focusing on the future, feedback allows individuals to benefit from learning while maintaining personal dignity.

FOCUS ON SPECIFICS

Avoid general assessments about team performance, such as "disorganized," "unfocused," or "on track." These terms mean different things to different people. The terms do not help the team understand what to do differently or what behaviors to repeat. A review of both problems and successes should be specific enough to identify the future course of action. This is especially true of successes. In general, if teams make assessments, they focus on recrimination rather than on what went well so that they can keep doing these things. Here's the principle: If you know what you did wrong, you still need to figure out what to do right. If you know what you did well, you just have to do it again and again. People and teams inherently want to succeed.

FOCUS ON LEARNING

As the team assesses its progress, it needs to match its performance with the organization's needs. Rather than focus on what its deficiencies might be, it needs to identify specifically what it needs to be able to do as a team. This draws the assessment full circle to focus on the purpose of the team. Focusing feedback of negative information on the learning needs of the team provides incentive to change. If feedback simply identifies deficiencies, team members are likely to attribute those deficiencies to individual team members or circumstances, and to miss important opportunities for the entire team to grow.

$\mathcal{F}$ollowership

$\mathcal{E}$xamples of Effective Followership

- A member of a new-product development team found out that no one was taking responsibility for coordinating engineering, marketing, and manufacturing. "She worked out an interdepartmental review schedule that identified the people who should be involved at each stage of development. Instead of burdening her boss with yet another problem, this woman took the initiative to present the issue along with a solution" (Kelley, 1988).

- A welder in a large railroad car assembly plant liked being a welder but avoided being a boss. "Although he stood on the lowest rung of the hierarchy in the plant, everyone knew Joe, and everyone agreed that he was the most important person in the entire factory. . . . The reason for his fame was simple: Joe had apparently mastered every phase of the plant's operation, and he was now able to take anyone's place if the necessity arose. Moreover, he could fix any broken-down piece of machinery, ranging from huge mechanical cranes to tiny electronic monitors. . . . Joe not only could perform these tasks, but actually enjoyed it when he was called upon to do them" (Kelley, 1992).

- Michael Eisner, CEO of Walt Disney Company, described one of his best followers. "[He] is a great devil's advocate. . . . He will ask the questions nobody ever thought of, and he will take the opposite side of everything. But he is a deal maker, not a deal breaker and that's very unique" (Kelley, 1992).

■ A leader described an effective follower as someone who was continuously mastering organizationally useful skills. Her personal standards for her own performance were generally higher than the organization required, and she continuously updated her skills in any way she could.

These incidents are examples of effective followership, which is an essential role in all leadership situations. The American Heritage Dictionary defines a follower as "one who subscribes to the teachings of another; an attendant, servant or subordinate; one who emulates . . . or agrees with another; one who accepts guidance or leadership of another" (The American Heritage Dictionary (1985)). As these examples demonstrate, the behavior of effective followers today is often more proactive than implied by these definitions.

A leader who embodies all the best traits and behaviors of classical and current theories of leadership probably does not exist. All leaders, successful or not, have weaknesses and gaps in their leadership styles. Effective followers fill in for these gaps and weaknesses. One researcher pointed out that followers contribute a lion's share of the effort that goes into achieving organizational goals (Kelley, 1992).

Leadership cannot exist without followers. Leadership takes place within the context of a specific group of followers (Hughes, Ginnett and Curphy, 1996)) and leadership and followership are interdependent (Heller and Van Til, 1982; Hollander, 1992). Leaders regularly adjust their own behavior to fit followers' characteristics and behaviors. Followers forgo rewards like money, status and fame that go with leadership and instead find meaning in working with their leader and coworkers. In Japan, the follower role is a highly valued tradition. Bushido is a traditional Japanese term for a faithful follower of one's lord. Although the lord has been replaced by the modern corporation, this traditional follower role is still associated with high social standing in Japan.

However, effective followers today are not "yes men" or "sheep" who do whatever the leader desires. Numerous factors influence the roles of followers in organizations. Today, these factors include scarce resources, increased foreign competition, higher operating costs, increasing education of the work force, changing attitudes toward formal authority, increased technology in the workplace, and reductions in the number of middle-management positions in large organizations. All these developments are causing followers to take on more responsibilities than in the past. Proactive followers who take responsibility for organizational tasks and improvements, who demonstrate self-management individually and in groups, and who carry out activities previously performed by leaders are increasingly common in many organizations (Lee, 1991; Kelley, 1992).

In today's organizations, followership is defined as an interactive role individuals play that complements the leadership role and is equivalent to it in importance for achieving group and organizational performance. The followership role includes the degree of enthusiasm, cooperation, effort, active participation, task competence, and critical thinking and individual exhibits in support of group or organizational objectives without the need for "star billing."

In formal organizations, most individuals (including leaders) spend much of their time as followers. No matter how many subordinates one has, she usually also has one or more bosses. Many military experts believe the first step in developing leadership potential is teaching individuals how to be good followers. Research shows that the same individuals who are nominated as most desired leaders are also nominated as most desired followers (Bass, 1990). The characteristics of good leaders are also characteristics of good followers, and one of the important skills of followers may be the ability to shift easily between leadership and followership roles (Hollander, 1992 and 1993; Chemers and Ayman, Eds.).

The following are effective followership behaviors:

1. Demonstrating job knowledge and competence while working without close supervision and completing work tasks on time

2. Demonstrating independent critical thinking by developing one's own opinions and ideas that show inventiveness and creativity

3. Showing initiative in taking on responsibilities, participating actively, seeing tasks through to completion, and taking responsibility for one's own career development

4. Speaking up frequently to offer information, share viewpoints, or take issue with decisions or actions that may be unethical or ill-advised

5. Building collaborative and supportive relationships with coworkers and the leader that result in partnerships for achieving organizational goals

6. Exerting influence on the leader in a confident and unemotional manner to help the leader avoid costly mistakes. Effective influence tactics often include logical persuasion, mobilizing coalitions, and being persistent and assertive. Flattery and praise of the leader are used sparingly

7. Showing up consistently when needed and accurately representing the leader's interests and views

8. Competently spanning group or organizational boundaries when needed to acquire resources, export products, manipulate or interpret the environment, and provide key information for the organization

9. Setting work goals that are action oriented, challenging, measurable, and aligned with group and organizational goals

10. Demonstrating proper comportment for the organization. This may include manner of speech, dress, grammar, and etiquette

11. Demonstrating a concern for performance as well as a supportive and friendly atmosphere within the work group (Gilbert and Hyde, 1988; Kelley, 1992; Gilbert and Whiteside, 1988; Hafsi and Misumi, 1992).

The followership role fulfills important personal needs for individuals. It provides for comradeship with valued others and thus helps satisfy one's social needs. It allows individuals to serve others and thus confirms a favorable self-concept and personal identity for many people. In addition, effective followers often identify with the leader and her mission. This identification with a respected leader and a worthwhile mission can enhance followers' self-concepts. By helping to reinforce one's self-concept, the followership role can also satisfy the needs for self-esteem and self-actualization. Finally, followership roles can provide for personal growth of individuals by helping them become more mature and effective performers or even future leaders, thus helping to satisfy human needs for competence and self-determination. Figure 5–1 summarizes the major followership behaviors.

Examples of Ineffective Followership

Some follower behaviors are very common but ineffective. Here are some examples:

- Hawkeye Pierce, in the TV series MASH, was a capable cynic who sarcastically criticized the leader's actions, often withheld his own efforts, and gradually sunk into disgruntled acquiescence (Kelley, 1992).

- Conformist followers are intellectually lazy because they "allow the leader to make the moral decisions for which they are responsible and . . . readily do what they are told" (Kelley, 1992).

- Passive followers "act morally only under someone else's prodding" (Kelley, 1992).

- Pragmatic followers "avert their eyes from wrongdoing rather than stop it or . . . are unwilling to disturb the status quo to do something worthwhile" (Kelley, 1992).

- Apathetic, passive, or cynical followers exhibit a spectator-like non-involvement that invites abuse by unethical leaders (Gardner, 1990).

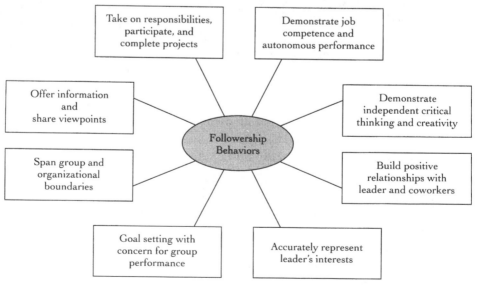

FIGURE 5-1

Followership Behaviors

FOLLOWERSHIP IN ACTION: TAKING RESPONSIBILITY IN A DIFFICULT SITUATION

Pilots of passenger airlines are operational leader-managers and their decisions have major impacts on cost and safety of the passengers. A major pilot error can cost tens of millions of dollars as well as hundreds of lives. Pilots must have the ability to rapidly evaluate complex situations and arrive at effective decisions. A case occurred where the captain on an international flight arrived for the preflight check in a drunken condition. The ground staff carefully ignored his condition and said nothing. When the first officer arrived, however, things were different. Drawing the older captain aside, the first officer asked him in a firm tone, "Captain, will you turn yourself in, or will I have to turn you in?" The captain went immediately to the chief pilot's office and voluntarily grounded himself. Getting control of his drinking problem took the captain six months, but he returned to flying without any further problems with alcohol. The effective followership behavior of the first officer demonstrated concern for the organization and the captain. The first officer demonstrated both job competence and autonomy. He took responsibility even though the captain was his superior in rank. After the captain got control of his alcohol problem, positive relations developed between the two pilots that lasted for years and contributed to organizational effectiveness. In this situation the followership behavior of the first officer was clearly in the best interest of the airline, the customers, and the two individuals involved.

- Ineffective followers expect training and development to be served to them. These individuals attend seminars and training experiences only if their organization sends them. They require a parental leader to care and feed their development or they become obsolete.

These followers are ineffective because they are not actively participating with the leader in individual and group development and performance. In contrast, the Followership in Action box shows an effective follower.

Importance of Followership

Followers have historically been thought of as dependent individuals who need to be told what to do. Followership was therefore viewed as a passive role like clay awaiting the leader's creative force. Organizations have emphasized leadership initiatives with rewards for outstanding leadership performance. Organizational researchers, university faculties, and management trainers have produced leadership programs, books, articles, and seminars offering leadership prescriptions to help guide groups and organizations toward higher performance.

But in the 1990s, many organizational members came to resent leaders with ridiculously high salaries and bonuses, extreme status symbols, and golden parachutes. Followers now want a larger role in making organizational decisions, in carrying out those decisions, and in reaping the benefits. In the next decades we will see followership roles being emphasized in organizations. The popularity of work teams, productivity improvement groups,

---

FOLLOWERSHIP IN PERSPECTIVE:
HOW TO INCREASE YOUR TECHNICAL COMPETENCE

1. Assess how your job contributes to organizational success.
2. Evaluate your current technical skills by seeking feedback from superiors and peers and reviewing past appraisals.
3. Seek out and attend formal education and training programs.
4. Observe others who handle work problems effectively and follow their examples.
5. Visit other parts of the organization and volunteer for different positions or roles to gain experience.
6. Work on team projects and volunteer for projects that expand relevant skills.

Source: Adapted from Kelley, R.E. (1992). *The Power of Followership.* New York: Doubleday.

---

employee ownership programs, and gainsharing all point to a larger role for followers in organizations of the future.

Followership roles provide growth and development experiences for individuals to prepare them for greater responsibilities. As individuals develop, they typically contribute more to group or organizational performance. They also increase their self-confidence and become more willing to make moral judgments about possible unethical actions contemplated or taken by their leaders. By becoming proactive regarding ethical issues, they may prevent major mistakes that could cause serious damage to their organization. As noted earlier, followership roles can satisfy psychological needs of comradeship, service to others, identification with a valued cause, self-determination, and self-esteem. Followership roles help organizations address increased competition, high costs of operation, and organizational downsizing (by taking over some management functions) that characterize many major industries today (Flower, 1991; Buhler, 1993). They also help their organizations by increasing their technical competence, as detailed in the box on how to increase your technical competence.

How to Be an Effective Follower

Although the research on followership is sparse, a few writers have suggested traits and skills that should help fulfill the followership role in formal organizations. When a follower develops a high degree of expertise or technical competence, often resulting from extensive education and/or relevant work experience, the follower is usually more capable of self-management and less reliant on a leader for direct guidance on the job. When followers develop good social skills, they can build cooperative relationships with leaders and coworkers. Cooperation builds cohesion and avoids cliques that subvert the group's objectives. Followers who are friendly and agreeable may also help the unit by building effective relationships with important outsiders (Kelley, 1992; Hughes, Ginnet and Curphy, 1996). Followers who share attitudes and val-

---

FOLLOWERSHIP IN PERSPECTIVE: FOLLOWERS' STRATEGIES FOR BUILDING EFFECTIVE RELATIONS WITH LEADERS

1. View your own and the leader's success as interdependent.
2. Try to understand the leader's personal and organizational objectives.
3. Recognize and complement the leader's weaknesses and limitations.
4. Keep the leader informed about activities, developments, and changes in the group.
5. Clarify your own role with the leader.
6. Adapt to the leader's style of leadership.
7. Show up prepared to perform.

Source: Adapted from Kelley, R.E. (1992). *The Power of Followership.* New York: Doubleday.

---

ues with their leader and coworkers are also likely to build effective relationships (Shamir, House and Arthur, 1993).

Flexible followers can adapt to changing demands and environments without being paralyzed by the stressful ambiguity that accompanies rapid change. Leaders usually appreciate a sense of humor and they rate this quality highly in followers.

Followers provide an audience of leaders. As such, a requirement for effective followership is a readiness to accept the leader's influence without being "yes men." This involves listening and learning without feeling threatened or sensing any loss of status. This readiness may result from the followers' maturity, including a sense of confidence and self-esteem. With charismatic leadership, however, the readiness may reflect followers' feelings of helplessness due to a perception that the situation is more than they can handle on their own. For whatever reason, effective followers must address the leader with a willingness to engage in a dynamic interaction of followership vis-à-vis leadership.

When followers are intelligent, competent, and possess critical thinking skills, others will probably view them as having expert power. If a follower's expertise is complemented with sociability, flexibility, and ability to handle stress, the follower will likely possess referent power. Both these sources of power can make followers more effective and influential with the leader and coworkers.

A leader's expectations and perceptions of the follower may influence the follower's willingness to engage in certain followership behaviors. For example, if a leader has high expectations for a follower, this can result in constructive follower behaviors, such as speaking up and exerting influence on the leader. By the same token, low expectations and perceptions can cause followers to be overly tentative, afraid to speak up, and unwilling to take unpopular (but needed) positions on important issues (Lippitt, 1982). A similar result may occur when a leader's beliefs, philosophy, or style are not compatible with those of followers. In this case, followers may not be willing to carry out the active followership behaviors needed to help the leader meet objectives. Certain leaders simply rub followers the wrong way. When this occurs, the follower should consider the followers' strategies for building effective relations with leaders, described in the box on followers' strategies for building effective relations with leaders. If the follower is unable or unwilling to attempt these strategies, then she had best seek another position with a leader who is more compatible.

Effects of Followership

A limited number of research studies have been carried out on the effectiveness of followership behaviors and skills described here. These studies show that followership behaviors resulted in higher performance ratings by superiors (Gardner, 1990; Gilbert and Hyde, 1988). We believe that these followership behaviors will also result in increased motivation, satisfaction, feelings of empowerment, and group cohesion. Much more research is needed to verify whether objective performance and productivity measures or other follower reactions are related to these followership behaviors.

Situational Factors and Followership

We believe that the active followership behaviors described in this chapter are valuable in virtually any leader-follower relationship. There are probably specific situations, however, in which the followership behaviors are especially needed and effective.

Enhancers of followership may be common in many organizations today. When the leader is frequently absent or distant from followers, the followership behaviors involving task competence, taking initiative, actively participating, and thinking independently may be especially critical for team performance. When followers' work tasks are highly complex or interdependent, then followers' task competence and activities that build cooperation with coworkers are probably especially important for group performance. When the followers' group faces frequent emergencies, high risk situations, or rapid change, then followership behaviors of speaking up, task competence proactive initiative, and concern for performance are probably especially important.

Because it is an essential role in the leadership process, there can be no complete replacement for followership. However, there may be replacements for specific followership behaviors. This might occur when the leader is very active in external boundary-spanning by gaining resources for the unit, building and maintaining networks with key outsiders, and facilitating important exchanges for the group. Here, the followers' external boundary-spanning behaviors may be unnecessary. When the leader is unusually adept at critical thinking, creativity, and inventiveness, this may at least partially alleviate the need for followers to demonstrate these characteristics. We have difficulty imagining, however, any replacements for followers' task competence, active participation, taking responsibility, building positive relations with coworkers, and several other followership behaviors.

One situational factor might possibly decrease (neutralize) the favorable effects of followership behaviors. A domineering, autocratic, and self-cen-

---

FOLLOWERSHIP IN PERSPECTIVE: FOLLOWERS' STRATEGIES FOR BUILDING COOPERATIVE RELATIONSHIPS WITH COWORKERS

1. Lend a hand to help others with problems.
2. Acknowledge shared interests, values, goals, and expectations.
3. Establish informal communication links with others.
4. Show a willingness to listen.
5. Think the best of others.

Source: Adapted from Kelley, R.E. (1992). *The Power of Followership.* New York: Doubleday.

---

tered leader may want nothing but "yes men" as followers, who flatter the leader and do not think for themselves. This type of leader may not value competent followers who show initiative and speak their mind. In these situations, the competent follower should work on building better relations with the leader or seek another position.

Although there is no research data, we suspect that neutralizers and replacements of followership behaviors are quite rare. Future research is clearly needed to better understand how followership behaviors interact with situational characteristics. The Followership in Perspective box above offers suggestions for building cooperative relationships with coworkers. These strategies may help create a cohesive group of followers, which can be an effective replacement for other leader behaviors described in this book.

*S*ummary

Followership is a necessary element in the leadership process. Most followership behaviors described in this chapter are needed to achieve group goals. However, certain followership behaviors may be especially important in specific situations. For example, when leaders are frequently distant from followers, when followers' tasks are complex or interdependent, or when followers face frequent high risks, emergency situations, or rapid change, the followership behaviors of speaking up, taking initiative, acting competently, building relationships with coworkers, and thinking independently can be especially important. Although research on these behaviors is sparse, we believe that nearly all leaders prefer this type of followership to having "yes men" or "sheep" who simply do as they are told. The changes occurring in organizations in the year 2000 and beyond will make these followership behaviors increasingly important. Because nearly all leaders in organizations report to higher-level leaders, these followership behaviors are useful for virtually all organizational members.

Figure 5-2 depicts a tentative process model of followership that summarizes much of the information in this chapter. Followership behaviors are shown at the top of figure 5-2 as affecting group and follower reactions, which in turn affect follower outcomes. Boxes at either side of figure 5–2 show how certain situational factors can increase or decrease the effectiveness of fol-

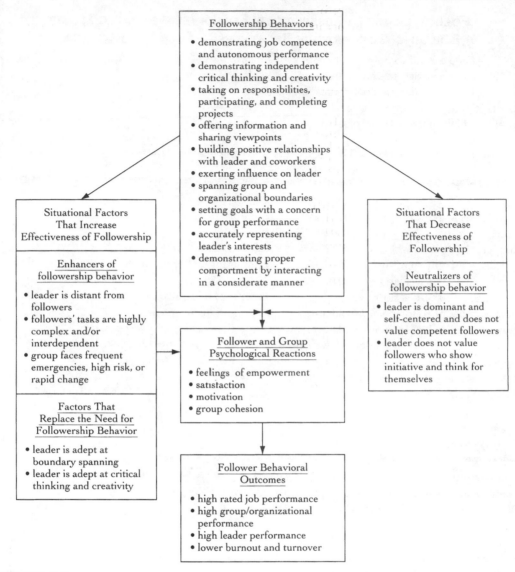

FIGURE 5-2

Tentative Process Model of Followership

lowership behaviors. Although the relationships shown in figure 5–2 are based on sparse research, we believe they will be strongly confirmed in the future.

Figure 5-3 shows how followers can apply the information contained in figure 5-2. The questions contained in box 1 at the top of figure 5-3 help identify situations where effective followership behaviors will be especially needed and effective. If the answer is "yes" to one or more of these questions, then the active followership behaviors shown in box 2 are needed, and followers should carry them out. The follower can then assess the situation to determine if modifications can be made to make the followership behaviors more effective (box 3). Enterprising followers can sometimes increase the distance from their leader, or identify rapidly changing environmental factors that will increase the leader's appreciation for their active followership. Once these situational factors are addressed, the follower then reevaluates the questions in box 1, provides the needed followership behaviors in box 2, and so on in a dynamic fashion.

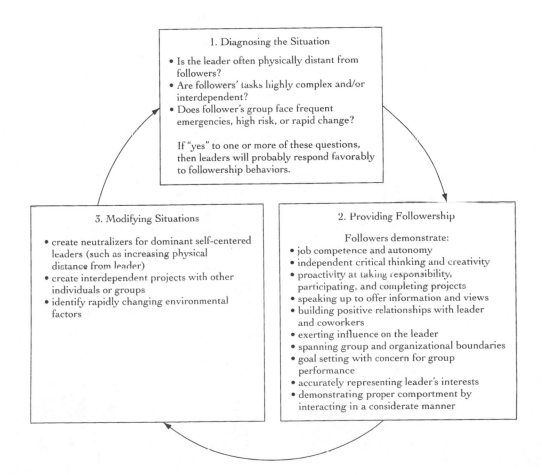

FIGURE 5-3

Applying the Tentative Model of Followership

APPENDICES

EDITOR'S NOTE:

Inside you'll find questionnaires, checklists, self-assessments, and tools to help individuals to become better team members and teams to perform at the highest levels. Each is self-explanatory and is designed to be used by itself or combined with others as you choose.

Appendix A

*T*eam-Maturity Scale

Based on your observations of your work unit, evaluate the maturity of your group as a mature team.

1. How are goals established in your work unit?

1	2	3	4	5
The group leader sets the goals for us.		We discuss goals, but finally the leader sets the goals.		We all work together to arrive at our goals.

2. How committed are the people in your unit to working hard to achieve the goals?

1	2	3	4	5
People demonstrate surface-level commitment to the goals.		People work at achieving the goals with which they agree.		Everyone is deeply committed to all of the goals.

3. How are decisions made in your unit?

1	2	3	4	5
The boss tells us what the decisions are.		We discuss issues, but the boss makes all final decisions.		We all make appropriate decisions by consensus.

4. How well do people collaborate with others?

1	2	3	4	5
Each person works independently of others.		There is some collaboration when people are pushed to it.		People easily work with others as needed.

5. How much do people trust each other—to carry out assignments, to keep confidences, to do their share, to help when needed?

1	2	3	4	5
There is almost no trust at all.		Some trust exists, but it is not widespread.		There is high trust among all.

6. How would you describe the unit leader's management style?

1	2	3	4	5
S/he is authoritarian—runs things his/her way.		S/he is consultative—consults with us, but has final say.		S/he is participative—is part of the team.

7. How open and free are communications in unit meetings?

1	2	3	4	5
Communication is very closed, guarded, and careful.		People will talk about matters that are safe.		Everyone feels free to say what they want.

8. When people have differences or conflicts, how are they handled?

1	2	3	4	5
Conflicts are ignored, or people are told not to worry about them.		Conflicts are sometimes looked at but are usually left hanging.		Conflicts are discussed openly and resolved.

9. What is the level of people feeling they are part of a team?

1	2	3	4	5
People really don't feel like they are part of a team.		Occasionally, there is a sense of team spirit.		There is a deep feeling of team pride and spirit.

10. To what extent do people in your work unit understand what people need from each other in order to achieve common goals?

1	2	3	4	5
People really don't understand what others need from them.		There is some understanding between some people.		Each person truly understands what others need from him/her.

11. To what extent do people really understand, accept, and implement decisions and assignments with commitment?

1	2	3	4	5
People just do what they are told. There is little personal commitment.		At times there is some commitment to decisions and assignments; at other times there is not.		There is full commitment by everyone to all decisions and assignments.

12. How supportive and helpful are the unit leaders and members toward one another?

1	2	3	4	5
There is little support among leaders and members.		There is some support and help some of the time.		There is high support and help most of the time.

13. Does your work unit ever stop and critique how well they are working together?

1	2	3	4	5
We never stop to critique how well we are doing.		We occasionally take time to critique how well we are doing.		We regularly take time to critique how well we are doing.

14. Generally how satisfied are you with the way your work unit functions as a team?

1	2	3	4	5
I am not satisfied at all.		Sometimes I'm satisfied; sometimes not.		I am very satisfied almost all of the time.

15. To what extent is the work unit dependent on the unit leader to move ahead and get work done?

1	2	3	4	5
Completely dependent on the leader.		Somewhat dependent.		Able to work independently as needed.

16. Is your unit leader capable of building your group into an effective team?

1	2	3	4	5
Not capable at all.		Somewhat capable.		Completely capable.

17. Do group members in your work unit have the knowledge and skills necessary to build an effective team?

1	2	3	4	5
Skills and knowledge are not there.		Some people have skills and knowledge.		Members have adequate skills and knowledge.

18. Are people willing to take a risk and try out new actions to make the team better?

1	2	3	4	5
No one is willing to risk.		Some willingness to risk.		High willingness to risk.

19. Group members are willing to make personal sacrifices for the good of the team.

1	2	3	4	5
Almost never.		Sometimes.		Almost always.

20. People feel they know how their work contributes to the goals of the total group.

1	2	3	4	5
No real understanding.		Some understanding.		Complete understanding.

21. Team members know how to get work done and maintain good relationships at the same time.

1	2	3	4	5
Don't do this well.		Have some ability.		Completely able to do this.

22. Team members are sensitive to the needs of other members of the team.

1	2	3	4	5
No sensitivity.		Some sensitivity.		Complete sensitivity.

Scoring: Each person should add up his or her score for the twenty-two items and divide that total by 22. This will give the perceived maturity score of the team by that member. If you add up all of the individual scores and divide by the number of members of the team, you will find the team's rating of its maturity. If the ratings are 3.75 or higher, there is evidence that there is an appropriate level of maturity. If the scores are between 2.5 and 3.75, this indicates that maturity is at a midlevel, and there is still work to be done by the team and team leader. If the score is between 1.00 and 2.50, the indications are that the team is at an immature level, and a great deal of team building is needed.

An item analysis, looking at the individual and team scores for each item, will help the team see the areas that need the most work to move the team to a higher level of maturity.

*This scale used with Permission of Novations, Inc. Provo, Utah.

$\mathcal{A}$ppendix $\mathcal{B}$

$\mathcal{L}$eaders Surround Themselves with Strong Staff

Most leaders seek advice from a few select, competent individuals on their staffs—people they can depend on for loyalty, competency, a broad perspective, and just plain good advice. It should be rather obvious, then, why staff selection is very critical to a leader's success. Many people have lost their opportunities to lead because they failed to surround themselves with the best advisers. Leaders who operate in a vacuum will not remain in leadership roles very long.

Successful leaders have the capacity to develop an inner circle of staff people who are loyal and competent. A strong staff is especially important when the leader has a large span of control (span of control is the total number of employees for whom the leader or manager is responsible).

Good communication skills help to create and maintain the close bond between a leader and his or her staff. Staff meetings should create an *esprit de corps*—a spirit that encourages loyalty and avoids dissension. Also, staff meetings should provide everyone with the opportunity to speak on all issues. And each staff meeting should contribute to the improvement of vertical relationships (between the leader and her or his staff) as well as of horizontal relationships (among staff members). Most importantly, participants should feel there was some value in the meeting, such as progress toward a goal or clarification of a point, process, or group understanding.

*Elmwood N. Chapman and Sharon Lund O'Neil, *Your Attitude is Showing: A Primer of Human Relations,* 9th Ed., Upper Saddle River, NJ: Prentice Hall, 1999.

MY SMALL-GROUP FACILITATION SKILLS

	Yes	No
Am I relaxed, comfortable, and effective when leading a small-group or team discussion?	☐	☐
Can I perceive and communicate group thinking patterns back to the members, for the best decision to be made?	☐	☐
Can I redirect a complacent group in the right direction, without discouraging contributions from one or more members?	☐	☐
Can I get all group members to contribute something to a discussion?	☐	☐

What percentage of improvement would you like to see in your small-group communication skills?

%

A good leader's staff becomes an extension of his or her image or leadership style. The staff's extension of the leader's style does not mean that everyone must become an image of the leader. It means that each staff member, in her or his own way, contributes to the leader's style. In turn, as the leader increases her or his effectiveness through a competent staff, the leader's overall impact is enhanced.

Some experts give staff selection top priority, but it is not only selection that counts. Leaders know that the development of good relationships with all individuals through group communication is an important rule to follow. All highly successful leaders—coaches, ministers, community leaders, corporate executives, and politicians—eventually become small-group communication experts. Many leaders take special seminars early in their development, as well as periodically, to enhance these skills.

Leaders Must Become Superior Speakers/Presenters

All leaders take advantage of opportunities to present to large groups. Some are inspirational, and their leadership image is greatly enhanced. Some are moderately inspirational, and their image is protected. Those who are credible (but noninspirational) speakers need to compensate by improving their image in other areas. Positive body language, or using good nonverbal skills, is an excellent way to create a positive reaction from an audience.

When it comes to leadership, becoming an outstanding speaker is a major advantage. If you work on making your attitude as positive as you can, you will have more confidence in making presentations to large groups. A positive attitude also is easily detected by audiences. Remember, *Your Attitude Is Showing** in everything you do!

Answer these questions about your presentation skills.

MY LARGE-GROUP PRESENTATION SKILLS

	Yes	No
Do I show confidence and a positive attitude when I speak to large audiences?	☐	☐
Am I good at audience analysis to determine how I am being perceived?	☐	☐
Am I skillful at receiving, interpreting, and answering difficult questions in large groups?	☐	☐
After speaking to a large group, do I feel good about myself and my presentation skills?	☐	☐

Write the percentage of improvement you would like to see its your large group presentation/speaking skills.

%

Elmwood N. Chapman and Sharon Lund O'Neil, *Your Attitude is Showing: A Primer of Human Relations,* 9th Ed., Upper Saddle River, NJ: Prentice Hall, 1999.

$\mathcal{A}$ppendix C

$\mathcal{H}$ ow Good Are My Listening Skills?

Respond to each of the 15 statements using the following scale:

1 = Strongly agree
2 = Agree
3 = Neither agree or disagree
4 = Disagree
5 = Strongly disagree

1. I frequently attempt to listen to several conversations at the same time.

   1   2   3   4   5

2. I like people to give me only the facts and then let me make my own interpretation.

   1   2   3   4   5

3. I sometimes pretend to pay attention to people.

   1   2   3   4   5

4. I consider myself a good judge of nonverbal communications.

   1   2   3   4   5

5. I usually know what another person is going to say before he or she says it.

   1   2   3   4   5

The Prentice Hall Self-Assessment Library: Insights into Your Skills, Abilities, and Interests, Edited by Stephen P. Robbins. Copyright © 2000 by Prentice Hall, Inc.

6. I usually end conversations that don't interest me by diverting my attention from the speaker.

   1   2   3   4   5

7. I frequently nod, frown, or provide other nonverbal cues to let the speaker know how I feel about what he or she is saying.

   1   2   3   4   5

8. I usually respond immediately when someone has finished talking.

   1   2   3   4   5

9. I evaluate what is being said while it is being said.

   1   2   3   4   5

10. I usually formulate a response while the other person is still talking.

    1   2   3   4   5

11. The speaker's "delivery" style frequently keeps me from listening to content.

    1   2   3   4   5

12. I usually ask people to clarify what they have said rather than guessing at the meaning.

    1   2   3   4   5

13. I make a concerted effort to understand other people's points of view.

    1   2   3   4   5

14. I frequently hear what I expect to hear rather than what is said.

    1   2   3   4   5

15. Most people feel that I have understood their point of view when we disagree.

    1   2   3   4   5

To obtain your score, add up all the ratings you circled for questions 1–15.

ANALYSIS

Effective communicators have developed good listening skills. This instrument is designed to provide you with some insights into your listening skills. Scores range from 15 to 75. The higher your score, the better listener you are. While any cutoffs are essentially arbitrary, few people score above 60. If you score 60 or above, your listening skills are fairly well honed. Scores of 40 or less indicate you need to make a serious effort at improving your listening skills.

Source: Reprinted from *Supervisory Management,* January 1989. © 1989 American Management Association, New York. http://www.amanet.org. All rights reserved.

How Good Am I at Giving Feedback?

For each of the following pairs, identify the statement that most closely matches what you normally do when you give feedback to someone else.

1. a. Describe the behavior
   b. Evaluate the behavior

2. a. Focus on the feelings that the behavior evokes
   b. Tell the person what they should be doing differently

3. a. Give specific instances of the behavior
   b. Generalize

4. a. Deal only with behavior that the person can control
   b. Sometimes focus on something the person can do nothing about

5. a. Tell the person as soon as possible after the behavior
   b. Sometimes wait too long

6. a. Focus on the effect the behavior has on me
   b. Try to figure out why the individual did what he or she did

7. a. Balance negative feedback with positive feedback
   b. Sometimes focus only on the negative

8. a. Do some soul searching to make sure that the reason I am giving the feedback is to help the other person or to strengthen our relationship
   b. Sometimes give feedback to punish, win, or dominate the other person

ANALYSIS

Along with listening skills, feedback skills comprise the other primary component of effective communication. This instrument is designed to assess how good you are at providing feedback.

In this assessment instrument, the "a" responses are your self-perceived strengths and the "b" responses are your self-perceived weaknesses. By looking at the proportion of your "a" and "b" responses, you will be able to see how effective you feel you are when giving feedback and determine where your strengths and weaknesses lie.

Source: Developing Managerial Skills in Organizational Behavior by Mainiero/Tromley, © 1994. Adapted by permission of Prentice-Hall, Inc., Upper Saddle River, NJ.

*A*m I a Team Player?

Use the following scale to identify the extent of your agreement with the 20 statements:

1 = Strongly agree
2 = Agree
3 = Slightly agree
4 = Neither agree or disagree
5 = Slightly disagree
6 = Disagree
7 = Strongly disagree

1. Only those who depend on themselves get ahead in life.

    1   2   3   4   5   6   7

2. To be superior, a person must stand alone.

    1   2   3   4   5   6   7

3. If you want something done right, you've got to do it yourself.

    1   2   3   4   5   6   7

4. What happens to me is my own doing.

    1   2   3   4   5   6   7

5. In the long run the only person you can count on is yourself.

    1   2   3   4   5   6   7

6. Winning is everything.

    1   2   3   4   5   6   7

7. I feel that winning is important in both work and games.

    1   2   3   4   5   6   7

8. Success is the most important thing in life.

    1   2   3   4   5   6   7

9. It annoys me when other people perform better than I do.

    1   2   3   4   5   6   7

10. Doing your best isn't enough; it is important to win.

    1   2   3   4   5   6   7

11. I prefer to work with others in a group rather than working alone.

    1   2   3   4   5   6   7

12. Given the choice, I would rather do a job where I can work alone rather than doing a job where I have to work with others in a group.

    1   2   3   4   5   6   7

13. Working with a group is better than working alone.

    1   2   3   4   5   6   7

14. People should be made aware that if they are going to be part of a group then they are sometimes going to have to do things they don't want to do.

    1   2   3   4   5   6   7

15. People who belong to a group should realize that they're not always going to get what they personally want.

    1   2   3   4   5   6   7

16. People in a group should realize that they sometimes are going to have to make sacrifices for the sake of the group as a whole.

    1   2   3   4   5   6   7

17. People in a group should be willing to make sacrifices for the sake of the group's well-being.

    1   2   3   4   5   6   7

18. A group is most productive when its members do what they want to do rather than what the group wants them to do.

    1   2   3   4   5   6   7

19. A group is most efficient when its members do what they think is best rather than doing what the group wants them to do.

    1   2   3   4   5   6   7

20. A group is most productive when its members follow their own interests and concerns.

    1   2   3   4   5   6   7

To obtain your score, add up all the ratings you circled for questions 1–20.

ANALYSIS

As organizations have redesigned jobs around teams, the ability to be a good team player has become increasingly important. This instrument can provide you with some insights into whether you'd fit well on a team, in contrast to working alone. It essentially taps individualistic vs. collectivist orientation. Your total score will be between 20 and 140. The higher your score, the higher your collectivist orientation, so high scores are more compatible with being a team player. For comparative purposes, 492 undergraduate students enrolled in an introductory management course at a large U.S. university scored an average of approximately 89. We might speculate that scores below 69 indicate a strong individualistic ethic, and scores above 109 indicate a strong team mentality.

Source: Reprinted with permission of Academy of Management, P.O. Box 3020, Briarcliff Manor, NY 10510–8020. "Studies of Individualism—Collectivism's Effects on Cooperation in Groups," J.A. Wagner III, 1995. Reproduced by permission of the publisher via Copyright Clearance Center, Inc.

*H*ow Good Am I at Building and Leading a Team?

Use the following rating scale to respond to the 18 questions on building and leading an effective team:

1 = Strongly disagree
2 = Disagree
3 = Slightly disagree
4 = Slightly agree
5 = Agree
6 = Strongly agree

1. I am knowledgeable about the different stages of development that teams can go through in their life cycles.

   1   2   3   4   5   6

2. When a team forms, I make certain that all team members are introduced to one another at the outset.

   1   2   3   4   5   6

3. When the team first comes together, I provide directions, answer team members' questions, and clarify goals, expectations, and procedures.

   1   2   3   4   5   6

4. I help team members establish a foundation of trust among one another and between themselves and me.

   1   2   3   4   5   6

5. I ensure that standards of excellence—not mediocrity or mere acceptability—characterize the team's work.

   1   2   3   4   5   6

6. I provide a great deal of feedback to team members regarding their performance.

   1   2   3   4   5   6

7. I encourage team members to balance individual autonomy with interdependence among other team members.

   1   2   3   4   5   6

8. I help team members become at least as committed to the success of the team as to their own personal success.

   1   2   3   4   5   6

9. I help members learn to play roles that assist the team in accomplishing its tasks as well as building strong interpersonal relationships.

   1   2   3   4   5   6

10. I articulate a clear, exciting, passionate vision of what the team can achieve.

    1   2   3   4   5   6

11. I help team members become committed to the team vision.

    1   2   3   4   5   6

12. I encourage a win/win philosophy in the team; that is, when one member wins, every member wins.

    1   2   3   4   5   6

13. I help the team avoid "groupthink" or making the group's survival more important than accomplishing its goal.

    1   2   3   4   5   6

14. I use formal process management procedures to help the group become faster, more efficient, and more productive, and to prevent errors.

    1   2   3   4   5   6

15. I encourage team members to represent the team's vision, goals, and accomplishments to outsiders.

    1   2   3   4   5   6

16. I diagnose and capitalize on the team's core competence.

    1   2   3   4   5   6

17. I encourage the team to achieve dramatic breakthrough innovations as well as small continuous improvements.

    1   2   3   4   5   6

18. I help the team work toward preventing mistakes, not just correcting them after-the-fact.

    1   2   3   4   5   6

To obtain your score, add up all the ratings you circled for questions 1–18.

ANALYSIS

The authors of this instrument propose that it assesses team development behaviors in five areas: diagnosing team development (items 1, 16); managing the forming stage (2–4); managing the conforming stage (6–9, 13); managing the storming stage (10–12, 14, 15), and managing the performing stage (5, 17, 18). Your score will range between 18 and 108.

    Based on a norm group of 500 business students, the following can help estimate where you are relative to others:

Total score of 95 or above	=	You're in the top quartile
72–94	=	You're in the second quartile
60–71	=	You're in the third quartile
Below 60	=	You're in the bottom quartile

Source: Adapted from D. A. Whetten and K. S. Cameron, *Developing Management Skills,* 3rd ed. (New York: HarperCollins, 1995), pp. 534–35.

$\mathcal{H}$ow Power-Oriented Am I?

For each of statement, select the response that most closely resembles your attitude. Use the following ratings scale for your responses:

1 = Disagree a lot
2 = Disagree a little
3 = Neutral
4 = Agree a little
5 = Agree a lot

1. The best way to handle people is to tell them what they want to hear.

   1   2   3   4   5

2. When you ask someone to do something for you, it is best to give the real reason for wanting it rather than giving reasons that might carry more weight.

   1   2   3   4   5

3. Anyone who completely trusts anyone else is asking for trouble.

   1   2   3   4   5

4. It is hard to get ahead without cutting corners here and there.

   1   2   3   4   5

5. It is safest to assume that all people have a vicious streak, and it will come out when they are given a chance.

   1   2   3   4   5

6. One should take action only when it is morally right.

   1   2   3   4   5

7. Most people are basically good and kind.

   1   2   3   4   5

8. There is no excuse for lying to someone else.

   1   2   3   4   5

9. Most people more easily forget the death of their father than the loss of their property.

   1   2   3   4   5

10. Generally speaking, people won't work hard unless they're forced to do so.

    1   2   3   4   5

ANALYSIS

This instrument was designed to compute your Machiavellianism (Mach) score. Machiavelli wrote in the 16th century on how to gain and manipulate power. An individual with a high-Mach score is pragmatic, maintains emotional distance, and believes that ends can justify means.

The National Opinion Research Center, which used this instrument in a random sample of American adults, found that the national average was 25.

High-Machs are more likely to manipulate more, win more, are persuaded less, and persuade others more than do low-Machs. High-Machs are also more likely to shade the truth or act unethically in ambiguous situations where the outcome is important to them.

Source: R. Christie and F. L. Geis, *Studies in Machiavellianism.* @Academic Press, 1970. With permission.

What's My Preferred Type of Power?

Respond to the 20 statements by thinking in terms of how you prefer to influence others. Use the following scale for your answers:

1 = Strongly disagree
2 = Disagree
3 = Neither agree or disagree
4 = Agree
5 = Strongly agree

To influence others, I would prefer to:

1. Increase their pay level

    1   2   3   4   5

2. Make them feel valued

    1   2   3   4   5

3. Give undesirable job assignments

    1   2   3   4   5

4. Make them feel like I approve of them

    1   2   3   4   5

5. Make them feel that they have commitments to meet

    1   2   3   4   5

6. Make them feel personally accepted

    1   2   3   4   5

7. Make them feel important

    1   2   3   4   5

8. Give them good technical suggestions

    1   2   3   4   5

9. Make the work difficult for them

    1   2   3   4   5

10. Share my experience and/or training

    1   2   3   4   5

11. Make things unpleasant here

    1   2   3   4   5

12. Make being at work distasteful

    1   2   3   4   5

13. Influence their getting a pay increase

    1   2   3   4   5

14. Make them feel like they should satisfy their job requirements

    1   2   3   4   5

15. Provide them with sound job-related advice

    1   2   3   4   5

16. Provide them with special benefits

    1   2   3   4   5

17. Influence their getting a promotion

    1   2   3   4   5

18. Give them the feeling that they have responsibilities to fulfill

    1   2   3   4   5

19. Provide them with needed technical knowledge

    1   2   3   4   5

20. Make them recognize that they have tasks to accomplish

    1   2   3   4   5

ANALYSIS

Five bases of power have been identified. Reward (based on the ability to distribute valuable rewards); coercive (based on fear); legitimate (based on formal position); expert (based on possessing knowledge or skill); and referent (based on others' desire to identify with you).

A high score (4 or greater) on any of the five dimensions implies that you prefer to influence others by using that particular form of power. A low score (2 or less) suggests that you prefer not to employ this power base.

Managerial positions come with legitimate, reward, and coercive powers. However, you don't have to be a manager to have power. If you're not in a position of formal authority, you can still be a powerful person in your organization if you focus on developing your expert and referent power bases.

Source: Adapted from T .R. Hinken and C.A. Schermerhorn, "Development and Application of New Scales to Measure the French and Raven (1959) Bases of Social Power," *Journal of Applied Psychology,* August 1989, pp. 561–67.

What's My Preferred Conflict-Handling Style?

When you differ with someone, how do you respond? Use the following rating scale to record your answers:

1 = Practically never
2 = Once in a great while
3 = Sometimes
4 = Fairly often
5 = Very often

1. I work to come out victorious, no matter what.

    1   2   3   4   5

2. I try to put the needs of others above my own.

    1   2   3   4   5

3. I look for a mutually satisfactory solution.

    1   2   3   4   5

4. I try not to get involved in conflicts.

    1   2   3   4   5

5. I strive to investigate issues thoroughly and jointly.

    1   2   3   4   5

6. I never back away from a good argument.

    1   2   3   4   5

7. I strive to foster harmony.

    1   2   3   4   5

8. I negotiate to get a portion of what I propose.

    1   2   3   4   5

9. I avoid open discussions of controversial subjects.

    1   2   3   4   5

10. I openly share information with others in resolving disagreements.

    1   2   3   4   5

11. I would rather win than end up compromising.

    1   2   3   4   5

12. I go along with suggestions of others.

    1   2   3   4   5

13. I look for a middle ground to resolve disagreements.

    1   2   3   4   5

14. I keep my true opinions to myself to avoid hard feelings.

    1   2   3   4   5

15. I encourage the open sharing of concerns and issues.

    1   2   3   4   5

16. I am reluctant to admit I am wrong.

    1   2   3   4   5

17. I try to help others avoid losing face in a disagreement.

    1   2   3   4   5

18. I stress the advantages of give-and-take.

    1   2   3   4   5

19. I agree early on, rather than argue about a point.

    1   2   3   4   5

20. I state my position as only one point of view.

    1   2   3   4   5

To obtain your score for each of the five categories mentioned, add the ratings for the items noted for that category.

ANALYSIS

Research has identified five conflict-handling styles. They are defined as follows:

> Competing = A desire to satisfy one's interests, regardless of the impact on the other party to the conflict. Items 1, 6, 11, and 16 in this instrument tap this style.
>
> Collaborating = Where the parties to a conflict each desire to satisfy fully the concerns of all parties. Items 5, 10, 15, and 20 in this instrument tap this style.
>
> Avoiding = The desire to withdraw from or suppress the conflict. Items 4, 9, 14, and 19 in this instrument tap this style.
>
> Accommodating = Willingness of one party in a conflict to place the opponent's interests above his or her own. Items 2, 7, 12, and 17 in this instrument tap this style.
>
> Compromising = Where each party to a conflict is willing to give up something. Items 3, 8, 13, and 18 in this instrument tap this style.

Your conflict-handling score within each category will range from 4 to 20. The category you score highest in is your preferred conflict-handling style. Your next-highest total is your secondary style.

Ideally, we should adjust our conflict-handling style to the situation. For instance, avoidance works well when a conflict is trivial, when emotions are running high and time is needed to cool them down, or when the potential disruption from a more assertive action outweighs the benefits of a resolution. In contrast, competing works well when you need a quick resolution on important issues where unpopular actions must be taken, or when commitment by others to your solution is not critical. However, the evidence indicates that we all have a preferred style for handling conflicts. When "push comes to shove," this is the style we tend to rely on. Your score on this instrument provides you with insight into this preferred style. Use this information to work against your natural tendencies when the situation requires a different style.

Source: Based on conflict dimensions defined in K. W Thomas, "Conflict and Conflict Management," in M. Dunnette (ed.), *Handbook of Industrial and Organizational Psychology* (Chicago: Rand McNally, 1976), pp. 889–935.

$\mathcal{A}$ppendix $\mathcal{D}$

$\mathcal{E}$xample Items from Peer Evaluations and 360-Degree Performance Evaluations

Some people, may be unfamiliar with what a typical 360-degree evaluation might look like. The fact is, there are no standards. In this appendix, we present examples of two 360-degree evaluation tools. The first one is a peer evaluation system; it is brief and is designed for students enrolled in a full-time M.B.A. program. The second one is much more extensive and designed to provide senior managers with confidential feedback about their leadership abilities and potential.

PETE: PERSONAL EFFECTIVENESS IN TEAM ENVIRONMENTS

Personal Effectiveness in Team Environments (PETE) is a Web-based peer evaluation system that enables students to give each other anonymous feedback on their team skills. The method is simple and completely automated. At the end of each academic quarter, students sign on to a Web page and provide anonymous feedback to their teammates by rating each other on 10 key criteria related to improving team-based outcomes (defined by Kellogg's Organization Behavior Department). The computer then compiles mean and standard deviation scores for each student. After all responses are compiled, students automatically receive a private e-mail with their personal scores from each of their teams. To enable them to track their progress in building their team skills over time, students also receive their scores from prior quarters.

Making the Team: A Guide for Managers, by Leigh L. Thompson. Copyright © 2000 by Prentice Hall, Inc.

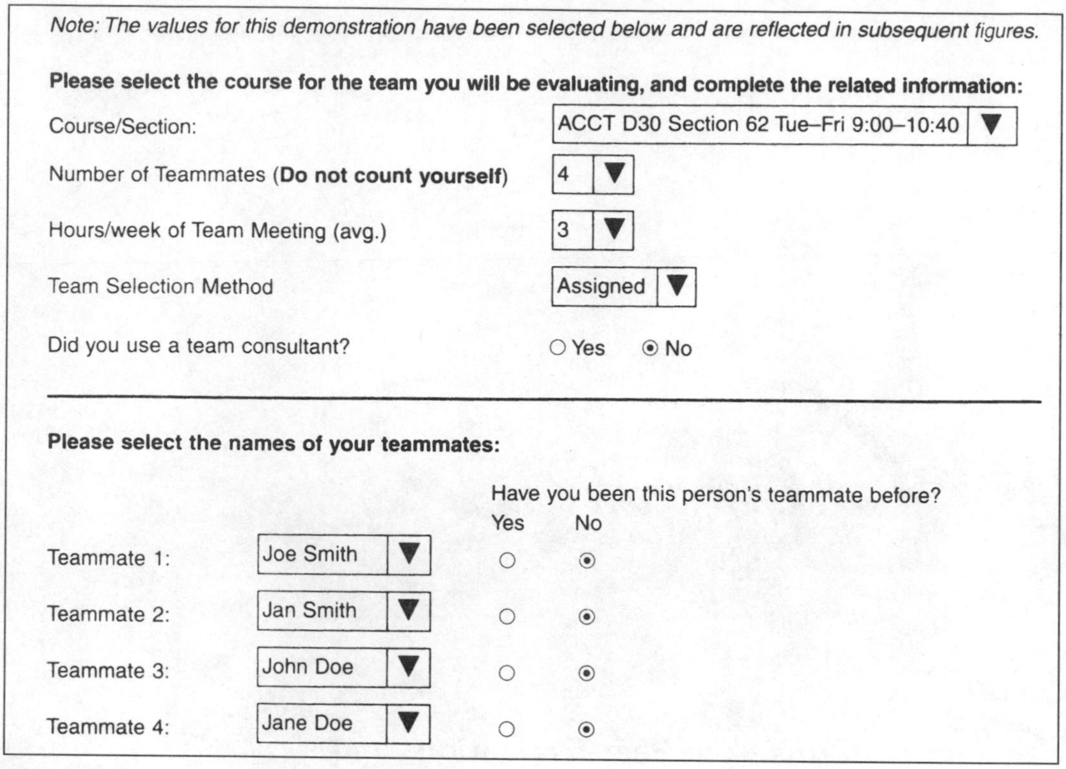

Note: The values for this demonstration have been selected below and are reflected in subsequent figures.

Please select the course for the team you will be evaluating, and complete the related information:

Course/Section: ACCT D30 Section 62 Tue–Fri 9:00–10:40 ▼

Number of Teammates (**Do not count yourself**)   4 ▼

Hours/week of Team Meeting (avg.)   3 ▼

Team Selection Method   Assigned ▼

Did you use a team consultant?   ○ Yes   ⊙ No

Please select the names of your teammates:

Have you been this person's teammate before?
Yes   No

Teammate 1:   Joe Smith ▼   ○   ⊙

Teammate 2:   Jan Smith ▼   ○   ⊙

Teammate 3:   John Doe ▼   ○   ⊙

Teammate 4:   Jane Doe ▼   ○   ⊙

FIGURE A-1

Selecting a Team to Evaluate Using PETE
Source: Adapted from PETE Web site at *http://faculty-web.at.nwu.edu/kellogg/pete/allenctr.html*

The system allows students to get direct and timely feedback on their team skills. They can track their skill development in particular areas (e.g., leadership) over time and across different teams and projects to focus on skill development. What's more, students learn how to use peer-based reviews. The automated process means that the information is collected and disseminated efficiently.

Figure A-1 illustrates how students using the PETE Web site can select the specific team and teammates they want to evaluate; Figure A-2 illustrates a sample matrix for evaluating a teammate and lists all 10 items on the PETE questionnaire; and Figure A-3 illustrates a sample of an output feedback that a student might receive from the PETE system.

INDUSTRIAL EXAMPLE OF 360-DEGREE EVALUATIONS

The questionnaire in Table A-1 from RHR Europe Company is designed to assess leadership behavior among senior employees. These behaviors encompass critical success factors in the company. The leaders choose at least nine people (one or two line managers; four or five peers; four or five subordinates) to complete the questionnaire, which is processed confidentially.

Each teammate receives feedback in the matrix below (one matrix per question; one question per Web site frame):

Teammate	Strongly Disagree 1	2	3	4	Neutral 5	6	7	8	9	Strongly Agree 10
Jane Doe	O	O	O	O	O	O	O	O	O	O
John Doe	O	O	O	O	O	O	O	O	O	O
Jan Smith	O	O	O	O	O	O	O	O	O	O
Joe Smith	O	O	O	O	O	O	O	O	O	O

Questions:

1. This teammate completed tasks on time and to specification.
2. This teammate encouraged innovation among teammates.
3. This teammate gave timely and honest feedback.
4. This teammate nondefensively accepted suggestions and critical comments.
5. This teammate shared essential information with teammates.
6. This teammate avoided destructive and divisive tactics, such as put-downs or playing games.
7. This teammate put self on the line to deal with difficult issues.
8. This teammate challenges the status quo when necessary.
9. This teammate communicates ideas efficiently.
10. This teammate balanced talking/telling with listening/hearing.

FIGURE A-2

PETE Questionnaire Items and Rating System

Source: Adapted from PETE Web site at *http://faculty-web.at.nwu.edu/kellogg/pete/allenctr.html*

The **Mean** and *Standard Deviaiton* of the evaluations you received for each class are listed below.

The aggregate statistics combine all of the peer evaluations you reveived for all your classes last term, including classes that lacked sufficient respondents to report individually; however, stats for sections in which you did not complete a PETE evaluation are not included and are omitted in the aggretate stats.

John Doe

Scale: 1-strongly disagree 10-strongly agree *Fall 1998–1999*	Completed timely and accurate work	Encouraged innovation	Focused on goal	Took suggestions and criticism	Respectful of individuals	Created atmosphere of trust	Challenged majority opinion	Changed own opinion as needed	Communicated ideas efficiently	Balanced talking and listening
Accounting D30	9.3 *0.6*	7.7 *2.3*	9.3 *0.6*	9.7 *0.6*	9.7 *0.6*	9.7 *0.6*	9.3 *0.6*	9.3 *0.6*	9.7 *0.6*	10 *0*
Economics D30	*Sorry, Since you did not complete a PETE evaluation for this section, you are unable to receive scores for this section.*									
Management & Strategy D30	9 *1.7*	8.7 *2.3*	9 *1.7*	8.7 *2.3*	9 *1.7*	9.3 *1.2*	9 *1.7*	9.3 *1.2*	9 *1*	9.3 *1.2*
Marketing D30	*Fewer than three responses; insufficient number to report for this section.*									
Org. Behavior D30	9 *1.7*	8.3 *2.1*	8.7 *2.3*	8.7 *2.3*	9.3 *1.2*	9.3 *1.2*	9 *1.7*	9.3 *1.2*	9.3 *1.2*	9.3 *1.2*
Aggregate	9.1 *1.3*	8.2 *2*	9 *1.5*	9 *1.7*	9.3 *1.1*	9.4 *0.9*	9.1 *1.3*	9.3 *0.9*	9.3 *0.9*	9.6 *0.9*

FIGURE A-3

Sample PETE Output Feedback Sheet

Source: Adapted from PETE Web site at *http://faculty-web.at.nwu.edu/kellogg/pete/allenctr.html*

TABLE A-1   360-DEGREE LEADERSHIP

Key Leadership Quality	Questions
Provide Vision: "Developing vision and demonstrating commitment to the company's strategies, and inspiring a sense of direction"	• Establishes initiatives that promote a global mindset organization • Creates a compelling scenario of the future involvement with the team and inspires buy-in • Identifies and applies models and processes that will stimulate behaviors in support of the company's vision • Puts the vision in practice by adopting desired behaviors and corresponding values • Actively gains information concerning markets and environment factors that can have an impact on strategies • Ensures that team and individual objectives support the company's vision • Creates a sense of team purpose according to vision and strategies • Shares insights and facilitates understanding and open communication around vision • Is able to imagine scenarios that are in discontinuity with the existing processes or products
Show Entrepreneurship: "Thinking ahead, seizing opportunities to develop new markets, products, or services and taking calculated risks to achieve growth"	• Demonstrates passion and energy to move forward • Invents strategies using various sources of data and individual experiences • Encourages proactive behaviors resulting in business growth • Takes calculated risks, then decides • Supports and rewards self-starting behaviors of collaborators • Seeks solutions beyond current practices • Demonstrates an action-oriented attitude • Explores and optimizes the use of resources and expertise available within the team • Communicates information and personal perceptions on new business opportunities for the company
Influence and Convince: "Persuading others to share a point of view, to adopt a specific position, or to take a course of action"	• Determines appropriate strategies to influence people • Builds networks and uses the authority or power of others to convince • Develops propositions tailored to the interest of the different parties involved • Builds a climate of trust • Expresses perspective with courage and integrity • Listens to others' viewpoints or objections and tests their ideas • Seeks to convince by underlining potential benefits of proposed solutions

- Negotiates proposals to determine common course of action
- Gains team adherence through effective communication

Achieve Results:
"Directing the activity of others by setting challenging goals for personal and team accomplishment and by controlling their achievements"

- Sets the example by showing high performance
- Sets challenging goals that require a "step change"
- Develops strategies and facilitates actions to overcome barriers
- Initiates corrective actions to address performance problems
- Supports and works alongside others to help improve performance and results
- Introduces and applies new methods within the company
- Communicates performance expectations to others
- Creates a performance-oriented spirit within the team
- Provides regular feedback on achieved performance
- Puts in place performance measurement tools

Focus on Customer.
"Managing proactively the various customer demands while maintaining a consistent level of effectiveness"

- Demonstrates a "customer first" attitude and meets with customers regularly
- Is involved in the customer's decision-making process
- Identifies customer needs and communicates relevant customer-related information
- Acts as an advocate by influencing the company on the customer's behalf
- Initiates actions that add value to the customer
- Ensures team priorities and cooperation are in line with customer service requirements
- Asks customers for feedback on service quality
- Ensures that performance matches the customer's needs
- Keeps close to customers' business evaluations
- Is responsive to customer complaints and keeps word

Enhance Cooperation and Adaptation:
"Managing people and teams across businesses and cultures"

- Creates an environment that fosters and rewards cooperation among diverse work teams
- Identifies interdependencies and understands the dynamics of bringing different cultures together
- Has gained credibility in managing outside home country
- Challenges self and others to consider issues from a wider and more global perspective
- Is sensitive and adaptable to other cultures
- Understands the challenges and opportunities of doing business globally
- Shares best practices, solutions, and a wide array of management processes across businesses
- Explores diverse methods of learning and acting
- Encourages relationships between people to enhance trust and communication across distances and differences

TABLE A-1 360-DEGREE LEADERSHIP *(CONTINUED)*	
Key Leadership Quality	**Questions**
Empower: "Allocating decision-making authority and creating sense of ownership of the job, missions, or project assignments"	• Sets the example in creating a collaborative team spirit to stimulate initiative • Facilitates the free expression of ideas by showing tolerance such that others are willing to act • Approves and facilitates decision-making among collaborators and is supportive in times of crisis • Exposes staff to situations or challenges outside their area of responsibility • Gives credit to others for what they have accomplished • Builds trust and openness with others • Recognizes creativity in others and allows them to experiment • Shows the willingness to delegate authority to the lowest possible level • Communicates standards or criteria by which team members can measure their progress
Manage Change: "Fostering innovation and questioning the existing while maintaining constant effectiveness"	• Addresses the needs for change by anticipating and acting upon trends affecting markets and customers • Determines and explains implications of change on the various components of the organization • Creates an environment that encourages people through continuous improvement processes • Recognizes own mistakes and uses these as a learning opportunity • Thinks outside the box and does not hesitate to change habits • Creates a sense of urgency in others to achieve change • Questions self or solicits feedback to adapt to change requirements, and encourages others to do the same • Maintains operational effectiveness while implementing agreed changes • Ensures persistent followup of change strategies • Allows new ideas to emerge and ensures their purposeful development through team effort
Develop Talents: "Creating a learning and continuous improvement climate with an appropriate level of coaching and organizational support"	• Links business and individual development needs • Identifies potentials and develops them • Identifies areas of need and opportunities for self-development • Actively deploys feedback, guidance, and coaching to support people development • Creates opportunities for others to practice new behaviors and to develop skills for current and future role • Measures progress and evaluates benefits of talent development

- Provides guidance, practical instructions, and directions in training activities
- Recognizes the achievements and development progress of others
- Takes charge of developing effective teams
- Supports the development of collaborators even for responsibilities outside the entity

Note: All questions answered on 4-point scale. I = almost never; 2 = sometimes; 3 = usually; 4 = almost always; CS = can't say

Source: 360 Degree Leadership. RHR International Co., @1998. Reprinted with permission from RHR International Co., Wood Dale, IL.

Appendix E

Reflection

Think of an example of team conflict that escalated out of control. What techniques were used to bring the situation back to a functional level of communication? Were the techniques helpful, or did they add to the conflict? Why?

PROBLEM-SOLVING WORKSHEET

Step 1: Identify the problem

What is happening now? _____

_____

How do you know this is a problem? _____

_____

What is the loss or waste? _____

_____

What are the costs? _____

_____

Teams: Structure, Process, Culture, and Politics, by Eileen K. Aranda, Luis Aranda, with Kristi Conlon. Copyright © 1998 by Prentice Hall, Inc.

What do you want to happen? _____

_____

Step 2: List the possible causes of the problem

_____

_____

_____

_____

_____

_____

Step 3: Categorize the causes

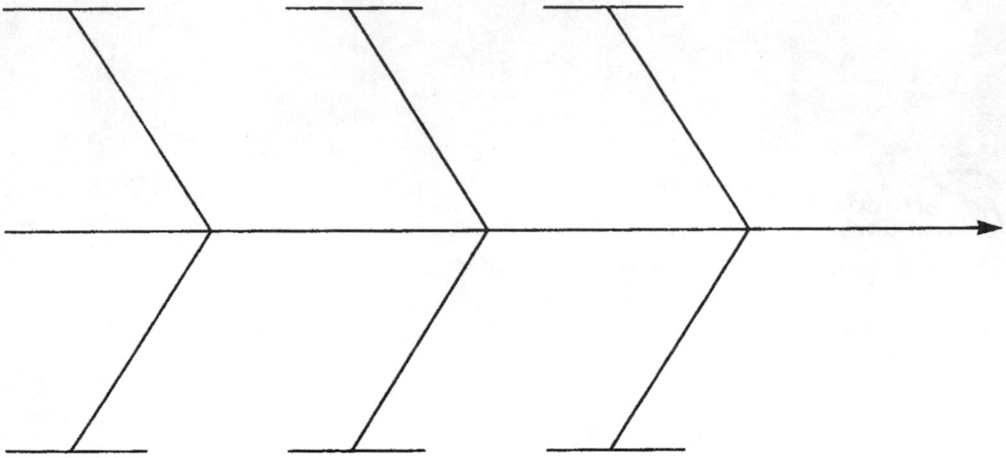

Step 4: Generate possible solutions

_____

_____

_____

_____

_____

_____

_____

_____

Define Criteria for a Good Solution (criteria might include time, cost, resources, career impact, visibility, politics, etc.)

Criteria	Weight
_____	_____
_____	_____
_____	_____
_____	_____
_____	_____

Step 5: Evaluate alternative and decide on solution

Fill in criteria and weight from information developed in Step 4. List each alternative. Then, on a scale from 1 to 10 (with 10 meaning the alternative completely meets the criteria) rate the alternative on each criteria and multiply by its weight. Add the weighted ratings to get the total score. The highest score indicates the most favorable alternative.

Alternative \ Criteria	#1	Wt.	#2	Wt.	#3	Wt.	#4	Wt.	Total

Chosen Solution:

_____

Step 6: Develop action plan for resolution

Action to be taken: _____

Plan:

Step	Priority	Preceding Action	Start and Finish Dates	Responsibility	Success Measure	Reward

Team Decision-Making Summary Sheet

Overview of the issue and desired outcome:

Data gathered (issues, costs, perspectives, etc):

•

•

•

•

•

•

Conclusions from data:

Options to consider:

1.

2.

3.

eflection

Consider a situation where you received team feedback. Was the team able to use the information?

Was there a focus on the future?

Was there a focus on specifics?

Was there a focus on learning?

Now consider your current team. Has the team received feedback? Was the information useful for course correction? How could feedback be more useful in the future?

Team Development Assessment

This form should be completed by individual team members on a regular basis to rate team progress. The forms should then be discussed by all team members.

Purpose

I	2	3	4	5

Purpose is clear.   Purpose is unclear.

Accountability

I	2	3	4	5

Team members are accountable.   Team members are not accountable.

Ground Rules

I	2	3	4	5

Ground rules are followed.   Ground rules are not followed.

Progress

I	2	3	4	5

Appropriate progress is being made.   Appropriate progess
                                                                    is not being made.

Feelings (inclusion vs. exclusion, commitment vs. noncommitment, loyalty vs. lack of loyalty, pride vs. embarrassment, trust vs. mistrust; see list following):

_____

_____

_____

_____

_____

"Feelings" of Effective Work Teams

Inclusion

- Team members get information that affects their jobs and their lives in the organization.
- New ideas are encouraged and treated with respect.
- Team members receive quick responses from other team members when they ask for help.

Commitment

- Team members make personal sacrifices to make sure the team succeeds.
- Team members care about team results.
- Team members are determined to succeed.

Loyalty

- Team members go out of their way to ensure the success of their peers.
- Team members give their colleagues the benefit of the doubt when they have apparently failed to fulfill a commitment.

Pride

- Feedback is sought out and taken seriously as a chance to improve.
- Team members believe that what they do is important and tied to organization goals.
- Team members have a strong orientation toward the future and expect to exceed their own current levels of performance.

Trust

- Team members do what they say they are going to do.
- Team members never conceal information from one another.
- Team members are willing to listen to one another and defer to one another because they expect reliable information and good ideas from one another.
- Team members view one another as having the knowledge and skills to perform.

Team Development Survey

Instructions: Using the numbers on the continuum below, select the number that best describes the team for all of the areas.

Don't Know	1	2	3	4	5	6	7	8	9	10
N/A for internal		Never				Sometimes				Always

Team Structure

_____ Goals are clearly stated and flexible.
_____ Initiating, planning, executing, and evaluating are shared by the team.
_____ The team is self-motivated.
_____ The skills of individual team members are suited to the task.

Team Climate

_____ Team members feel a sense of unity and cohesion.
_____ Team members express themselves freely but consider the welfare of the whole team.
_____ Responsibilities are shared.
_____ Team leadership is shared among members at different times.

Team Process

_____ Progress toward goals can be seen.
_____ The team follows a problem-solving process.
_____ The team performs regular self-checks.

Team Politics

_____ The team maintains an external focus.
_____ The team is growing in its ability to identify and meet the needs of constituents.
_____ Team members understand the importance of conflict in teams and organizations.
_____ The team is growing in the skills of influencing, persuasion, negotiation, and conflict resolution.

Team Effectiveness Review

Things I like about this team:
1.
2.
3.
4.
5.
6.

Things I do not like about this team:
1.
2.
3.
4.
5.
6.

ACTION STEP

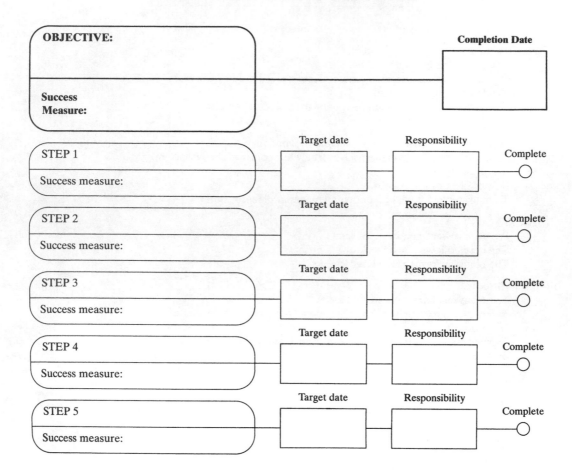

OBJECTIVE:

Completion Date

Success Measure:

STEP 1

Success measure:

Target date

Responsibility

Complete

STEP 2

Success measure:

Target date

Responsibility

Complete

STEP 3

Success measure:

Target date

Responsibility

Complete

STEP 4

Success measure:

Target date

Responsibility

Complete

STEP 5

Success measure:

Target date

Responsibility

Complete

Index